DO YOU KNOW—

1. which pronouns to use when referring to a nation or a ship?

2. which is the currently preferred spelling of a commonly used adverb—*backward* or *backwards*?

3. which is the politically correct usage—*man and wife* or *husband and wife*?

4. what *A.D.*, *CARE*, and *d/b/a* stand for?

5. what a Gopher and a Knowbot are on the Internet?

6. what *DDFWM* and *S/DA/BF* stand for in personal classified ads?

7. what a newborn whale is called?

This authoritative book answers these and thousands of other questions you may have about correct and current usage of our complex language. Build the powerful skills and self-confidence you need with . . .

SMART ENGLISH
It's got it all!

Answers: 1. *it* or *its*—not *she* or *her.* 2. backward. 3. husband and wife. 4. [*anno Domini*] in the year of (our) Lord; Cooperative for American Relief Everywhere; doing business as. 5. a menu-based system for exploring Internet resources, an experimental robotic information-retrieval tool. 6. drug and disease free white male, single or divorced Asian or black female. 7. calf.

SMART
ENGLISH

The Easy-to-Use, Instant-Access Guide to Proper Written and Spoken English

Annette Francis

A SIGNET BOOK

SIGNET
Published by the Penguin Group
Penguin Books USA Inc., 375 Hudson Street,
New York, New York 10014, U.S.A.
Penguin Books Ltd, 27 Wrights Lane,
London W8 5TZ, England
Penguin Books Australia Ltd, Ringwood,
Victoria, Australia
Penguin Books Canada Ltd, 10 Alcorn Avenue,
Toronto, Ontario, Canada M4V 3B2
Penguin Books (N.Z.) Ltd, 182–190 Wairau Road,
Auckland 10, New Zealand

Penguin Books Ltd, Registered Offices:
Harmondsworth, Middlesex, England

First published by Signet, an imprint of Dutton Signet,
a division of Penguin Books USA Inc.

First Printing, October, 1995
10 9 8 7 6 5 4 3 2 1

*To English teachers everywhere . . .
and especially to the memory of my own
English teachers who revealed to me
the riches of the language*

Acknowledgments

I would like to express grateful acknowledgment to Jack Sawyer Harris of New York for reading the manuscript and contributing constructive comments.

In addition, I am most indebted to three Massachusetts professionals who aided me in areas of their special competence: computer software engineer and researcher Philip H. Bailey Jr. of Arlington and technical editor Stephen D. Pratt of Framingham for the chapter titled "Computer & Internet Terms"; and Steven L. Fuchs, Esq., of Newton for reviewing the legal terms in the chapter titled "Frequently Misused Words."

I also wish to thank my son, Alan Benjamin, network manager at a major telecommunications company in Princeton, New Jersey, and Boston Computer Society volunteer Ron Cook of Saugus, Massachusetts, for their input on "Computer & Internet Terms," and Dr. Bryn Mader, Collections Registrar, Department of Mammalogy, American Museum of Natural History, New York, for his help on "Names of Animals & Their Families" in the Appendices.

My special gratitude goes to Marc L. Makos and David Korchin of Boston for their invaluable assistance in many phases of the book's development and for encouraging me in my objectives—and to many on-site and telephone reference librarians of the Boston Public Library for their graciousness and expertise.

Contents

APPENDICES

Preface

When Julius Caesar landed on the coast of Britain with his Roman legions in 55 and 54 B.C., the English language did not exist. Within five hundred years, rudimentary *Englisc* was developed and spoken by a small number of inhabitants. Nearly a millennium later, during the period that William Shakespeare flourished, English had become the native speech of between five and seven million English men and women in their own country.

In the next four hundred years, countless and diverse speakers of English, traveling to every part of the globe on missions of exploration, conquest, and commerce, brought their mother tongue and made it the most widely spoken and written language in history. English, now used by close to a billion people, is the first truly *global* language and is used internationally in the fields of business, entertainment, medicine, science, sports, and telecommunications.

While a good command of the English language has always been an invaluable asset in getting ahead in life, the use of *proper* English has become an *essential* for succeeding in today's highly competitive marketplace. First and lasting impressions are made by our written and spoken use of language. Nothing is more powerful or permanent than words—a fact recognized by the world's greatest intellects for more than two thousand years. Among them:

"Words are healers of the sick tempered."
—Aeschylus (525–456 B.C.),
from *Prometheus Bound,* line 380

"Words are, of course, the most powerful drug used by mankind."
—Rudyard Kipling (1865–1936),
from a speech on February 14, 1923

"Words and magic were in the beginning one and the same thing, and even words today contain much of their magical power. By words one can give to another the greatest happiness or bring about utter despair."
—Sigmund Freud (1856–1939),
from *A General Introduction to Psychoanalysis*
(twenty-eight lectures from 1916–17)

Perhaps the most significant of all aspects of language is its impact on history. The most powerful nation in the modern world was born in Philadelphia on July 4, 1776, when our founding fathers signed the Declaration of Independence, one of the most eloquent and meaningful examples of American writing, another being Lincoln's Gettysburg Address on November 19, 1863.

What fixes that most dramatic technological achievement of the twentieth century in our minds are the first words spoken on the moon by American astronaut Neil Armstrong on July 20, 1969, at 4:17:40 P.M. EST: "That's one small step for a man, one giant leap for mankind."

As an admirer of well-crafted prose and a seasoned editor and published author, I care about the correct use of the English language (which is in jeopardy in America today, as frequently demonstrated in the media). With that in mind I simplified thousands of pointers along the road to good English and compiled them uniquely into *Smart English*—a concise, up-to-date, and instantly accessible supplement to a dictionary—incorporating my "real-life" experiences editing the words of other authors, CEOs, attorneys, politicians, physicians, and scientists.

Combining the fundamentals and the finer points, *Smart English* will help build new confidence in your writing ability; lessen your dependency on computer spell-checkers which, at the present, cannot detect numerous basic errors; and unravel many of the mysteries of our complex language.

I hope *Smart English* will not only prove to be a handy reference for those who desire to hone their linguistic skills, but will also help to raise their level of language competence and effectiveness—the most valuable tools of human communication.

PART ONE

THE FUNDAMENTALS

Our language is well known not to be primitive or self-originated, but to have adopted words of every generation, and either for the supply of its necessities, or the encrease of its copiousness, to have received additions from very different regions; so that in search for the progenitors of our speech, we may wander from the tropic to the frozen zone, and find some in the valleys of Palestine, and some upon the rocks of Norway.

—Samuel Johnson (1709–84), from *The Plan of A Dictionary Of the English Language* (1747)

· 1 ·

Capitalization

Capital letters in writing or printing have two basic purposes: to denote the beginning of a sentence, a sentence fragment, a line of poetry, or other constructions— and to signal a proper noun or a pronoun or adjective derived from a proper noun.

A *noun* is a naming word that is used to identify anything that can be named, from people and places to ideas and emotions.

Proper nouns—words that name *specific* persons, places, or things—are always capitalized, or *uppercased*.

Common nouns—words that do *not* refer to specific names of persons, places, or things—are *not* capitalized, or *lowercased*.

Uppercase and *lowercase* are terms derived from seventeenth-century compositors' practice of keeping capital letters in the upper part of a type case and small capitals, fractions, symbols, and accents in the lower part.

The following pages demonstrate the use of *full* capital letters, which are more common than *small* capital letters. Some examples of the use of small caps can be found in Chapter 2, "Punctuation," and include calendar and time designations and, in play scripts, the names of characters. Additionally, small caps are used for the opening of book chapters, with mathematical copy, in certain quotations, and in tables. (In typed material or if small caps are unavailable, use full caps.)

Capitalize the first word of:

1. **a sentence or sentence fragment.**

   > The dictionary is on my desk.
   > Are you going to the library today?
   > Bravo!

2. **a parenthetical sentence (a sentence contained within parentheses) if it does not occur within another sentence.**

   > I prefer the Bard's poetry to that of all other poets. (His sonnets are my favorites.)

   Do *not* capitalize the first word of a parenthetical sentence within another sentence.

   > After spending a week in New Orleans (the restaurants there cannot be surpassed), we each gained five pounds.

3. **a direct quotation, except when the quotation is split.**

   > Jack asked, "Was the book a good read?"
   > "Yes," I replied, "it was very engrossing."

4. **each line in a poem in traditional verse.**

   > O, learn to read what silent love hath writ:
   > To hear with eyes belongs to love's fine wit.
   > —W. Shakespeare
   > from *Sonnet XXIV*

   In twentieth-century poetry, the line beginnings are frequently lowercased.

5. **the first word after a colon if the material introduced consists of more than one sentence—or is a formal statement, a quotation, or a speech in dialogue; otherwise use a lowercase letter.**

In the nucleus of every single human cell are forty-six threadlike particles, the chromosomes: Every chromosome is composed of hundreds and perhaps thousands of genes, the basic units of heredity. The forty-six chromosomes consist of twenty-three pairs, one member of each pair having come from the father, the other from the mother.

"I wish to make an announcement: The store will close in fifteen minutes," the manager said.

Her answer took him by surprise: "Because I don't love you anymore."

Now Harwood had his second inspiration: the lynx-hare cycle corresponded with the cycle of sunspot activity.

6. **enumerations, run-in enumerations that form complete sentences, and vertical lists.**

Do the following if someone is exhibiting dangerous or violent behavior: 1. Try not to become excited. 2. Do not try to argue, reason, restrain, or fight back with a person in this state. 3. Get away as quickly as possible, taking any children with you and warning any adults so they will follow you. 4. Call the police or your doctor as soon as you are safely away.

Shorter enumerations, such as words or phrases run in with the introductory text, are usually lowercased unless first word is a proper noun.

Today's schedule will include (1) Statue of Liberty, (2) lunch in Chinatown, (3) SoHo art galleries, (4) off-Broadway show.

This is today's schedule:
    Statue of Liberty
    Lunch in Chinatown
    SoHo art galleries
    Off-Broadway show

7. **the salutation of a letter and a complimentary close.**

    Dear Carolyn,
    Yours sincerely,

8. **an outline heading.**

    I. The three B's
      A. Bach
      B. Beethoven
      C. Brahms

Capitalize the names of people, places, and things listed in the following alphabetized categories (unless lowercase is specified):

ACADEMIC DEGREES, DEPARTMENTS, SUBJECTS, TITLES & YEARS:

Degrees abbreviated only after a full name (not after a last name alone) and set off by commas:

BA	BFA
BS	LLD
MA	PhD

Kathryn Vincent, PhD, was the guest speaker.
   but
Kathryn Vincent, who has a doctorate in
   psychology, was the guest speaker.

Her brother Jeffrey holds a master's degree in
   medical laboratory science.

Do not use in the same reference a courtesy title before a name that is followed by the abbreviation for a degree:

Dr. Fulton Bernstein, an immunologist
   not
Dr. Fulton Bernstein, PhD

Departments only for those words that are proper nouns or adjectives:

the department of English
the English department
the department of sociology
the sociology department

Subjects only when referring to a specific course or words that are proper nouns or adjectives:

Spanish
Business 204
Art Appreciation
a business course
a communication skills class
my sophomore year French teacher

Titles (chairman, chancellor, professor, etc.) only when they precede a name—modifiers that are not proper nouns should be lowercased:

Professor David Leigh
philosophy Professor Margo Black
department Chairman Albert Cunningham

Years—freshman, sophomore, junior, and senior—are lowercased.

AIRCRAFT & SPACE VEHICLES:

Air Force One	*Apollo 18*
Lindbergh's *Spirit of St. Louis*	*Columbia*
F-4 Phantom 2	*Endeavour*

ANIMAL BREEDS OR TYPES (when named for people or places):

King Charles spaniel	Saint Bernard
African elephant	Persian cat
Siamese fighting fish	Grant's gazelle
Baltimore oriole	Great Pyrenees
Columbian black-tailed deer	Bengal tiger
Tasmanian devil	Yorkshire terrier

ANIMAL GENERA (capitalize genus but not species names in binomial nomenclature):

lobster (*Homarus americanus*)
lion (*Panthera leo*)
llama (*Lama guanico*)
gazelle (*Gazella subgutturosa*)

ARMY (and other military terms when used with full titles but lowercase when used alone or are not part of an official title):

United States Army *but* the army, the American army, the armed forces
Fifth Army *but* the Fifth, the army
Army Corps of Engineers
Allied armies
National Guard, the guard

See also "Military Units," p. 17.

AWARDS, PRIZES & OTHER HONORS:

Academy Awards (also known as the *Oscars*)

Lowercase *the academy* and *the awards* if not used together.

Nobel Prizes

Nobel Peace Prize
Nobel Prize in chemistry
Nobel Prize in literature
Nobel Prize in physics
Nobel Prize in physiology *or* medicine
the Nobel Prize award ceremonies
She is a Nobel Prize winner.
He is a Nobel Prize-winning scientist.

Lowercase *prize* when used without the word *Nobel:*

The chemistry prize was awarded yesterday.

Pulitzer Prizes

Pulitzer Prize in fiction
Pulitzer Prize in public service
He is a Pulitzer Prize winner.
She is a Pulitzer Prize-winning author.

Other Honors

Distinguished Flying Cross
Distinguished Service Order (DSO)
Medal of Honor (*not* Congressional Medal of
   Honor)
Purple Heart
Silver Star
Victoria Cross
   but
croix de guerre

BUILDINGS & OTHER STRUCTURES:

the Alamo   Independence Hall
Paramount Theater   Empire State Building
Golden Gate Bridge   Leaning Tower of Pisa

CAPITOL BUILDING (Washington, D.C.):

U.S. Capitol, the Capitol, Capitol Hill

The word *capital* refers to the city in which a seat of
government is located.

(When used in a financial sense, *capital* describes
money, equipment, or property used in a business by
a person or corporation.)

COMMITTEES & CONFERENCES:

Senate Foreign Relations Committee
House Ways and Means Committee
Republican National Committee

U.S. Conference of Mayors *but* mayors'
    conference
Democratic Governors' Conference

COMPASS POINTS & DIRECTIONS (when referring to a geographical region or its inhabitants, or are
parts of a street name—lowercase when referring to
simple directions):

up North — a north course
the North Atlantic — a northerly gale
the North End (of — a northern constellation
    Boston) — northern Italy
Northerners — northern pike
the North Woods — northern states

back East — an eastern Congressman
the East (the Orient) — the island's eastern half
the East Coast — an eastern route
East End Avenue — east of the Mississippi
East-West relations — an eastwardly wind

Deep South — a souther
down South — a southerly direction
Park Avenue South — a southern exposure
Southern-fried chicken — southern lights
the South Pole — southernmost

out West — the west coast of Florida
the West Bank — a western migration
the Western Hemisphere — western omelet
West Siders — western shirt
Middle West *or* — the western branch
    Midwest — office
Middle East, Northern Ireland, South Korea
    but northern France, eastern Canada

The West Coast is having a heat wave.
A blizzard is headed for the Northeast.
A cold front is moving south.
She is a Northern liberal.

Although the North won the Civil War, some dyed-in-the-wool Southerners think the South will rise again.

The leaders of Eastern Europe are meeting to discuss oil from Southeast Asia.

Abbreviations

cardinal: N, E, S, W
intercardinal: NE, SE, SW, NW
others: NNE, ENE, ESE, SSE, SSW, WSW, WNW, NNW

CONGRESS (Washington, D.C.):

U.S. Congress, Congress
1st Congressional District, the 1st District

Lowercase *district* when used alone and *congressional* unless part of a proper name:

congressional salaries
the *Congressional Quarterly*
the *Congressional Record*

The titles *congressman* and *congresswoman* refer to members of the U.S. House of Representatives. Capitalize only before a name. (See "Titles," p. 21.)

CONSTELLATIONS, PLANETS & STARS:

Milky Way	Saturn
Sirius, the Dog Star	Nova
Big and Little Dippers	Orion

Earth, when used as the proper name of our planet:

The astronauts returned to Earth.
The space shuttle can carry people and cargo into Earth orbit.

Lowercase nouns and adjectives derived from the proper names of planets and other heavenly bodies:

martian   jovian
lunar   venusian

COURTS (the full proper names at all levels):

Federal

> the Supreme Court of the United States, the U.S. Supreme Court, the Supreme Court

> chief justice of the United States (*not* of the Supreme Court): Chief Justice William Rehnquist

> associate justices: Justice Ruth Bader Ginsburg *or* Associate Justice Ruth Bader Ginsburg

> the U.S. Court of Appeals for the Federal Circuit
> U.S. Court of Customs and Patent Appeals
> 7th U.S. Circuit Court of Appeals
> 3rd District Court

State

> the state Superior Court, the Superior Court, Superior Court
> the state Supreme Court, the Supreme Court, Supreme Court

> (Titles for jurists on state courts vary.)

County

> County Court
> County Judge (before a name)

Courthouse

> Courthouse (with the name of a jurisdiction):
> the U.S. Courthouse
> the Cook County Courthouse

Court House (two words) is used in the proper names of some communities.

Lowercase *the county courthouse, the courthouse, the federal courthouse,* and *judicial branch.*

DECLARATIONS & TREATIES:

Declaration of Independence
Balfour Declaration
Magna Carta *or* Magna Charta
Panama Canal Treaty
Treaty of Versailles
North Atlantic Treaty Organization (NATO)

DERIVATIVES OF PROPER NAMES (except in their extended senses):

Rome, Roman nose *but* roman numerals
Bohemia *but* bohemian attitude
Don Quixote *but* quixotic idea
Hercules *but* herculean feat
Queen Victoria *and* Victorian era
Byzantine Empire *but* byzantine office politics
William Shakespeare *and* Shakespearean tragedies

DISEASES (when named for people or places):

Bright's disease
Asiatic cholera
Legionnaires' disease
Parkinson's disease
German measles (rubella)

EPITHETS & NICKNAMES

An *epithet* is a word or phrase applied to a person, place, or thing that describes an actual or attributed quality, and may either accompany or be used in place of the original name. (*Epithet* can also mean an insult.)

Stonewall—Thomas Jonathan Jackson (1824–63), Confederate general during the Civil War

Honest Abe—Abraham Lincoln (1809–65), 16th president of the United States

Swedish Nightingale—Jenny Lind (1820–87), Swedish soprano

Ivan the Terrible—Ivan IV (1530–84), first czar of Russia

A *nickname* is a name added to or substituted for the proper name of a person, place, or thing—or a familiar form of a proper name, such as *Tom* for *Thomas*.

President Bill Clinton
President Jimmy Carter
Edwin E. "Buzz" Aldrin Jr.
Catfish Hunter
Dizzy Gillespie

Old Glory
the Lone Star
  State
Motown
the Windy City

FAMILY RELATIONSHIPS (when used with a person's name as a title):

Aunt Marjorie *but* my aunt Marjorie Leigh
I spoke to Mother *but* my mother called
Uncle David *but* my uncle David Bauer

FOODS (named for places):

baked Alaska
Boston cream pie
Thousand Island dressing
  but
brussels sprouts, french fries

French toast
Spanish rice
Swiss cheese

FOREIGN PARTICLES (such as *de, la,* and *von* when the last name starts a sentence):

De Gaulle organized French resistance in World War II and led the establishment of the Fifth Republic of France in 1958.

GEOGRAPHIC NAMES:

Brazil	Seattle
Sault Sainte Marie	West Virginia
Andes Mountains	Niagara Falls
Bermuda Triangle	North Pole
Pacific Ocean	Mt. Fuji
Mediterranean Sea	Lake Superior

Hudson River *but* the Hudson valley
Canary Islands *but* canary seed
Philippine Islands *or* the Philippines *but* the islands
Sri Lanka (formerly Ceylon)
Mali (formerly Sudanese Republic)
Mozambique (formerly Portuguese East Africa)

NOTE: The worldwide political upheavals of the late twentieth century have resulted in many countries changing their names. If you are uncertain about the current name (or spelling) of a country, consult a reference librarian or a local newspaper office before using it in written material.

GEOLOGIC ERAS & PERIODS:

Age of Reptiles	Mesozoic era
Triassic period	Bronze Age

GOVERNMENTAL BODIES—assemblies, houses of representatives, legislatures, senates (when referring to a specific one):

the California Assembly, the state Assembly
the Colorado Legislature, the state Legislature
the U.S. House of Representatives, the U.S. House
the Alabama House of Representatives, the Alabama House
the U.S. Senate, the Senate
the Oklahoma Senate, the state Senate
the Florida Department of Human Resources

Lowercase all plural uses: *the California and New York assemblies, the Oklahoma and South Carolina*

senates—and references to nongovernmental bodies:
the student senate at Princeton.

HISTORICAL PERIODS & EVENTS:

the Roman era	the Boston Tea Party
the Middle Ages	the Battle of Waterloo
the Atomic Age	the Yalta Conference
D-Day	the Vietnam War
the War of 1812	the Persian Gulf War

HOLIDAYS & HOLY DAYS:

Columbus Day	Easter
Thanksgiving	Ascension Day
Christmas	Passover
New Year's Eve	Yom Kippur
New Year's Day	Hanukkah

HORSES, RACES & RACETRACKS:

Man o' War	Kentucky Derby
Seattle Slew	Preakness
Gulfstream Park	Belmont Stakes

LAWS, ACTS & AMENDMENTS (but not bills):

Sherman Antitrust Law
Taft-Hartley Law
Clean Air Act of 1990
Equal Rights Amendment
U.S. Constitution, the Constitution
Massachusetts Constitution *but* the state
   constitution
Fifth Amendment, *colloquial* the Fifth
10th Amendment
Bill of Rights (the first 10 amendments to the
   Constitution)

MILITARY UNITS:

First Infantry Division *but* the division
Fifth Battalion *but* the battalion
395th Field Artillery *but* the artillery
Task Force Fifty-six *but* the task force

NATIONALITIES, RACES, TRIBES & LANGUAGES:

Caucasian	Maori
Cherokee	Gypsy
Chinese	Zulu
Portuguese	Nordic

ORGANIZATIONS & INSTITUTIONS:

Boy Scouts of America: Cub Scouts *or* Cubs, Boy Scouts *or* Scouts, Explorers (not *Explorer Scouts*), Sea Explorers

Girl Scouts of the U.S.A.: Brownie Girl Scouts *or* Brownies, Junior Girl Scouts *or* Juniors, Cadette Girl Scouts *or* Cadettes, Senior Girl Scouts *or* Seniors

American Medical Association
First Presbyterian Church
Yale School of Drama
Massachusetts Institute of Technology (formal name of MIT)
College of the Holy Cross *or* Holy Cross College
Harvard School of Dental Medicine *or* Harvard Dental School

PEOPLE:

Julius Caesar	Golda Meir
Alexander the Great	Nikita S. Khrushchev
Ludwig van Beethoven	Eleanor Roosevelt
Marie Antoinette	Tennessee Williams

PERSONIFICATIONS:

A *personification* is the attribution of personal nature or character to inanimate objects or abstract notions.

Father Time	Grim Reaper
Mother Nature	John Barleycorn

PLACES, DISTRICTS & REGIONS:

the Main Line (Philadelphia)
the French Quarter (New Orleans)
the Combat Zone (Boston)
Greenwich Village (New York)
The Strip (a section of Hollywood's Sunset Boulevard)
Haight-Ashbury (San Francisco)
SoHo (New York)
Soho (London, England)
Left Bank (Paris, France)

PLANTS & VEGETABLES (containing proper names):

African violet	Chinese cabbage
Easter lily	Belgian endive
Boston fern	Spanish moss

POLITICAL PARTIES & PHILOSOPHIES (when referring to a specific party or member):

the Democratic Party, a Democrat
the Liberal Party, a Liberal
the Republican Party, a Republican

Lowercase *all* political philosophies (e.g., *communism, conservatism, fascism, liberalism, socialism*) unless derived from a proper name: *Marxism, Marxist; Nazism, Nazi.*

RELIGIOUS TERMS & SACRED WORKS:

Judeo-Christian

the Almighty
the Bible (when referring to the Scriptures in the
    Old Testament or New Testament)
Bible Belt
the books of the Old Testament* and New
    Testament†
the branches of Judeo-Christian religions
the Gemara
God
Gospels, Gospel of St. Mark
Hades
He, His (when referring to God)
he, his (when referring to Jesus Christ)
the Holy Scriptures
the Holy Spirit
Jesus Christ (and major events in his life)
the Messiah
the Mishnah
the Pentateuch
Satan
the Scriptures
Son of God
the Supreme Being
the Talmud
the Ten Commandments
the Torah
the Twelve Apostles

* Old Testament (in order): Genesis, Exodus, Leviticus, Numbers, Deuteronomy, Joshua, Judges, Ruth, 1 Samuel, 2 Samuel, 1 Kings, 2 Kings, 1 Chronicles, 2 Chronicles, Ezra, Nehemiah, Esther, Job, Psalms, Proverbs, Ecclesiastes, Song of Solomon, Isaiah, Jeremiah, Lamentations, Ezekiel, Daniel, Hosea, Joel, Amos, Obadiah, Jonah, Micah, Nahum, Habakkuk, Zephaniah, Haggai, Zechariah, Malachi.

† New Testament (in order): Matthew, Mark, Luke, John, Acts, Romans, 1 Corinthians, 2 Corinthians, Galatians, Ephesians, Philippians, Colossians, 1 Thessalonians, 2 Thessalonians, 1 Timothy, 2 Timothy, Titus, Philemon, Hebrews, Epistles of James, 1 Peter, 2 Peter, 1 John, 2 John, 3 John, Jude, Revelation.

Lowercase *bible* in nonreligious references; *biblical* in all uses; *catholic* when used in its generic sense of general or universal; and *angel, cherub, deity, devil, heaven, hell, icon,* and *satanic.*

Other

Islam
Allah
One God
Mohammed
His Prophet
Koran
Moslem, Muslem, Muslim

Hinduism
Brahman
Hindu
Brahma
Vishnu
Siva

Buddhism
Gautama Buddha
Nirvana

Jainism
Mahavira

Confucianism
Confucius
the Five Classics

Taoism
Lao-tse (the Old Master)
Tae Te Ching (The Way and Its Power)

Shinto (the Way of the Gods)
Shintoist
Sect Shinto
State Shinto

Sikhism
Sikh
Guru Nanak
Granth

Zoroastrianism
Zoroaster
Ahura-Mazda
Zend-Avesta
Parsi

Bahá'í
Ali-Mohammed (*the Bab*)
Hussein Ali (*Baha Ullah*)

SHIPS & FLEETS:

the *Titanic*
U.S.S. *Arizona*
Delta Queen

Spanish Armada
Royal Navy
Pacific Fleet (U.S., World War II)

SPORTS EVENTS, PLACES & TEAMS:

Boston Marathon	Yankee Stadium
U.S. Tennis Open	Rose Bowl
Indianapolis 500	St. Louis Cardinals
World Series	Harlem Globetrotters
Masters Tournament	Oakland Raiders
Super Bowl	Princeton Tigers
Meadowlands	Montreal Canadiens

TITLES—CIVIL, JUDICIAL, MILITARY, RELIGIOUS (when preceding a name):

President Mandela	Senator Rainbolt
acting Mayor Daly	Representative Mendes
King Edward	Justice Marshall
Lord Mountbatten	District Attorney Alberts
Pope John Paul II	Rabbi Marks
General Schwarzkopf	Reverend Billy Graham

With the *exception* of the President and Vice President of the United States, lowercase *all* formal titles if not used before a name—including those above and others such as *admiral, ambassador, commander in chief, commissioner, detective, sheriff, constable, congressman, congresswoman, archbishop, pope* (*pontiff, priest, minister, executor, astronaut, cosmonaut,* and *attaché* are not formal titles and are never capitalized).

TITLES—ITALICIZED CREATIVE WORKS & PUBLICATIONS:

Italicize the titles and capitalize the *keywords* in the titles of ballets, books, epic poems, major musical works, magazines, motion pictures, newspapers, paintings, plays, radio and television series, and sculpture.

Tchaikovsky's *Swan Lake*
Emily Brontë's *Wuthering Heights*
Homer's epic poems, the *Iliad* and the *Odyssey*
Time magazine

Mozart's *The Magic Flute*
Schubert's *Unfinished Symphony*
Rodgers & Hammerstein's *The Sound of Music*
Orson Welles's *Citizen Kane*
the Miami *Herald*
Botticelli's *The Birth of Venus*
Ibsen's *Hedda Gabler*
PBS's *Mystery!*
Rodin's *The Thinker*

TRADEMARKS:

Dr Pepper (no period after *Dr*)	Popsicle
	Rolls-Royce
Kleenex	Sucaryl
Mace	Valium
Mailgram	Vaseline
Musak	Windbreaker
Plexiglas (single *s*)	Xerox

Kmart (lowercase *m*, all one word)
Orlon *but* nylon and rayon (not trademarks)

Lowercase former trademarks that are now generic terms such as cellophane, kerosene, linoleum, mimeograph, pacemaker, and yo-yo.

It is unnecessary to use the symbols ™ and ®—frequently accompanying registered trademark names on product packaging and in advertisements—in text (body copy).

· 2 ·
Punctuation

The function of punctuation, a system of using conventional marks or characters in writing to separate groups of words, is to help clarify the thought that is being expressed. These marks signal to the reader, for example, that he or she has come to the beginning of a list or quoted material, or to the end of a sentence or question.

The trend in recent years is to punctuate less, except in the use of hyphens in forming compound words previously written as two or more separate words. Correct punctuation, however, is as important as ever—your choice of punctuation should be considered as carefully as your choice of words. Incorrect punctuation can change the meaning of a sentence, possibly leading to far-reaching consequences. Overpunctuation can make writing as confusing as no punctuation, obscuring the sense and making the reader's task difficult and time-consuming.

Use punctuation only where you need it. If any mark of punctuation does not help to make clear what you have written, delete it. If a long sentence gets bogged down with punctuation, rephrase the entire sentence or replace it with two or more shorter sentences.

The guidelines offered in this chapter regarding the use of standard punctuation marks illustrate general rules that apply only to American usage and are presented, not in alphabetical order as are other listings in this book, but in order of common usage.

PERIOD $\boxed{\,\cdot\,}$

Use a period:

1. **after a complete declarative sentence.**

   The library is closed Saturdays in July and August.

2. **after a mildly imperative sentence.**

   Return my thesaurus when you can.

3. **after an indirect question.**

   She asked me what the time was.

4. **after some rhetorical questions.**

   Why don't we read more classics.

5. **after some abbreviations.**

A.M.	Ave.
P.M.	Blvd.
Jan.	St.
Sat.	Co.
Tenn.	Inc.

   Franklin D. Roosevelt *but* FDR

6. **after numerals or letters used to enumerate items in a vertical list.**

1. Neanderthal	A. holidays
2. Cro-Magnon	B. festivals

Omit a period:

1. **after items in a vertical list unless one or more listings are complete sentences.**

   Wintergreen oil serves as a flavoring for:
   candy
   chewing gum

medicine
tooth powder

After interviewing the applicant, I had concerns that
1. he is not well-organized;
2. he would not work well under pressure; and
3. he would step on his boss to get ahead.

2. **after a sentence within a sentence *unless* the included sentence comes last, in which case a period goes outside the closing parenthesis or bracket and inside the close-quote marks.**

The rock band's new bass player (I heard him practicing backstage) sounds better than the first one.

Sheila's comment, "You strike a hard bargain," took me by surprise.

Christopher announced last night that he's leaving for Hollywood next week (he's quitting the field of sportscasting for acting).

Attributed to Hannibal (247–183 B.C.), Carthaginian general who crossed the Alps and invaded Italy, are the words, "We will either find a way or make one."

COMMA ,

Use a comma:

1. **to set off an appositive (one or more words that explain or give additional information about a preceding expression)—**

Barbara Samuels, 47, was elected mayor today by a wide margin.

The company president, Mr. Harrington, is in the Far East.

—but *not* between two nouns whereby one identifies the other.

> The accountant Quinn finished my tax return early this year.

2. (also called *serial* or *series comma*) to separate three or more words in a series before the conjunction connecting the last two elements, except in headings or before an ampersand.

> Foremost Spanish painter Pablo Picasso also gained fame as a sculptor, draftsman, engraver, and ceramist.

> Thomas Jefferson collected books that became the basis of the Library of Congress, wrote a manual of rules for parliamentary procedure, and compiled a dictionary of Indian dialects.

3. to separate two or more adjectives of equal rank—

> a dark, deserted alley
> a loyal, longtime, and supportive friend

—but *not* when the last adjective before a noun outranks its predecessor due to its being an integral element of a noun phrase (the equivalent of a single noun).

> a picturesque covered bridge
> a diamond engagement ring

4. to separate the name of a city from the name of a state *and* to separate the following state name from the rest of a sentence.

> Cincinnati, Ohio, is my hometown; but Boston, Massachusetts, is where I live now.

5. to separate an introductory word or words from the rest of the sentence.

> Yes, there is a Sunday matinée.

6. **when writing figures with four or more digits—**

4,500 $85,640.25

—but *not* in street addresses, room or suite numbers, broadcast frequencies, serial numbers, telephone numbers, and years.

> 1529 Summit Avenue Room 2102 Suite 5600
> P.O. Box 3435 1540 kilohertz 737-2882 1492

7. **on the inside of quotation marks.**

> Sometimes called "Little Paris," Brussels is the capital of Belgium.

8. **to set off direct quotations—**

> Mother said, "Drink eight glasses of water a day."
> "Drink eight glasses of water a day," Mother said.

—but *not* if a question mark is needed at the end of the quotation.

> "When is the best time to call you?" she asked.

9. **to precede and follow parenthetical words or phrases—**

> In addition, I will order a garden salad.

> If, on the other hand, the fruit is fresh, I will have the fruit salad.

—but *not* if the connection is sufficiently close and does not call for a pause in reading.

> He was probably the finest guitarist I ever heard.

> The music was dissonant and therefore did not appeal to the more conservative members of the audience.

10. **after a closing parenthesis if the sentence construction requires it.**

> While many mammals are able to take care of themselves from birth (for example, colts and calves), others need parental training.

11. **to separate the independent clauses of a compound sentence preceding the conjunction *unless* the thoughts expressed require a more emphatic form of punctuation—**

> English is used by at least 750 million people today, and barely half of those speak it as a mother tongue.

—but *not* if the clauses are short and closely connected in thought.

> My father leaves for the country today and my mother will join him tomorrow.

12. **to indicate an ellipsis (the omission from a sentence or other construction of one or more words unnecessary to the meaning).**

> Mary Ellen brought the birthday cake; John, the candles and paper hats.

13. **to set off a nonrestrictive phrase or clause (also called *descriptive clause*), one that adds a thought to the sentence but is not essential to its meaning—**

> The blue whale, the world's largest animal, weighs more than 150 tons.

> This whale, which is also called the sulfur-bottom, may reach a length of 111 feet.

—but *not* to set off a restrictive phrase or clause (one that *is* essential to the meaning of the sentence).

The pianist who won last year's competition is going on a worldwide tour.

SEMICOLON $;$

Use a semicolon:

1. **to link independent clauses in a compound sentence when no connective word is used.**

   The word *irregardless,* a double negative, is non-standard English; use *regardless* instead.

2. **to link clauses joined by a conjunctive adverb** *(accordingly, also, besides, consequently, even so, furthermore, hence, however, indeed, likewise, moreover, nevertheless, otherwise, similarly, so, still, then, therefore, thus, yet).*

   The word *unique* means one of a kind; therefore, do not describe something as *very unique* or *most unique.*

3. **to link clauses joined by a coordinating conjunction** *(and, but, for, nor, or)* **if one of the clauses has internal punctuation or is long and involved.**

   The word *definitely* is overused as a vague intensifier (a linguistic element that increases the degree of emphasis or force); and one should avoid using it.

4. **before clauses that introduce expansions** *(e.g., for example, for instance, i.e., that is).*

   The word *scenario* has been overused for years; for example, as in *worst-case scenario.*

5. **to separate phrases that contain commas.**

   Our company has sales offices in eight capital cities: Austin, Texas; Providence, Rhode Island; Springfield, Illinois; Columbus, Ohio; Columbia,

South Carolina; Baton Rouge, Louisiana; Hartford, Connecticut; and Albany, New York.

6. **for clarity between items in a complex or lengthy enumeration in a sentence.**

My favorite ghost stories are (1) "The Gray Champion" by Nathaniel Hawthorne, author of *The Scarlet Letter;* (2) "The Phantom 'Rickshaw" by Rudyard Kipling, author of *Captains Courageous;* and (3) "Ligeia" by Edgar Allan Poe, who wrote "The Gold Bug."

7. **outside quotation marks and parentheses.**

The longest word I recall seeing is "honorificabilitudinitatibus"; it is from Shakespeare's comedy, *Love's Labour's Lost* (1594–95?), which satirized the manners and mores of the day.

Shakespeare was a country boy (born 1564 in Stratford, in the heart of Warwickshire, then a town of some 1,500 inhabitants); much of his poetry reflects his delight in the English countryside.

COLON :

Use a colon:

1. **to introduce a series, lists, tabulations, texts, examples, or extracts at the end of a sentence.**

You must know how to recognize these poisonous plants: poison ivy, poison oak, and poison sumac.

The following is a synopsis of Eugene O'Neill's *Desire Under the Elms:*

2. **for dialogue in plays, court proceedings, and question-and-answer interviews.**

HAMLET: Madam, how like you this play?
QUEEN: The lady protests too much, methinks.

OLIVER: Where were you on the night of the
          robbery?
GIBSON: Working out at the gym.

Q: Why did you choose this career?
A: I always enjoyed working in a bookstore.

3. to emphasize or express a strong contrast.

She had only one interest: art.

God creates: man destroys.

4. to introduce a long quotation, statement, or question.

John Adams wrote: "The preservation of the means
of knowledge among the lowest ranks is of more
importance to the public than all the property of all
the rich men in the country."

Colons go outside quotation marks unless they are
part of the quotation itself.

5. to separate hours, minutes, and seconds in indicating time.

2:45:15   7:30 P.M. *or* 7:30 p.m. *or* 7:30 PM

6. to separate parts of a citation (quotation), such as volume, chapter, page, and verse.

Ex. 7:8 *or* Ex. 7.8 (seen in current works)

Journal of Astrophysics 8:181–202

Do *not* italicize references to the Judeo-Christian Bible and its parts or include page numbers; abbreviate
book names.

7. to follow a formal salutation, as in a business letter or speech.

Dear Madam Attorney General:

Dear Mr. President:

To Whom It May Concern:

My Fellow Americans:

QUESTION MARK ?

Use a question mark:

1. **at the end of a direct question.**

   Did you know that George Eliot and George Sand are pen names of two women novelists?

2. **at the end of a question in the form of a declarative sentence.**

   You ran for governor?

3. **at the end of an interpolated (inserted) question.**

   You told me—Didn't you promise me?—that you would stop smoking.

4. **at the end of a question within a question.**

   Were you present when she asked the boss, "When do I get a raise?"

5. **at the end of a question in a question-and-answer format.**

   Q: What are your hobbies?
   A: Chess, photography, and skiing.

6. **to indicate doubt or uncertainty.**

   Tutankhamen was a king of Egypt from 1366–1357? B.C.

7. **with quotation marks, depending upon the meaning.**

> Who wrote "The Emperor's New Clothes"?
> She asked, "When will my car be ready?"

APOSTROPHE   '

Use an apostrophe:

1. **to indicate the possessive case of nouns.**

> See Chapter 3, "Possessives."

2. **to indicate plural forms of certain letters and figures.**

> See Chapter 4, "Plural Forms."

3. **to indicate omission of letters in contractions.**

> nat'l   we're   haven't

4. **to indicate omission of figures in dates.**

> the Roaring '20s   the Spirit of '76
> the class of '89   the '49ers

QUOTATION MARKS   " "

Use quotation marks:

1. **in direct quotations to enclose the exact words of a speaker or a writer.**

> "I'll be happy to meet you for dinner," she replied.

> "I hope," he said, "that you remembered to lock the front door."

> In an address to Congress, January 8, 1790, George Washington said, "To be prepared for war is one of the most effective means of preserving peace."

Henry David Thoreau wrote, "How many a man has dated a new era in his life from the reading of a book!"

2. **to enclose a quotation within a quotation, in which case single quotation marks are used.**

Reading Alan's letter, Sherry said, "Listen to this! 'I've just received notice that I've been promoted to network manager.' Isn't that great?"

Joan confided, "When Ralph proposed, he simply said, 'Please marry me.' "

3. **to enclose a word or phrase used in an ironical sense.**

Steve's summer "vacation" consisted of two weeks of cleaning out the garage, basement, and attic.

4. **to enclose an unusual word or trade term the first time it appears in copy.**

The cub reporter was stunned when the editor ordered a prompt "kill" of her first major story.

5. **to enclose titles of creative works and publications when italics are not available.**

See "Titles—Italicized Creative Works & Publications" in Chapter 1, "Capitalization," pp. 21–22.

6. **to enclose titles of articles, chapters or parts of books, brochures, pamphlets, plays (when part of a collection), poems, songs, and stories.**

Francis Scott Key, a well-known Washington lawyer, became famous for writing the words of our national anthem, "The Star-Spangled Banner."

"The Gift of the Magi" is an excellent example of O. Henry's mastery of the surprise ending.

EXCLAMATION POINT !

Use an exclamation point (also called *exclamation mark*):

1. **to express astonishment, distress, or other strong emotions.**

   "I hate you!" she screamed.

   Place the exclamation point *inside* quotation marks when it is part of the quoted material; *outside,* when not part of the quoted material. Do not use more than one mark at a time and avoid overuse.

   I loved hearing Horowitz's recording of Chopin's "Fantaisie-Impromptu"!

2. **to add, in casual writing, a tone of amusement, amazement, or outrage.**

   And he calls himself a pro!

   My new skating partner is 6'4" (!) and speaks with a Finnish accent.

SLASH /

Use a slash (also called *diagonal, slant, solidus,* or *virgule*):

1. **between two words to denote *or* or *and/or,* whichever is appropriate to complete the sense of the sentence.**

   She is a highly successful singer/songwriter.

   A prospective employee should bring at least six copies of his/her résumé to a job interview.

2. **as a dividing line in dates, fractions, and time signatures in music.**

His notes, dated 12/12/93, stated that the waltz was developed from the *ländler,* an Austrian peasant dance, and is written in 3/4 time.

ELLIPSES   `... or ....`

Use ellipsis points or dots (also called *suspension points*)—three or four consecutive periods—to indicate that one or more words in a quotation, text, or document has been omitted. At the beginning or middle of the sentence—or between sentences—use three dots; at the end of a sentence, use four dots.

> "Theseus seemed ... to resemble Romulus. ... Both of them, born out of wedlock and of uncertain parentage, had the repute of being sprung from the gods."
>
>   —From *Plutarch's Lives*

> "The results of these trials proved this method [of reducing lower back pain] to be nearly 100 percent effective. ..."

Ellipsis points are usually separated from each other and from the text by a space.

HYPHEN   `-`

Use a hyphen:

1. **to form certain compound nouns and compound modifiers.**

    See Chapter 9, "Compound Words & Phrases."

2. **to divide a word into syllables.**

    hip-po-pot-a-mus

3. **to spell out a word or name.**

    c-o-p-i-o-u-s   J-o-n-a-t-h-a-n

4. **to form suspensive hyphenation.**

Both men received 5- to 10-year prison sentences.

5. **to avoid ambiguity.**

My husband is at a meeting of small-business men.

6. **to connect a word ending in _y_ to another word when spelling out numbers.**

thirty-two　　　　fifty-fifty　　　　ninety-four

7. **to separate figures in odds, ratios, and scores.**

The odds were 3-1 against his winning the race.

The ratio was 5-2.　a 5-2 ratio　a ratio of 5-2

The Cowboys scored a 12-6 victory over the Dolphins.

8. **to simplify pronunciation when a prefix doubles a vowel or a suffix triples a consonant.**

anti-intellectual　de-energize　shell-like

9. **to separate a prefix followed by a proper noun.**

mid-Atlantic　pre-Columbian　un-American

10. **when _mid-_ precedes a figure.**

The senator is in his mid-40s.

DASH ── ─

There are several kinds of dashes which differ in length and use—em dashes, en dashes, and 2- and 3-em dashes. An _en dash_ (–) is half the length of an _em dash_ (—) but longer than a _hyphen_ (-). The 2- and 3-em dashes are the length of two em dashes and three em dashes, respectively.

Use an em dash or a pair of dashes:

1. **to denote an emphatic pause or abrupt change in thought.**

   I'm off to college next fall—if I get a scholarship.

   Max proposed to me—it was so unexpected—on the Staten Island ferry.

2. **to set off a series, within a phrase, that would ordinarily be set off by commas or parentheses.**

   She listed the qualities—a sense of humor, intelligence, consideration, and loyalty—that she's looking for in a husband.

3. **before an author's name at the end of a quotation to denote attribution.**

   "I love the ground under his feet, and the air over his head, and everything he touches, and every word he says. I love all his looks, and all his actions, and him entirely and altogether."
   —From Emily Brontë's *Wuthering Heights*

4. **to suggest faltering speech.**

   "Well—er—I—uh—just really don't know," he stammered.

   (When typing, use two hyphens for an em dash.)

Use an en dash:

1. **to connect continued (inclusive) numbers such as dates, time, or page references.**

   1900–94
   9:30 A.M.–5:00 P.M.
   March–April 1988
   pp. 14–36
   17 June 1975–25 August 1986

    but
from 1990 to 1994
from March to April, 1988
between 1991 and 1994
between 9:30 A.M. and 5:00 P.M.

2. **after the first number when the concluding date of a time period is in the future.**

    Dr. Kim Chan (1942–) was appointed chairman.

3. **instead of a hyphen in a compound adjective when one of the elements is an open (unhyphenated) compound, e.g., *Rhode Island*; or when two or more of the elements are hyphenated compounds.**

    New Jersey–Pennsylvania border
post–World War II baby boom
quasi-public–quasi-private project

(When typing, use a hyphen for an en dash.)

Use a 2-em dash to indicate missing letters, leaving no space between the dash and the existing part of the word—but where the dash represents the end of a word, insert a normal letter space.

    W——l [Warhol?]

    "What the h—— is going on here?"

Use a 3-em dash, inserting a space on each side, to indicate the omission of a whole word or one that will be supplied.

    A prominent social figure in Palm ——— held a press conference. . . .

    A ship that sailed for ——— in May. . . .

PARENTHESES ( )

Use parentheses:

1. **to enclose numbers or letters that list elements in a series.**

   Famous Shakespearean actors include (1) Sarah Bernhardt, (2) David Garrick, (3) Julia Marlowe, (4) Sir Laurence Olivier, and (5) the Barrymore family.

   She is considering specializing in (a) internal medicine, (b) gynecology, or (c) ophthalmology.

2. **to enclose, for confirmation, a numerical figure immediately following a spelled-out number.**

   Enclosed is a check for one hundred dollars ($100.00) for my annual dues.

3. **to enclose relevant material that is not part of the main sentence.**

   The two volumes of Liszt's *Hungarian Rhapsodies* (published by G. Schirmer) were awarded to the prizewinners.

4. **to enclose an amplifying element.**

   Jung's concept (see p. 9) was more cogent.

5. **to enclose clarifying information.**

   My college roommate got married last month and moved to Paris (Texas).

BRACKETS [ ]

Use brackets (also called *square brackets*):

1. **to enclose an insertion, usually an explanatory or editorial comment in quoted material, that was not part of the original quotation.**

According to the *Herald* art critic, "This [Botticelli's *Birth of Venus*] is one of the most famous paintings of the Italian Renaissance."

2. **to enclose stage directions, usually italicized, in the scripts of plays, motion pictures, or radio or television broadcasts. (Parentheses may also be used for this purpose.)**

THE GENERAL [*markedly*]: I hope you will always tell me the truth, my darling, at all events.

EDITH [*complacently coming to the fireplace*]: You can depend on me for that, Uncle Boxer.
   —From Bernard Shaw's *Getting Married*

3. **to enclose a correction of an error in a quotation.**

"Texas was an independent republic from 1836 to 1844 [1845—Ed.] and became the 28th state on December 29, 1845."

4. **to enclose the Latin word *sic*, meaning "thus," an editorial acknowledgment of deliberately quoting—for the sake of accuracy—an error in spelling, punctuation, or fact as it appeared in the original statement.**

"Gibraltar, which occupies a rocky peninsula on the southern shores of Spain, is separated from the African coast by the narrow Straits [*sic*] of Gibraltar." (*Straits* should be *Strait*.)

5. **to enclose a parenthetical expression within a parenthetical expression.**

[1]See "The Musical Impressionists" (Howard D. McKinney and W. R. Anderson, *Music in History—The Evolution of an Art* [New York, American Book Company, 1940]).

AMPERSAND   &boxed;&

Use an ampersand (a symbol that stands for the word *and*) when it is part of a company's formal name.

> Steinway & Sons

> Dun & Bradstreet Corp.

> Dow Jones & Co.

> Merrill Lynch & Co. Inc.

> American Telephone & Telegraph Co.
> (*AT&T* is acceptable on second reference, i.e., the second time the company is mentioned in copy.)

> Standard & Poor's Corp.

> Chesapeake & Ohio Railway Co.

> Great Atlantic & Pacific Tea Co. Inc.
> (*A&P* is acceptable on second reference.)

An ampersand may also be used in headings as the one for Chapter 8 in this book—"Abbreviations, Acronyms & Initialisms"—and is *not* preceded by a comma that usually separates the conjunction connecting the last two elements in a series.

• 3 •

Possessives

In English, nouns change form or *case* to become possessive by the addition of an apostrophe and an *s* (in most usages) to denote possession, ownership, origin, the performer of an act, or a type of item.

There are many variations in the use of the apostrophe as it indicates the possessive form for common and proper nouns, pronouns, compound words, joint and individual possession, descriptive names and phrases, and more. In addition to the following rules governing the possessive form, there is a quick-reference list of examples—including holidays, well-known phrases, organizations, and medical conditions—at the end of this chapter.

RULES FOR FORMING POSSESSIVES

1. For **singular nouns *not* ending in *s*,** add *'s: the dog's leash, a month's vacation.*

   EXCEPTION: For expressions in which a word ending in an *s* sound is followed by a word that begins with an *s*, use an apostrophe only: *for appearance' sake, for conscience' sake* but *her appearance's effect, my conscience's voice.*

2. For **singular nouns ending in *s*,** add *'s: the lioness's paws, the witness's testimony* unless the next word begins with an *s: the lioness' shoulder, the witness'*

story. The same applies to proper nouns: *James's book* but *James' schoolbooks.*

EXCEPTIONS: Ancient or classical proper names that would be awkward to pronounce with an added *'s* use only an apostrophe—*Moses' Laws, in Jesus' name*—or change the compound into a phrase using the preposition *of*—*Xerxes' chariot* or *the chariot of Xerxes, Isis' temple* or *the temple of Isis.*

3. For **plural nouns ending in** *s*, add an apostrophe only: *the churches' choirs, the potatoes' eyes.*

4. For **plural nouns** *not* **ending in** *s*, add *'s: children's games, the radii's measurements.*

5. For **nouns spelled the same in singular and plural**, treat as plurals regardless of whether the meaning is singular or plural: *a sheep's wool, the corps' drill.*

6. For **compound words**, add *'s* or an apostrophe alone to the word closest to the object possessed, whether the compound is singular or plural: *the attorney general's files, the attorneys general's files; the chief justice's files, the chief justices' files.*

   See Chapter 4, "Plural Forms," for guidelines governing plurals of compound words.

7. For **joint, multiple, or individual possession**, use a possessive form after the last word *only* if ownership is joint: *Bob and Carol's boat, Bob and Carol's Seafood Restaurant.* If possession is shared by three or more nouns, use the possessive case for the last noun in the series: *Ann, John, and David's father.*

   If the objects are individually owned, use a possessive form after both words: *Bob's and Carol's CD collections, Bob's and Carol's paintings.* The same applies to personal or family relationships: *Bob's and Carol's children from previous marriages.*

8. For **pronouns** designated as personal, interrogative, or relative pronouns—*my, mine, our, ours, your,*

yours, his, her, hers, its, their, theirs, whose—an apostrophe is not used. However, *'s* or an apostrophe alone is needed to form the possessives of indefinite pronouns: *another's desire, others' decisions, somebody else's hat, someone's dream.*

9. For **descriptive phrases**, an apostrophe is not required when the phrase is used in a descriptive sense: *a Boston Bruins goalie, a teachers college, the musicians union* (American Federation of Musicians).

   However, if the term includes a plural word not ending in *s*, add *'s: women's rights, a children's playground, the New York Philharmonic Young People's Concerts.*

10. For **descriptive names in possessive form** used by organizations of any kind, maintain the organizations' established styles: *Diners Club, National Governors' Association, PGA Seniors' Championship.*

11. For **modifying gerunds**, when a noun or pronoun is used before a gerund (a verb form ending in *-ing* that is used as a noun), the rules for possessive nouns apply: *the baby's walking so suddenly, the President's decision making.*

12. For **nouns involving time or money**, when used as possessive adjectives, the rules for possessive nouns apply: *after four months' therapy, buying one dollar's worth of candy.*

13. For **inanimate objects**, which do not normally "possess" anything, the possessive form using the preposition *of* is the accepted way to express a quality, arrangement, or part of an inanimate thing or things: *the gloom of night*, rather than *the night's gloom; the effects of AIDS*, rather than *the AIDS' effects.*

   The recent trend, however, has allowed more inanimate things to take the possessive form: *the razor's edge, the film's success, education's failure.*

14. For **personifications**, the rules for possessive nouns
    apply: *life's meaning, the breeze's murmur.*

COMMONLY MISPUNCTUATED POSSESSIVES

Achilles' heel
Achilles tendon
Actors' Equity Association
Adam's apple
Adam's rib
All Fools' Day
All Hallows' Day
All Saints' Day
All Souls' Day
Alzheimer's disease
Americas Cup *golf*
America's Cup *yachting*
April Fools' Day
arm's-length *adj*
arm's length *n*
athlete's foot

baby's breath
bachelor's
bachelor's degree
baker's dozen *thirteen*
baker's yeast
beeswax
Bell's palsy
bird's-eye, bird's-eyes
bird's-eye view
bird's-nest fern
bird's nest soup
Brill's disease
Brussels lace
bull's-eye, bull's-eyes
buyers' market

cashier's check
cat's cradle
cat's-eye, cat's-eyes
cat's meow
cat's-paw, cat's-paws

children's
child's play
citizens band
Cleopatra's Needle
cobbler's bench
collectors' item
Cook's tour
Cooley's anemia
crow's-foot, crow's-feet
crow's nest
Cupid's arrows
Cupid's bow

Davy Jones's locker
dead man's float
dean's list
death's-head
devil's advocate
devil's paintbrush
Diners Club
director's chair
dog's age
dog's life
Dow-Jones average
Down's syndrome
driver's license
driver's seat

Einstein's theory of
    relativity
elephant's-ear
elephant's-foot

farmers cooperative
farmer's lung
Father's Day
foolscap *or* fool's cap
fool's errand

fool's gold
fool's paradise
fuller's earth

gentleman's agreement
gentleman's gentleman
goatsbeard
God's acre
God's gift
Grant's Tomb

Halley's comet
harm's way
Harpers Ferry *or* Harper's
  Ferry
Hell's Kitchen
Hodgkin's disease
hornet's nest
horse's mouth
hound's-tooth check
hunter's moon
hunter's pink
Huntington's chorea

International Ladies'
  Garment Workers Union
International
  Longshoremen's and
  Warehousemen's Union

Jacob's ladder
Jehovah's Witnesses

king's English
king's-pawn openings
king's ransom

Ladies Professional Golf
  Association
ladies' room
lamb's wool
Lincoln's Birthday
Lions Club

lion's share
Lord's Prayer
Lord's Supper
lovers' lane
lover's leap
Love's Labour's Lost
  Shakespeare

maiden's-tears
mama's boy
man's man
mare's nest
master's
master's degree
Masters Tournament
Mendel's law
Ménière's disease
men's room
menswear
mind's eye
monkshood
Mother's Day
mother's helper
Murphy's Law

National Governors'
  Association
Newton's law of
  gravitation
New Year's, New Year's
  Day, New Year's Eve
no-man's-land
numbers game
numbers racket
nurse's aide

Pandora's box
Parkinson's Law
Parsons table
People's Republic of China
PGA Seniors'
  Championship
physician's assistant

pigs' feet
Pikes Peak
planter's punch
potter's clay
potter's wheel
Presidents' Day
Professional Golfers'
  Association of America

Queen Anne's lace
queen's English
queen's-pawn openings

rabbit's foot
Reserve Officers' Training
  Corps
robin's-egg blue
rogues' gallery

sailor's knot
Saint Agnes' Eve
Saint Andrew's cross
Saint Anthony's fire
Saint Elmo's fire
Saint John's bread *carob*
Saint Martin's summer
Saint Patrick's Day
saint's day
Saint Valentine's Day
Saint Vitus' dance *or* Saint
  Vitus's dance
savings and loan
  associations
sellers' market
shepherd's pie
ship's papers
snail's pace
state's evidence
states' righter
states' rights
stockmen's advisory

stone's throw
swimmer's ear
swimmer's itch

teachers college
teacher's pet
The Winter's Tale
  Shakespeare
tiger's-eye *or* tigereye
travelers' advisory
traveler's check

United Nations Day

Valentine's Day *or*
  Valentine Day
Venus's-flytrap
Veterans Administration
Veterans Day

Washington's Birthday
winner's circle
wit's end
wolfsbane
Woman's Christian
  Temperance Union
woman's rights, women's
  rights
Women's Army Corps
womenswear
workers' compensation
  insurance

Young Men's Christian
  Association
Young Men's Hebrew
  Association
Young Women's Christian
  Association
Young Women's Hebrew
  Association

• 4 •
Plural Forms

While most English words are spelled according to established rules, the exceptions to the rules—especially in forming plurals—make it difficult for even professional writers to apply automatically. A quick reference is often helpful. When a word has two or more plural forms, the first listed is the preferred one.

Most Nouns
Add *s: dogs, airplanes, skyscrapers.*

Nouns Ending in a Sibilant Sound: ch (soft), s, sh, ss, x, z
Add *es: benches, lenses, fetishes, kisses, taxes, quizzes.*
EXCEPTION: *monarchs,* which has a hard *ch.*

Nouns Ending in *f* or *fe*
Some add *s: briefs, roofs;* others add *s* or remain the same: *proofs* or *proof.* Most change the *f* or *fe* to *v* and add *es: elves, knives, loaves, sheaves, shelves, wives.* Others either add *s* or change the *f* to *v* and add *es: calves* or *calfs, dwarfs* or *dwarves, handkerchiefs* or *handkerchieves, hooves* or *hoofs, leaves* or *leafs.*

Nouns Ending in *is*
See "Nouns with Latin or Greek Roots" on the following page.

Nouns Ending in *o*
Some add *s: albinos, armadillos, kudos, memos, pianos, radios, ratios, rodeos, weirdos.*

Others add *es: heroes, potatoes, tomatoes, torpedoes, vetoes.* Some remain the same or add either *s* or *es: buffalo, buffaloes,* or *buffalos; dominoes* or *dominos; halos* or *haloes; tornadoes* or *tornados; zeros* or *zeroes.* **EXCEPTION:** *fiascoes* or *fiaschi.*

Nouns Ending in *y*
Add *s* if the *y* is preceded by a vowel: *bays, toys, monkeys.* If preceded by a consonant or *qu,* change the *y* to *i* and add *es: bevies, centuries, dictionaries, navies, soliloquies.*

Nouns with Latin or Greek Roots
Most **ending in *a*** change the *a* to *ae: alumna, alumnae.* Some ending in *a* either add *s* or change the *a* to *ae: amoeba, amoebas* or *amoebae; antenna, antennae* or *antennas; formula, formulas* or *formulae.*

Those **ending in *ex*** add *es* or change *ex* to *ic* before adding *es: apex, apexes* or *apices; index, indexes* or *indices.* **EXCEPTION:** *ibex, ibex* or *ibexes.*

Those **ending in *is*** change *is* to *es: analysis, analyses; basis, bases; crisis, crises; hypothesis, hypotheses; parenthesis, parentheses.* **EXCEPTION:** *ibis, ibis* or *ibises.*

Those **ending in *ix*** add *es* or change the *x* to *c* and add *es: appendix, appendixes* or *appendices; helix, helices* or *helixes; matrix, matrices* or *matrixes.*

Those **ending in *o*** (e.g., Italian musical terms) remain the same, change *o* to *i,* or add *s: cello, cello* or *celli; concerto, concerti* or *concertos.*

Those **ending in *on*** change *on* to *a* or add *s: criterion, criteria* or *criterions; phenomenon, phenomena* or *phenomenons.*

Those **ending in *um*** change *um* to *a* or add *s: addendum, addenda; atrium, atria* or *atriums; bacterium, bacteria; bacteria* (a genus, species, or strain), *bacterias; centrum, centrums* or *centra; compendium, compendiums* or *compendia; consortium, consortia* or *consortiums; continuum, continua* or *continuums; curriculum, curricula* or *curriculums; datum* (outdated word, *fact* preferred when referring to a single piece of data), *data* or *datums;*

erratum, errata; medium, mediums or *media; memorandum, memorandums* or *memoranda; podium, podiums* or *podia; referendum, referenda* or *referendums; sanitarium, sanitariums* or *sanitaria; stadium, stadia* or *stadiums.*

Most **ending in *us*** change *us* to *i: alumnus, alumni; bacillus, bacilli; stimulus, stimuli.* Others may also add *es: radius, radii* or *radiuses.*

Unusual Plural Forms

Among plurals formed irregularly are: *ox, oxen; brother, brethren; child, children.* Others change the vowel or double vowels: *man, men; woman, women; goose, geese; foot, feet; tooth, teeth.*

Some change form in other ways: *die, dice* or *dies; louse, lice; mouse, mice.* Some are spelled the same in singular *and* plural, and only the use of a singular or plural verb conveys the meaning of a particular sentence: *aircraft, corps, moose, offspring, sheep, species.*

Plural Nouns & Singular Usage

When a noun that is plural in meaning denotes a group or quantity that is regarded as a unit, it is called a *collective noun* and takes singular verbs and pronouns: *band, class, committee, crowd, data, family, group, herd, jury, orchestra, panel, team, trio.*

The band was playing my favorite song.
The committee is meeting today to set its August
    agenda.
The data (a unit) presented at yesterday's conference is
    sound.

EXCEPTION: The data (individual items) have been collected from the department heads.

Other words in this category that take singular verbs are: *measles, mumps, news.* However, others take singular or plural verbs, depending upon the sense of the sentence: *grits, scissors, tweezers.*

Plural Non-Nouns

Most add an *s* without an apostrophe; some use *s* or *'s*:

> There were too many "ifs," "ands," and "buts" in his proposal.

> the dos and don'ts (*or* do's and don'ts) of first aid

Compound Words

Some solid compounds—those without hyphens—add *s* at the end or make the most significant word plural: *cupfuls* or *cupsful, handfuls* or *handsful.*

Other compounds composed of separate words or words joined by a hyphen make the most significant word plural: *assistant attorneys, deputy sheriffs, aides-de-camp, mothers-in-law.*

Proper Names

Most add *s—two Alans and three Barbaras in my class, the Clintons, the O'Donnells*—including those ending in *y,* even if preceded by a consonant: *the Murphys, the two Amys, the eight King Henrys.* **EXCEPTIONS:** *Alleghenies* and *Rockies.*

A proper name ending in a sibilant adds *es: March, Marches; Harris, Harrises; Charles, Charleses; Jones, Joneses; Tesh, Teshes; Gless, Glesses; Max, Maxes; Lopez, Lopezes.* NOTE: Do not use an apostrophe to denote the plural form of personal names.

Letters

For a single letter, add *'s*:

> He knew his p's and q's.
> She received all A's on her report card.
> He played the three B's on the piano by age eight.

For multiple letters and abbreviations, add *s* except for academic degrees:

> He learned the ABCs of golf from his father.
> I gave him two IOUs.
> Two PhD's and four VIPs with high IQs were there.

(Some stylebooks add 's or s to single or multiple letters and abbreviations; others add s alone to single or multiple letters and abbreviations.)

Italicized Words
For italicized names such as newspapers and book titles that are singular in form, the s at the end is not italicized. If the name is itself plural, no other ending is required. Plural forms of italicized foreign words are set entirely in italics.

two *Boston Globe*s   three *New York Times*
journal, journaux

SINGULAR & PLURAL FORMS

addendum, addenda
adjutant general, adjutants general
agenda, agendas
    Agenda takes singular verb and pronoun.
aircraft, aircraft
albino, albinos
alley, alleys
alumna, alumnae *f*
alumnus, alumni *m*
    Use *alumni* when referring to a group of men and
    women.
ambassador-at-large, ambassadors-at-large
amoeba, amoebas *or* amoebae
analysis, analyses
and, ands
anecdote, anecdotes *or* anecdota
antenna, antennae *or* antennas
apex, apexes *or* apices
appendix, appendixes *or* appendices
armadillo, armadillos
assistant attorney, assistant attorneys
assistant attorney general, assistant attorneys general
assistant corporation counsel, assistant corporation
    counsels
assistant counsel, assistant counsels
atrium, atria *or* atriums
attorney-at-law, attorneys-at-law

attorney general, attorneys general *or* attorney generals
attorney general-designate, attorneys general-designate *or*
    attorney generals-designate
auto, autos
ax, axes
axis, axes

bacchanal, bacchanalia
bacillus, bacilli
bacteria, bacterias
bacterium, bacteria
bagful, bagfuls *or* bagsful
barrelful, barrelfuls *or* barrelsful
basis, bases
basketful, basketfuls *or* basketsful
battle royal, battles royal *or* battle royals
bevy, bevies
biceps, biceps *or* bicepses
bichon frise, bichons frises
bill of lading, bills of lading
biscuit, biscuits *or* biscuit
bison, bison
box, boxes
brief, briefs
brigadier general, brigadier generals
bronco, broncos
brother, brothers *or* brethren
brother-in-law, brothers-in-law
bucketful, bucketfuls *or* bucketsful
buffalo, buffalo *or* buffaloes *or* buffalos
bull's-eye, bull's-eyes
bus, buses *or* busses
buss, busses
but, buts
butt, butts
buzz, buzzes

cactus, cacti *or* cactuses *or* cactus
calf, calves *or* calfs
calypso, calypsos *or* calypsoes
cargo, cargoes *or* cargos
carp, carp *or* carps
carrying-on, carryings-on

carte blanche, cartes blanches [F, lit., blank document] *full discretionary power*

carte du jour, cartes du jour [F, lit., card of the day] *menu*

casino, casinos

castle in the air, castles in the air

catch-22, catch-22's *or* catch-22s (*often cap*)

cat's-eye, cat's-eyes

cat's-paw, cat's-paws

cease-fire, cease-fires (verb form: *cease fire*)

cello, cello *or* celli (short for *violoncello* [It])

centrum, centrums *or* centra

chantey, chanteys *or* chanties

charge-off, charge-offs

chassis, chassis

château, châteaus *or* châteaux

cheetah, cheetahs *or* cheetah

cherub (a celestial being or angel), cherubim

cherub (a beautiful or innocent person), cherubs

chief justice, chief justices

child, children

chili, chilies

citrus, citrus *or* citruses

city, cities

cloverleaf, cloverleafs *or* cloverleaves

coat of arms, coats of arms

coat of mail, coats of mail *armor*

commander in chief, commanders in chief

compendium, compendia *or* compendiums

concerto, concerti *or* concertos

condominium, condominiums

congressman at large, congressmen at large

congresswoman at large, congresswomen at large

consortium, consortia *or* consortiums

consul general, consuls general

continuum, continua *or* continuums

controller general, controllers general

cookie, cookies

corgi, corgis

corps, corps [F, fr. L *corpus* body]

councilman at large, councilmen at large

councilwoman at large, councilwomen at large

coup d'état, coups d'état *or* coup d'etat, coups d'etat

[F, lit., stroke of state] *a violent change in government* (The word *coup* or *coups* usually is sufficient.)

court-martial, courts-martial *or* court-martials

covey, coveys

coyote, coyotes *or* coyote

cranium, craniums *or* crania

crêpe suzette, crêpes suzette *or* crêpe suzettes

crisis, crises

criterion, criteria *or* criterions

crux, cruxes *or* cruces

cul-de-sac, culs-de-sac *or* cul-de-sacs [F, lit., bottom of the bag] *a street closed at one end; a blind alley*

cupful, cupfuls *or* cupsful

curriculum, curricula *or* curriculums

curriculum vitae, curricula vitae

datum, data *or* datums

daughter-in-law, daughters-in-law

deer, deer

deputy chief of staff, deputy chiefs of staff

deputy sheriff, deputy sheriffs

dictionary, dictionaries

die, dice *or* dies

dinghy, dinghies

dingo, dingoes

doctor of philosophy, doctors of philosophy

doe, does

dominatrix, dominatrices

domino, dominoes

donkey, donkeys

dry, drys *n*

dwarf, dwarfs *or* dwarves

echo, echoes

editor in chief, editors in chief

ego, egos

elf, elves

elk, elk *or* elks

ellipsis, ellipses

Emmy, Emmys *television award*

enfant terrible, enfants terribles [F, lit., terrifying child]

erratum, errata

fait accompli, faits accomplis [F, lit., accomplished fact]
　a thing already done and presumed irreversible
falling-out, fallings-out *or* falling-outs
father-in-law, fathers-in-law
faux pas, faux pas [F, lit., false stop] *a social blunder*
fee simple, fees simple
fiasco, fiascoes *or* fiaschi
fish, fish *or* fishes
fizz, fizzes
fly, flies
focus, foci
folk, folk *or* folks
foot, feet *or* foot
formula, formulas *or* formulae
forum, forums *or* fora
fowl, fowl *or* fowls

gazelle, gazelles *or* gazelle
gentleman farmer, gentlemen farmers
get-together, get-togethers
ghetto, ghettos
go-between, go-betweens
godchild, godchildren
goose, geese
governor-general, governors-general *or* governor-generals
grande dame, grandes dames *or* grande dames [F, lit.,
　great lady]
grant-in-aid, grants-in-aid
gravy, gravies
grotto, grottoes *or* grottos
gymnasium, gymnasiums *or* gymnasia

hairdo, hairdos
halo, halos *or* haloes
handful, handfuls *or* handsful
handkerchief, handkerchiefs *or* handkerchieves
hanger-on, hangers-on
heir apparent, heirs apparent
helix, helices *or* helixes
hero, heroes
history, histories
hole-in-the-wall, holes-in-the-wall
holiday, holidays

hoof, hooves *or* hoofs
hypothesis, hypotheses

ibis, ibis *or* ibises
Idaho (potato), Idahos *or* Idahoes
index, indexes *or* indices
injury, injuries
Inuit, Inuit *or* Inuits
ivy, ivies

jack-of-all-trades, jacks-of-all-trades
Joint Chief of Staff, Joint Chiefs of Staff
judge advocate, judge advocates
judge advocate general, judge advocates general
jury, juries
justice of the peace, justices of the peace

kangaroo, kangaroos
knife, knives
kudo, kudos

l, ll *abbreviation for* line(s)
leaf, leaves *or* leafs
lean-to, lean-tos
lens, lenses
lieutenant colonel, lieutenant colonels
lieutenant governor, lieutenant governors
limbo, limbos
loaf, loaves
locus, loci
looker-on, lookers-on
louse, lice

MA, MA's
maestro, maestros *or* maestri
maître d' *or* maitre d', maître d's *or* maitre d's
maître d' hôtel, maîtres d'hôtel [F, lit., master of (the)
   hotel] *headwaiter*
major general, major generals
man, men
master of arts, masters of arts
matrix, matrices *or* matrixes
maximum, maxima *or* maximums

medium, mediums *or* media
medley, medleys
memo, memos
memorandum, memorandums *or* memoranda
millennium, millennia *or* millenniums
million, millions *or* million
minimum, minima *or* minimums
minister resident, ministers resident
mink, mink *or* minks
minnow, minnows *or* minnow
monarch, monarchs
monkey, monkeys
moose, moose
mother-in-law, mothers-in-law
motto, mottoes
mouse, mice
mover and shaker, movers and shakers
Mr., Messrs.
Mrs., Mmes.
Ms., Mss. *or* Mses.
MS, MSS *abbreviation for* manuscript(s)

n, nn *abbreviation for* note(s)
nevus, nevi
newborn, newborn *or* newborns
nexus, nexuses *or* nexus
nitro, nitros
nouveau riche, nouveaux riches [F, lit., new rich]
nucleus, nuclei

oasis, oases
Obie, Obies *theater award*
opossum, opossums *or* opossum
ox, oxen

p, pp *abbreviation for* page(s)
palazzo, palazzi [It, fr. L *palatium* palace]
parenthesis, parentheses
passer-by, passers-by
patina, patinas *or* patinae
patois, patois
peccadillo, peccadilloes *or* peccadillos
person, people

PhD, PhD's
phenomenon, phenomena *or* phenomenons
piano, pianos
piccolo, piccolos
pièce de résistance, pièces de résistance [F, lit., piece of resistance] *special or prized feature*
podium, podiums *or* podia
poet laureate, poets laureate *or* poet laureates
postmaster general, postmasters general
potato, potatoes
POW, POWs
president-elect, presidents-elect
princess royal, princesses royal
prisoner of war, prisoners of war
prix fixe, prix fixes [F, lit., fixed price] *a complete meal offered at a fixed price; the price charged*
proof, proofs *or* proof
proviso, provisos
provost marshal, provost marshals
pulley, pulleys

quail, quail *or* quails
quality, qualities
quantity, quantities
quantum, quanta
quarto, quartos
queen consort, queens consort
quiz, quizzes

radio, radios
radius, radii *or* radiuses
radix, radices *or* radixes
ratio, ratios
referendum, referenda *or* referendums
rendezvous, rendezvous
right-of-way, rights-of-way *or* right-of-ways
rodeo, rodeos
roof, roofs
runner-up, runners-up

salmon, salmon *or* salmons
salvo, salvos
sanitarium, sanitariums *or* sanitaria

scarf, scarves *or* scarfs
scenario, scenarios
schema, schemata *or* schemas
scherzo, scherzos *or* scherzi
secretary-general, secretaries-general
seed, seed *or* seeds
self, selves
sergeant-at-arms, sergeants-at-arms
sergeant major, sergeants major *or* sergeant majors
shampoo, shampoos
sheaf, sheaves
sheep, sheep
shelf, shelves
shih tzu, shih tzus *or* shih tzu
silo, silos
sister-in-law, sisters-in-law
soliloquy, soliloquies
son-in-law, sons-in-law
son of a gun, sons of guns
stadium, stadia *or* stadiums
stigma, stigmata
stimulus, stimuli
Stradivarius, Stradivari *violin(s)*
swine, swine
symposium, symposia *or* symposiums

tablespoonful, tablespoonfuls *or* tablespoonsful
tam-o'-shanter, tam-o'-shanters
tango, tangos
taxi, taxis *or* taxies
teaspoonful, teaspoonfuls *or* teaspoonsful
theater-in-the-round, theaters-in-the-round
thesis, theses
thing-in-itself, things-in-themselves
thousand, thousands *or* thousand
tomato, tomatoes
Tony, Tonys *theater award*
tooth, teeth
tornado, tornadoes *or* tornados
torpedo, torpedoes
torso, torsos *or* torsi
tour de force, tours de force [F, feat of strength or skill]
  a feat requiring unusual strength, skill, or ingenuity

tuna, tuna *or* tunas
turf, turfs *or* turves
tuxedo, tuxedos *or* tuxedoes

UFO, UFO's *or* UFOs
umbilicus, umbilici *or* umbilicuses
utopia, utopias

vacancy, vacancies
vagary, vagaries
valley, valleys
vertex, vertices *or* vertexes
vertigo, vertigoes *or* vertigos
veto, vetoes
viola da gamba, violas da gamba *or* viole da gamba [It,
    lit., viol for the leg]
violoncello, violoncello *or* violoncelli [It, equiv. to
    violon(e) VIOLONE + -*cello* dim. suffix]
volcano, volcanoes *or* volcanos
volley, volleys
vortex, vortices *or* vortexes

weirdo, weirdos
wheeler and dealer, wheelers and dealers
whiz *or* whizz, whizzes
wife, wives
wolf, wolves
woman, women

yak, yaks *or* yak

zebra, zebras *or* zebra
zero, zeros *or* zeroes

Expressing Numbers

*N*umbers, words that denote *quantity*, have been used since prehistoric times when human beings first found it necessary to count their possessions—initially, by simple tallying methods, making marks or collecting objects such as pebbles and shells. Later, people began using words for this purpose and developed an assortment of written symbols to stand for numbers—*numerals*.

Of the many numerical systems developed by early civilizations, two remain in widespread use, *roman* (200 B.C.) and *arabic* (A.D. 800), the familiar 1, 2, 3, etc. While it is simple to add and subtract with roman numerals, the system proved inconvenient and cumbersome for other types of calculations and was replaced by the easier arabic-numeral system in the late 1500s.

ROMAN NUMERALS

The roman numeral system uses capital letters to express its seven basic numerals: I(1), V(5), X(10), L(50), C(100), D(500), and M(1,000)—there is no numeral for *zero* or *million*. Today, roman numerals are used mainly to: establish sequence of wars and personal sequence for people and animals; number the faces of timepieces, volumes and chapters of books, and division of plays; list important topics in outlines; and record dates on monuments and public buildings.

Lowercase roman numerals are frequently used for page numbers and headings in the opening and closing sections of books, for subheading lists in outlines, and scene division of plays.

World War I	WWI
Native Dancer II	WWII
King Henry VIII	
Pope John XXIII	
Frank Edward	
Wainwright III	

Act I, Scene ii (*or* Act I, Scene 2 *or* Act 1, Scene 2 *or* act 1, scene 2)

Some individuals prefer to use the notation *II* or *2nd* instead of *Jr.* However, *II* or *2nd* may refer to a grandson or nephew, as well as to a son.

Roman numerals are written left to right, starting with the thousands, then the hundreds and tens, and finally the units. The principles of addition and subtraction are applied in designating the numerical symbols.

Added—the value of a letter that *follows* another letter of equal or greater value: III=3, VI=6, XII=12.

Subtracted—the value of a letter that *precedes* another letter of greater value: 4=IV (or 5 minus 1), 9=IX (or 10 minus 1).

The same principle applies to any number beginning with a 4 or 9: 40=XL, 90=XC, 400=CD, 900=CM.

Thus, the arabic number *3,867* is written in roman numerals as *MMMDCCCLXVII*, arrived at by the following steps:

1. MMM (3,000)
2. DCCC (500+300=800)
3. LX (50+10=60)
4. VII (7)

ROMAN	ARABIC	ROMAN	ARABIC
I	1	XL	40
II	2	L	50
III	3	LX	60
IV	4	LXX	70
V	5	LXXX	80
VI	6	XC	90
VII	7	C	100
VIII	8	CC	200
IX	9	CCI	201
X	10	CCC	300
XI	11	CD	400
XII	12	D	500
XIII	13	DC	600
XIV	14	DCC	700
XV	15	DCCC	800
XVI	16	CM	900
XVII	17	M	1,000
XVIII	18	MCMXCIII	1993
XIX	19	MCMXCIV	1994
XX	20	MM	2,000
XXX	30	MMI	2001

To write larger numbers, a *vinculum,* or bar, is sometimes placed over a number to multiply it by 1,000.

$\overline{\text{DCCLVI}}$CCLXXXI   756,281

(To demonstrate the clumsiness of using roman numerals for large numbers, multiply 283×54. The answer in arabic numerals is 15,282; in roman, MMMMMMMMMMMMMMMCCLXXXII.)

ARABIC NUMERALS

Arabic numerical figures—*1, 2, 3, 4, 5, 6, 7, 8, 9, 10*—are used in two ways: as cardinal numbers or ordinal numbers.

Cardinal numbers are any numbers or combination of numbers that express *amount,* such as: one (1), two (2), three (3). Their corresponding words may be used as nouns, pronouns, or adjectives.

She counted to ten.
Ten attended the meeting.
The Egyptians developed a 365-day year.
According to the Bible, Moses gave the Ten
    Commandments on Mount Sinai.

Ordinal numbers are used as adjectives to express degree, quality, or position in an order of succession regarding such entities as names, objects, and periods of time.

to the nth degree
the 10th Amendment
the tenth row center
the tenth century
the 38th parallel (Korean War)

WHEN TO USE FIGURES OR WORDS

What determines the choice between using figures or spelling out any particular number depends upon such factors as:

(1) whether the text in which the number appears is humanistic (i.e., literary or philosophical), scientific, or technological; (2) whether the number is large, small, a fraction, an approximation, or an exact quantity; and (3) the essential nature of the number enumerated. Authorities on style—such as publishers of books, newspapers, and scholarly journals—are not always in agreement on this subject. However, the following guidelines are commonly used.

In *formal writing,* whole numbers from *one through ninety-nine* are spelled out, as are hyphenated numbers (such as *twenty-one through twenty-nine*) when used alone or part of a larger number that is spelled out.

The first talking picture was made over eighty years
    ago.
My daughter will be thirty-two years old in December.

Also spelled out are whole numbers followed by *hundred, thousand, hundred thousand, million, billion,* etc.

My ancestors came from England over three hundred
years ago.

If a number between one thousand and ten thousand can
be expressed in terms of hundreds, spelling it out is preferable.

She wrote her autobiography in less than ninety-five
hundred words.

In *casual writing,* the numbers *one* to *nine* are spelled
out, and larger numbers are expressed in numerals.

Two's company, three's a crowd.
I fell overboard on my 20th day at sea.

In *casual expressions,* spell out numbers.

A million thanks!
A cast of thousands

In writing *dates or other serial numbers,* generally do not
spell out. Write them in arabic figures (without *nd, rd, st,*
or *th*) or in roman notation according to which is appropriate.

June 6, 1944   Chapter XII *or* Chapter 12
Rule 5   Napoleon III

Spell out when they occur in *dialogue.*

"I arrived home from Europe on August ninth."
"I was married in 1970 on my twenty-first birthday."
"I shall read Chapter Twelve tonight."

In writing *fractions,* spell out amounts less than one and
hyphenate.

one-third   one-half   seven-eighths

In writing *percentages,* use figures (even those with dec-
imals) and repeat *percent* with each figure. For amounts

under 1 percent, place a zero before the decimal. In tables or statistical reporting, the symbol % may be used.

    0.4 percent   4.5 percent
    1 percent   99.4 percent
    The weatherman predicted a 20 percent to 30 percent chance of more rain for today.

In *organizational names that contain numbers,* spell out or use numerals according to the organizations' established styles.

    Century 21
    Twentieth Century Fund, Inc.
    First Trade Union Savings Bank

In writing *addresses,* it is preferable, space permitting, to spell out the names of numbered streets of one hundred or less.

    Fifty-seventh Street
    Third Avenue

Building numbers are written in numerals unless a building's name is its address, in which case the number is often spelled out.

    4903 Tenison Court, Austin, Texas 78731
    One Longfellow Place   Two Fifth Avenue

In writing *highway designations,* all numbers should be written as figures.

    U.S. Highway 1
    State Route 1, Box 20
    Interstate Highway 495
    Interstate 495 *or* Interstate I-495

When *a letter or letters follow a number,* use capitals but no hyphens.

    Route 1A *or* A1A (for alternate route)

In writing *years,* use figures unless the year is the first word of a sentence.

the 1990s, the '90s
Nineteen ninety was a year for great technological advances.

In writing *words in a series,* use the guidelines listed previously.

My family had two horses, four pigs, and 10 dogs.

In expressing *ages,* usually use figures and hyphenate those in adjectival form before a noun or when used as a substitute for a noun.

The race at Churchill Downs today is for 3-year-olds.

I started playing the piano when I was 7 years old.

My sister, 15, began ballet lessons at age 8.

My 9-year-old best friend took accordion lessons.

My son's violin teacher is in his 40s.

There is a large diversity in expressing numbers—ranging from court decisions, monetary units, and scores (using cardinal numbers) to geographic, military, and political designations (using ordinal numbers). The following sentences contain a sampling of common numerical and capitalization usages:

The U.S. Court of Appeals is divided into 13 circuits including the Federal Circuit and the Second Circuit based in New York that include three states: Connecticut, New York, and Vermont.

I attended Public School 3.

Boston University was my No. 1 choice.

My sister was one of 835 first-year students who entered the teachers college in 1993.

Our mother graduated from Ohio State University one year after our uncle.

It was a 6 to 5 board decision to cut the annual budget by $15 million.

Bake in an 8-inch × 12-inch pan in a 350-degree oven for 20 to 30 minutes.

Samuel Morgan was a first lieutenant in World War II who served with the 103rd Infantry ("Cactus") Division during the French Liberation. His brother, Petty Officer First Class Leo Morgan, served two years with the Seventh Fleet in the South Pacific.

· 6 ·

Redundancies & Clichés

To achieve the goal of writing clear, fresh, and effective prose, two types of expressions should be avoided—redundancies and clichés.

Redundancy, a word used since Shakespeare's time, means the needless repetition or overlapping of words or ideas. Occasionally a redundancy is permissible, as in the case of *OPEC countries* (OPEC is the acronym for *Organizations of Petroleum Exporting Countries*). There are also some redundant phrases, such as *false pretenses* and *joined together,* that have withstood the test of time.

To eliminate redundancy, delete the italicized elements in the phrases:

> assemble *together* ("assemble" means to bring or
>   gather together);
> big *in size* ("big" means of considerable size);
> *fellow* colleagues ("colleague" means a fellow member
>   of a profession, staff, or academic faculty).

Cliché, a French word [lit., printer's stereotype] in English usage for over a century, means a trite, time-worn phrase, usually expressing a common thought or idea that has lost its originality. Occasionally a cliché is permissible—when there is no better way to express a thought or for emphasis. Using a redundancy could be described as *gilding the lily,* an antiquated cliché.

In the following lists are several phrases that are also termed *oxymoronic*—referring to a figure of speech called an *oxymoron,* a combination of contradictory or incongruous words.

REDUNDANCIES

ABM missiles
absolutely conclusive
active consideration
advance planning
agricultural crop
AIDS syndrome
all-time record
anthracite coal
ascend upward
assemble together

basic fundamental
big in size
bisect in two
blend together

capitol building
chief *or* leading *or* main protagonist
close proximity
coalesce together
collaborate jointly *or* together
competitive contest
completely full
completely unanimous
congregate together
connect together
consensus of opinion
continue to persist
controversial issue
courthouse building
current *or* present incumbent

descend downward
doctorate degree

endorse (a check) on the back
enormous giant
erupt violently
explode violently

factual information
fellow colleague
few and far between
few in number
finish completing
first beginning
forcible rape
founder and sink
free gift
from where
fuse together
future planning
future potential

gather together
general consensus
giant jumbo shrimp *also oxymoronic*
great masterpiece
great masterwork

habitual custom
hoist up
hollow tube
hollow tunnel
hostile attack

individual person

join together

knots per hour

large in size

merge together
monstrous ogre
more *or* most flawless
more *or* most ideal
more *or* most perfect
more *or* most unique

new innovation
new record
new recruit

old antique
old cliché
opening gambit
original prototype

passing fad
past history
personal remembrance
pointed barb
potential future
protrude out

rarely ever
real fact
reason why
recall back
recur again *or* repeatedly
refer back
rescue ambulance
Rio Grande River [Sp, lit.,
    river large river]

scuba apparatus
self-confessed
short in length *or* height
shuttle back and forth
Sierra Nevada Mountains
    [Sp, lit., *mountain range
    snow-clad* mountains]
skirt around
small dwarf
small in size
smile on your face

tall in height
temporary reprieve
10 a.m. in the morning
10 p.m. at night
three triplets
total entirety
totally demolished
totally destroyed
true reality
12 midnight
12 noon
two twins

unexpected surprise
universal panacea
uphill struggle

viable alternative
violent explosion
visible to the eye

widow of the late
widower of the late

How many redundancies are in the following sentences?

It was absolutely conclusive that the violent explosion in the hollow tunnel was in close proximity to the completely full trucks carrying agricultural crops.

He was an enormous giant of a man, a brilliant genius who almost never made a mistake.

It was virtually necessary, although an uphill struggle, to set a new record in the competitive contest for being the leader in her field.

CLICHÉS

acid test
according to Hoyle
add insult to injury
afraid of his/her own
    shadow
age before beauty
aid and abet
all in a day's work
all over but the shouting
all things (being)
    considered
all things being equal
all things to all people
all work and no play
American as apple pie
ancient history
another fish to fry
apple of one's eye
arm and a leg
armed to the teeth
as cute as a button
asleep at the switch
asleep at the wheel
as luck would have it
as young as you feel
at a loss for words
at arm's length
at a tender age
at first blush
at one fell swoop
avoid like the plague
ax to grind

babe in the woods

backhanded compliment
bad blood (between them)
bag and baggage
bald as a billiard ball
bald as a coot
ball of fire
bane of one's existence
banker's hours
bark up the wrong tree
be-all and end-all
beat a dead horse
beat a hasty retreat
beat around the bush
beauty and the beast
beck and call
bed of roses
beg the question
bend over backward
benefit of the doubt
best foot forward
best-laid plans
better late than never
between a (the) rock and a
    (the) hard place
between the devil and the
    deep blue sea
betwixt and between
beyond the call of duty
beyond the shadow of a
    doubt
big as a house
big as all outdoors
bigger than life
bigger than the both of us

bite off more than one can chew
bite the bullet
bite the dust
bits and pieces
bitter end
black as pitch
black as the ace of spades
blazing inferno *also redundant*
blessed event
blessing in disguise
blew up like a balloon
blind as a bat
blissful ignorance
bloody but unbowed
blow hot and cold
blow off steam
blow one's mind
blow one's top
blow the whistle
blue in the face
blunt and brutal
blushing bride
bolt from the blue
bone of contention
bottomless pit
bound and determined
brave as a bull
brave as a lion
breathe a sigh of relief
breath of fresh air
breath of spring air
bright and early
bright-eyed and bushy-tailed
bring home the bacon
broad daylight
brown as a berry
budding genius
bull in a china shop
burning issue
burning question

burning the candle at both ends
burn one's bridges
burn the midnight oil
bury the hatchet
busman's holiday
busy as a beaver
busy as a bee
by leaps and bounds
by the same token
by word of mouth

calm before the storm
came out smelling like a rose
can't beat a dead horse
can't see the forest for the trees
capacity crowd
cardinal sin
caught red-handed
checkered career
cherished belief
chip off the old block
clean as a hound's tooth
clean as a whistle
clear and simple
clear as a bell
clear as mud
clear the decks
clever like a fox
coin a phrase
cold as ice
colorful scene
come on like gangbusters
comfortable as an old shoe
confused and bewildered
conspicuous by one's absence
cool as a cucumber
coveted award
crack troops
crazy as a bedbug

crazy as a coot
crazy as a loon
crazy like a fox
cried like a baby
cross as a bear
cruel kindness *also
    oxymoronic*
crux of the matter
crying need
curvaceous blonde
cut a long story short
cute as a bug's ear
cute as a button
cute as pie

damned if you do, damned
    if you don't
dead as a doornail
dead giveaway
deaf as a post
deep as the ocean
delicate as a flower
depths of despair
diamond in the rough
dictates of conscience
different as apples and
    oranges
different as night and day
discreet silence
disgraced and dishonored
do one's thing
down and out
down in the dumps
down in the mouth
down one's alley
down the primrose path
dramatic new move
drastic action
draw the line
dread disease
dream come true
drink like a fish
drop in the bucket

dropped it like a hot potato
dropping like flies
drunk as a lord
drunk as a skunk
dry as a bone
dry as dust
dull as dishwater (*actually*
    ditchwater)
dull thud
dumb as an ox

each and every
each individual
ear to the ground
easier said than done
easy as falling off a log
easy as pie
easy pickings
eat like a bird
eat like a pig
eat like there was no
    tomorrow
eat one's hat
eat one's heart out
eat one's words
eloquent silence
epic struggle
eternal reward

face that could stop a clock
face the music
fair and just
fair and square
fair sex
fall on deaf ears
fame and fortune
far be it from me
far cry
fast and loose
fast as lightning
fat as a pig
fate worse than death
feast or famine

feather in one's cap
feel one's oats
few and far between
fickle fortune
fight like cats and dogs
fill the bill
fine kettle of fish
first and foremost
fit as a fiddle
fits and starts
fits like a glove
fit the bill
fix it like new
flash in the pan
flat as a pancake
flea in one's ear
flesh and blood
food for thought
foot in one's mouth
for all intents and purposes
foregone conclusion
foreseeable future
free as a bird
free as the air
fresh as a daisy

generation gap
generous to a fault
gentle as a lamb
gentle hint
get down to brass tacks
get one's back up
get one's dander up
gift of gab
gild the lily
give it one's best shot
glaring omission
glutton for punishment
go against the grain
goes without saying
good as gold
gory details
grain of salt

green as grass
green-eyed monster
grew like a weed
grief-stricken
Grim Reaper
grin and bear it
grind to a halt
guilty as sin

hairy as an ape
hammer out (an agreement)
hand in glove
hand over fist
handwriting on the wall
hapless victim
happy as a clam
happy as a lark
happy couple
hard as a rock
hard row to hoe
haul over the coals
have a foot in the door
have a leg up
have a shoo-in
head over heels (in love)
healthy as a horse
heart of gold
heart of the matter
heave a sigh of relief
here today, gone tomorrow
high and dry
high as a kite
high on the hog
hit her/him like a ton of
    bricks
hit the nail on the head
hit the spot
honest as the day is long
hook, line, and sinker
hook or crook
hot as an oven
hot as a pistol
hot as blazes

hue and cry
hungry as a bear
hungry as a horse

in close proximity *also redundant*
in like Flynn
innocent as a lamb
innocent as a newborn babe
in no uncertain terms
in on the ground floor
in seventh heaven
intensive investigation
in the final analysis
in the long run
in the nick of time
in the twinkling of an eye
in this day and age
iron out (problems)
irons in the fire
irrelevant and immaterial
irreparable damage
irreparable loss

jig is up
just deserts
just what the doctor ordered

keep a low profile
keep one's chin up
knock on wood

labor of love
lady luck
lash out
last but not least
last-ditch stand
last straw
lean and hungry look
lean over backward
leaps and bounds

leave in the lurch
leave no stone unturned
left-handed compliment
lend a helping hand
let nature take its course
let one's hair down
let the cat out of the bag
let well enough alone
lick into shape
lie like a rug
light as a feather
light at the end of the tunnel
lightning speed
like a house afire
like a house on fire
like pulling teeth
limp as a dishrag
limp into port
lit up like a Christmas tree
live like a king
load off my mind
lock, stock, and barrel
long arm of coincidence
long arm of the law
loose as a goose
lower than a snake's belly

mad as a hatter
mad as a hornet
mad as a wet hen
mad dash
madder than hell
make a long story short
make bricks without straw
make (both) ends meet
make hay while the sun shines
make no bones about it
make out like a bandit
man in the street
marvels of science
matrimonial bliss

matrimonial knot
matter of life and death
meager pension
meet one's Waterloo
melts like butter
memory like an elephant('s)
memory like a sieve
method in one's madness
mince words
miraculous escape
miss the boat
month of Sundays
moot point
moot question
more than meets the eye
more the merrier
Mother Nature
motley crew
move into high gear

naked as a jaybird
naked as the day you were born
naked truth
neat as a pin
necessary evil
needle in a haystack
neither fish nor fowl
neither here nor there
neither hide nor hair
nervous and distraught
nervous as a kitten
nervous in the service
never a dull moment
never rains but it pours
never say die
newborn babe
new lease on life
new wrinkle
nice as can be
nip in the bud
no holds barred

none the worse for wear
nook and cranny
no sooner said than done
not a moment too soon
nothing new under the sun
null and void
nutty as a fruitcake

odds and ends
off (out of) one's gourd
off one's rocker
old as Methuselah
Old Man Winter
once and for all
once in a blue moon
on cloud nine
on the horns of a dilemma
open secret *also oxymoronic*
opportunity knocks
other side of the coin
out like a light
out of harm's way
out of the frying pan and into the fire
over a barrel
over the hill
own worst enemy

paint a grim picture
paint the town red
pale as a ghost
part and parcel
pay the piper
pay the supreme penalty
penny for one's thoughts
penny-wise, pound-foolish
perfect gentleman
pet peeve
phony as a three-dollar bill
pick and choose
picture of health
piece of cake

pillar of society
pillar of the church
pillar of the community
pinpoint the cause
plain as day
plain as the nose on your
 face
play it by ear
point with pride
police dragnet
pool of blood
poor as a churchmouse
poor but honest
poor excuse for a man/
 woman
posh resort
powder keg
powers that be
predawn darkness
prestigious law firm
pretty as a picture
pretty penny
proud as a peacock
proud heritage
proud parents
psychological moment
pure and simple
pure as the driven snow
pursuit of excellence
put the cart before the
 horse

quick as a bunny
quick as a flash
quick as a wink
quiet as a mouse

racing heart
rack one's brains
radiant bride
rain cats and dogs
raise Cain
read (someone) the riot act

ready and willing
red as a beet
red as a lobster
red-faced, red faces
red-letter day
reign supreme
reins of government
reliable source
render a decision
rich as Croesus
right and proper
right as rain
ring true
ripe old age
rolls off her/him like water
 off a duck's back
rough as sandpaper
rub one the wrong way
run like a deer
run like the wind
rushed to the scene

sadder but wiser
safe and sound
save for a rainy day
scantily clad
scarce as hen's teeth
scintilla of evidence
seal one's doom
seal one's fate
second to none
seething mass of humanity
sell(ing) like hotcakes
separate the men from the
 boys
separate the women from
 the girls
serve one right
set one's teeth on edge
shake a leg
shaking like a leaf
sharp as a tack
shoot your wad

shot in the arm
show one's hand
shun like the plague
shy and withdrawn
sick and tired
sick as a dog
sigh of relief
sight for sore eyes
silent as a tomb
silly as a goose
six of one and half-dozen
   of the other
skeleton in one's closet
skinny as a rail
slept like a baby
slept like a log
slept like a top
slippery as an eel
slow as molasses (in
   January)
sly as a fox
small world
smell a rat
smoke like a chimney
smooth and silky
smooth as a baby's behind
smooth as silk
snug as a bug in a rug
soar like an eagle
so far, so good
soft as butter
soft as velvet
solid as a rock
solid as the Rock of
   Gibraltar
sooner or later
sophisticated technology
sour grapes
sow one's wild oats
spearheading the campaign
spend money like a
   drunken sailor

spend money like it was
   going out of style
spirited debate
spitting image *also* spit and
   image
spotlessly clean
sprawling base, facility
spreading like wildfire
square peg in a round hole
stark raving mad
start from scratch
steal one's thunder
steaming jungle
stick out like a sore thumb
stick to one's guns
stiff as a board
stiff upper lip
stir up a hornet's nest
stole away like a thief in
   the night
storm of protest
straight and narrow
straight as an arrow
straight from the shoulder
strange bedfellows
stranger than fiction
straw in the wind
straw that broke the
   camel's back
strong as a bull
strong as an ox
stubborn as a mule
sturdy as an oak
sum and substance
supreme sacrifice
surprise move
swear like a trooper
sweat of one's brow
sweet as honey
sweet as pie
sweet as sugar
sweet harmony
sweetness and light

sweet sixteen
swing of the pendulum

take a dim view of
take it or leave it
take the bull by the horns
talk through one's hat
tempest in a teapot
tender mercies
terror-stricken
that is to say
the whole ball of wax
thick as molasses
thick as thieves
thin as a rail
thin as a toothpick
this day and age
this point in time
throw caution to the wind
throw down the gauntlet
throw in the sponge
throw in the towel
throw the book at
tie the knot
tight as a drum
tight as a spring
tight as a tick
time immemorial
time of one's life
time will tell
tip of the iceberg
tip the scales
tired as a dog
tit for tat
too big for his/her britches
too cute for words
too funny for words
too good to be true
took to it like a duck to water
too little, too late
tools of the trade
too numerous to mention

tough as a boot
tough as nails
tower of strength
trail of blood
trail of death and destruction
treat like dirt
trials and tribulations
tried and true
true blue
true colors
turn over a new leaf
turn over in one's grave

ugly as sin
uncharted seas
unrequited love
untimely end
up a creek (without a paddle)

vale of tears
vanish in(to) thin air
various and sundry
view with alarm

wail like a banshee
walking encyclopedia
warm as toast
warts-and-all
wash one's hands of
watch like a hawk
wax poetic
wealth of information
wear and tear
wear two hats
wee (small) hours
wend one's way
went off like clockwork
went over like a lead balloon
when all is said and done
when push comes to shove

when the cows come home
when you come right down to it
whirlwind campaign
whirlwind courtship
white elephant
whole ball of wax
whole nine yards
wide as a house
wide-open spaces
wild as a buck
wise as an owl
wishful thinking
with bated breath
without further ado

wolf in sheep's clothing
word to the wise
work like a charm
work like a dog
work one's fingers to the bone
worn to a frazzle
worse for wear
wouldn't touch it with a 10-foot pole
wreak havoc
wrinkled as a prune

yesterday's news
younger than springtime

7

Preferred Usage

A language develops through usage, which determines the appropriateness of specific expressions in specific grammatical situations.

Today's ubiquitous *like,* for example, historically in standard English was assigned only the grammatical function of a preposition. The double negative—a construction of syntax in which two negative words are used in the same clause to express a single negative—has long been considered nonstandard English, although it was standard in English through Shakespeare's time and is used in French. Today some uses of double negatives are fully standard, sometimes even suggesting an affirmative alternative.

The following examples illustrate a variety of confusing points in current usage.

WORDS & PHRASES

For	*Use*
accused with a crime	accused of a crime
acknowledged leader	leader
ad nauseum	Always two words.
almost never	seldom *or* hardly ever
ameliorate	improve
angry	angry at *or* with someone
announced the names of	identified
approximately	about

For	*Use*
arrested for killing	arrested on a charge of killing
arrive	arrive at
as respects	as regards
as though	as if
as to whether	whether
augur for	augur
average *n*	an average of 95
avowed	promised *or* pledged
basically	Usually superfluous.
because (to show cause-effect relationship)	as
beside *adv*	besides
cabaret	nightclub
can't hardly (*double negative* implied)	can hardly
catalogue	catalog
commence	begin
comparative	Usually superfluous.
conduct a poll	poll
convicted for a crime	convicted of a crime
couple *n*	a couple of apples
deactivate	close *or* shut off
defense spending	military spending
definitely	Usually superfluous.
depart	depart from
different than	different from
dove (past tense and past participle of *dive*)	dived
drunk *adj*	after a form of *to be*
drunken *adj*	before nouns
en route	Always two words.
endeavor *v*	try
equally as	equally *or* as
erenow	heretofore
essentially	Usually superfluous.

For	*Use*
few ones *avoid*	few
finalize	end *or* complete
first annual *avoid*	An event is not annual until it is held in at least two successive years: *The organizers plan to hold an event annually.*
flyer (aviator *or* handbill)	flier
fortnight	two weeks
fundamentally	Usually superfluous.
graduated	graduated from *or* was graduated from the university
healthcare	health care
held a meeting	met
Holy Ghost	Holy Spirit
hospital facilities	hospitals
impact *v*	affect
implement *v*	carry out
initiate	begin
injuries received	injuries suffered *or* sustained
in spite of	despite
interface	work together
jury	Takes singular verbs and pronouns.
kind of	Restrict it to its literal sense—except in familiar style—not as a substitute for *rather* or *something like.*
legislation	Bills are *passed.* Laws are *enacted.*
methodology	method

For	*Use*
Near East	Middle East
not yet known	unknown
objective	aim *or* goal
off of	off
opt	choose
option	choice
the pope *or* the pontiff	Holy Father
presently	in a little while *or* shortly (not *now*)
prior to	before
proliferation	spread
purchase *v*	buy
recreational activities	recreation
relatively	Usually superfluous.
remuneration	pay
rosary	*recited* or *said*, not *read* (always lowercase *rosary*)
skincare	skin care
so (*so* happy)	An intensifier to be avoided.
sort of	Restrict it to its literal sense—except in familiar style—not as a substitute for *rather* or *something like*.
specifically	Usually superfluous.
stated	said
thanking you in advance	Will you please *or* I shall be obliged
theretofore	until then
these ones *avoid*	these
three-D	3-D
touch base with	call
utilize	use

For	Use
very	Usually superfluous.
whereabouts	Takes a singular verb.
worrisome matter	worry

AUXILIARY VERBS

Among the most confusing aspects of English is the usage of *auxiliary* or *helping verbs*—due mainly to disagreement among grammarians for over 300 years. Also, many traditional rules of usage, still followed in Britain, are no longer observed by most educated native-American users of English.

The following list presents a summation of current usage. For a more detailed review, consult a dictionary.

Auxiliary Verbs	*Use*
shall (present tense)	Historically, for first-person construction to express determination: We *shall* overcome. and simple futurity: When *shall* I expect you?
will (present tense)	Historically, for second- and third-person construction, unless determination is stressed: You *will* enjoy the movie. She *will* find the film too violent. We *shall* attend the annual meeting. *also* We *will* attend the annual meeting.

To avoid sounding biblical or pompous, *will* is used in all three persons construction of all types of speech and writing for the simple future as well as to express determination. There are, however, alternatives to *shall* and *will*: in expressing volition, *I promise to attend;* in stating what is predictive, *I expect to attend;* and for describing what is mandatory, *We must obey the laws.*

Auxiliary Verbs	*Use*
should (past tense of *shall*)	For the *subjunctive mood*—a verb form used to express contrary-to-fact conditions and expressions of doubts, wishes, or regrets: If Bill *should* move out of the house, his mother would be beset with worry. To express an obligation: We *should* help those less fortunate than ourselves. To express futurity from a point of view in the past: He *should* be home before rush hour.
would (past tense of *will*)	To express a customary action: Every fall I *would* look forward to attending school. In constructing a conditional past tense: If I had not had such a good job offer, I *would* not have moved abroad. In place of *could*: My new portable rack *would* hold 30 CDs. In place of *should*: Dan thought I *would* enjoy the new play.
may (present tense)	To imply uncertainty: It *may* rain tonight. To express contingency: He'll finish law school come what *may*.

Auxiliary Verbs	*Use*

To indicate giving permission to (used interchangeably with *can*):
> You *may* borrow my car tonight.

In law, along with *shall* or *must*, where the sense, purpose, or policy requires this interpretation:
> Publisher may postpone publication or *may*, by written notice to the Author, decline to publish the work.

might
(past tense of ***may*****)**

To express less probability than *can, could,* or *may*:
> The delivery *might* get here by closing time.

As a polite alternative to *may*:
> *Might* I ask you a favor?

As a polite alternative to *ought* or *should*:
> You *might* have called to say you'd be late for dinner.

can
(present tense)

To indicate knowing how to:
> Audrey *can* drive a stick shift.

To indicate being physically or mentally able to:
> She *can* read and speak Russian.

To indicate being inherently able or designed to:
> Gerald has the best home entertainment center that money *can* buy.

To indicate giving permission to (used interchangeably with *may*):
> You *can* borrow my car tonight.

Auxiliary Verbs	*Use*
could (past tense of *can*)	To imply ability but with conditions attached: We *could* take the 6 o'clock train if you *could* leave the office early.
	To politely ask a question: *Could* you change my appointment to next week?

PRONOUNS

Pronouns comprise a small set of words that are used as noun substitutes. Three pronouns—*that, which,* and *who*—are used with essential and nonessential sentence elements, which may be a word, phrase (a group of words), or a clause (a group of words containing a verb).

An *essential* element—also called a *restrictive* element—*cannot* be deleted from a sentence without changing the basic meaning. A *nonessential* element—also called a *nonrestrictive element*—*can* be deleted from a sentence without changing the basic meaning, as it provides descriptive detail only. Commas are *not* used with essential elements, but are needed to set off nonessential elements, as shown in the following examples.

While the use of *which* for *that* is common in written and spoken English, *that* is generally preferable to *which*. *Who* has its own uses, which are discussed farther on in this chapter.

Pronouns	*Use*
that	To refer to a person, idea, or feeling: Love is an emotion *that* Ryan has never felt.
	To refer to an inanimate object: It was the dishwasher *that* needed repair.

Pronouns	*Use*
	To refer to an animal without a name: The German shepherd is one breed of dogs *that* is often used for police work.
which	To introduce a nonessential element that refers to an inanimate object: I have a great recipe for Texas chili, *which* is easy to make.
	To introduce a nonessential element that refers to an animal without a name: My first dog, *which* was a French poodle, lived to be 17 years old.
	To avoid the unwanted repetition of *that*: Natalie said that the concert *which* her trio is giving tonight is free.
who	To represent a person or an animal with a name as the subject of a sentence, clause, or phrase: *Who* is the fairest of them all?
	In essential or nonessential clauses, to represent a specified or implied antecedent—a person, animal, or personified thing: Any student *who* wants to can improve her or his vocabulary.
whom (objective case of *who*)	To represent a person or animal with a name as the object of a verb: *Whom* do you want to see in the White House next year?

Pronouns	*Use*
	To represent a person as the object of a preceding preposition: The man to *whom* I was engaged just came through the door.
he/him/his	When referring to human males and to animals whose sex has been established or who have a name: The bull pawed the ground with *his* hooves. Archie the Yorkie always used to beg at *his* owner's dinner table.
she/her/hers	When referring to human females and to animals whose sex has been established or who have a name: The mare stayed close to *her* foal. My 90-pound rottweiler Brünnhilde disturbed the neighbors with *her* barking.
it/its	When referring to inanimate objects and to animals whose sex has not been established: The lamp had an unusual design on *its* base. Paula's cat was scared, and *it* ran to *its* basket.

PART TWO

THE
FINER POINTS

If language is not correct, then what is said is not what is meant; if what is said is not what is meant, then what ought to be done remains undone; if this remains undone, morals and art deteriorate; if morals and art deteriorate, justice will go astray; if justice goes astray, the people will stand about in helpless confusion. Hence there must be no arbitrariness in what is said.

—Confucius
(551–479 B.C.)

8

Abbreviations, Acronyms & Initialisms

An *abbreviation* is any shortened form of a written word or phrase used in place of the whole, especially a form that does not fall into the categories of *acronyms* or *initialisms*—such as *Ave.* (Avenue).

An *acronym* is formed from the initial letter or letters of each of the successive or major parts of a compound term and is *read or spoken as a word*—such as *Amtrak* (American Track).

An *initialism* is formed from the initial letters of an expression and is *pronounced letter by letter*—such as *SRO* (standing room only *or* single-room occupancy).

Some acronyms and initialisms such as *AIDS* and *A.D.,* respectively, are acceptable in all references. As a general rule, however, an expression should be written out in its entirety the first time it is used and its acronym or initialism on second or succeeding references. To maintain clarity in writing, avoid the overuse of *all* forms of abbreviation.

The following list of abbreviations, acronyms, and initialisms—while not intended to be all-inclusive—contains many of those most commonly used. There is considerable variation in today's use of periods and in capitalization (as *rpm, r.p.m., Rpm,* and *RPM*), and stylings other than those presented in this book are often acceptable. It is, however, important to maintain *consistency* in the styling of your choice throughout a single written piece of material. (The styling in this chapter is

from *Merriam-Webster's Collegiate Dictionary,* Tenth
Edition, 1993.)

a   absent; acre; adult; answer; area

AA   Alcoholics Anonymous

AAA   American Automobile Association

AAAL   American Academy of Arts and Letters

AAAS   American Association for the Advancement
                of Science

AARP   American Association of Retired Persons

ABA   American Bar Association

ABC   American Broadcasting Companies

ABD   all but dissertation

A-bomb   atomic bomb

AC   air conditioner; air conditioning; alternating
                current; [ML *ante Christum*] before Christ;
                area code; athletic club

AC/DC   alternating current/direct current; *slang*
                bisexual

ACLU   American Civil Liberties Union

ACT   Action for Children's Television; American
                College Test; American Conservatory
                Theater; Association of Classroom Teachers

ACTH   adrenocorticotropic hormone, produced by
                the pituitary gland and stimulates the cortex
                (outer layer) of the adrenal glands, located
                above the kidneys

A.D.*	[L *anno Domini*] in the year of (our) Lord goes *before* the figure for the year: A.D. *86.* Do not write: *The fifth century* A.D. *The fifth century* is sufficient.
ADA	American Dental Association
ADAMHA	Alcohol, Drug Abuse, and Mental Health Association
ADC	advanced developing countries; Aid to Dependent Children
ADD	attention deficit disorder
ad lib	[L *ad libitum*] at will
ADR	alternative dispute resolution
ADT	Alaska daylight time; Atlantic daylight time
ad val	[L *ad valorem*] according to the value (imposed at a rate percent of value)
AEC	Atomic Energy Commission
AF	air force; audio frequency; auto focus
AFC	American Football Conference
AFDC	Aid to Families with Dependent Children
AFL	American Football League
AFL-CIO	American Federation of Labor and Congress of Industrial Organizations
AFT	American Federation of Teachers
AFTRA	American Federation of Television and Radio Artists

* Exception to *Webster's.*

AG	adjutant general; attorney general
AGI	adjusted gross income
AH	arts and humanities
A.H.*	[L *anno Hebraico*] in the Hebrew year; [L *anno Hegirae*] in the year of the Hegira
AHL	American Hockey League
AHSA	American Horse Shows Association
AI	Amnesty International
AIA	American Institute of Architects
AID	Agency for International Development; artificial insemination by donor
AIDS	acquired immune deficiency syndrome *or* acquired immunodeficiency syndrome
aka	also known as
AKC	American Kennel Club
AL	American League; American Legion
ALS	advanced life support; amyotrophic lateral sclerosis (also called *Lou Gehrig's disease*)
A&M	agricultural and mechanical (university)
AM	amplitude modulation (of radio wave)
A.M.*	[L *anno mundi*] in the year of the world; [L *ante meridiem*] before noon; [NL *artium magister*] master of arts
AMA	American Medical Association

* Exception to *Webster's*.

Amer	America; American
AMPAS	Academy of Motion Picture Arts and Sciences (awards *Oscars* each year since 1927 for outstanding filmmaking)
Amtrak	American Track (National Railroad Passenger Corporation)
AMVETS	American Veterans (of World War II and more recent wars)
ANA	American Nurses Association
ans	answer
AOR	album-oriented rock (music on radio)
AP	American plan; Associated Press
APB	all points bulletin
APC	armored personnel carrier; aspirin, phenacetin, and caffeine
APEX	Advance Purchase Excursion (type of international air fare)
APO	army post office
APR	annual percentage rate
AQ	as quoted
A&R	artists and repertoire (record company department)
AR	annual return
ARC	AIDS-related complex; American Red Cross
ARM	adjustable rate mortgage

ASA	American Society on Aging; American Standards Association
ASAP	as soon as possible
ASCAP	American Society of Composers, Authors & Publishers
ASE	American Stock Exchange (*also* AMEX *or* Amex)
ASEAN	Association of Southeast Asian Nations
ASPCA	American Society for the Prevention of Cruelty to Animals
assn	association
assoc	associate; associated
ASSR	Autonomous Soviet Socialist Republic
asst	assistant
AST	Alaska standard time; Atlantic standard time
AT	advanced technology; automatic transmission
ATC	air traffic control
ATE	automatic test equipment
ATF	(Bureau of) Alcohol, Tobacco, and Firearms
ATM	asynchronous transfer mode; automated (*or* automatic) teller machine
attn	attention
atty	attorney

ATV	all-terrain vehicle
AV	audiovisual
AVC	automatic volume control
AWACS	airborne warning and control system
AWD	all wheel drive
AWOL	absent without leave
AWP	average wholesale price
AZT	azidothymidine (a drug approved by the FDA to fight AIDS)
BA	[NL *baccalaureus artium*] bachelor of arts
BAC	blood alcohol concentration
B&B	bed-and-breakfast
BBB	Better Business Bureau
BBC	British Broadcasting Corporation
BBQ	barbecue
B.C.*	before Christ—As the full phrase would be *in the year 94 before Christ*, the abbreviation goes *after* the figure for the year: *94 B.C.*
BCW	Bureau of Child Welfare
B&D	bondage and discipline
B&E	breaking and entering

* Exception to *Webster's*.

BFA	bachelor of fine arts
BIA	Bureau of Indian Affairs
BLT	bacon, lettuce, and tomato (sandwich)
blvd	boulevard
BMI	Broadcast Music Inc.
BMOC	big man on campus
BMR	basal metabolic rate
BMW	[G *Bayerische Motoren Werke*] Bavarian Motor Works
BO	back order; *informal* body odor; box office; branch office
BP	beautiful people; blood pressure
BS	bachelor of science
BSA	Boy Scouts of America
BSE	breast self-examination
Btu	British thermal unit
b/w, b&w	black and white (film, movie, or television screen)
BW	bacteriological warfare; biological warfare
BYOB	bring your own bottle
C	(degrees) Celsius (replaces *centigrade*)
CA	cancer; chronological age
ca	[L *circa*] about

CAD coronary artery disease

CAP Civil Air Patrol

CARE Cooperative for American Relief Everywhere

CATV community antenna television

CB citizens band (shortwave radio); continental breakfast

CBAT College Board Achievement Test

CBC Canadian Broadcasting Corporation; complete blood count

CBD central business district

CBS Columbia Broadcasting System

CBT Chicago Board of Trade

CC community college; country club

CCR Commission on Civil Rights

CCTV closed-circuit television

CCU coronary care unit

CD certificate of deposit; civil defense; compact disk; [F *corps diplomatique*] diplomatic corps

CDC Centers for Disease Control

CDT central daylight time

CE chemical engineer; civil engineer

CEA Council of Economic Advisors

CEC	Commodity Exchange Commission
CED	Committee for Economic Development
CEEB	College Entrance Examination Board
CEMA	Council for Economic Mutual Assistance
CEO	chief executive officer
CETA	Comprehensive Employment and Training Act
CF	centrifugal force; cystic fibrosis
CFNP	Community Food and Nutrition Program
CFO	chief financial officer
CFS	chronic fatigue syndrome
CFTC	Commodity Futures Trading Commission
CG	coast guard; commanding general
CHD	coronary heart disease
CIA	Central Intelligence Agency
C in C	commander in chief
CIS	Commonwealth of Independent States (formed by 11 of the 15 former republics of the USSR after its breakup in 1991)
CJ	chief justice
CLEP	College Level Examination Program
CLI	cost-of-living index
CM	command module (spacecraft); Common Market

COD	cash on delivery; collect on delivery
C of C	Chamber of Commerce
COLA	cost-of-living adjustment
Conrail	Consolidated Rail Corporation
COO	chief operating officer
CORE	Congress of Racial Equality
CP	cerebral palsy; chemically pure; command post; communist party
CPA	certified public accountant
CPB	Corporation for Public Broadcasting
CPI	consumer price index
CPR	cardiopulmonary resuscitation
CPSC	Consumer Product Safety Commission
CRC	camera-ready copy; Civil Rights Commission
crim con	criminal conversation
CS	civil service; conditioned stimulus; county seat
CSE	child support enforcement
C-section	*informal* Caesarean section
CST	central standard time; convulsive shock treatment
CV	cardiovascular; [L *curriculum vitae*] a brief biographical résumé of one's career

CVA	cerebrovascular accident (stroke); Columbia Valley Authority
C&W	country-and-western
CY	calendar year
DA	district attorney; don't answer
DARE	Drug Abuse Rehabilitation Enterprise; Drug Abuse Resistance Education
DAV	Disabled American Veterans
DBA	doctor of business administration
d/b/a	doing business as
DBS	direct broadcast satellite
D&C	dilation (of the cervix) and curettage (of the uterus)
DC	direct current; doctor of chiropractic
DDR	[G *Deutsche Demokratische Republik*] German Democratic Republic
DDS	doctor of dental surgery
DEA	Drug Enforcement Administration; Drug Enforcement Agency
DEFCON	defense readiness condition (U.S. military forces)
Dem	Democrat; Democratic
dim	dimension; diminish; diminutive
DINK	double income, no kids

DJ	disc jockey
DMD	[NL *dentariae medicinae doctor*] doctor of dental medicine
DMV	Department of Motor Vehicles
DMZ	demilitarized zone
DNA	deoxyribonucleic acid (genetics)
DNF	did not finish
DNR	do not resuscitate (hospital order)
DO	doctor of optometry; doctor of osteopathy
DOA	dead on arrival (describing a person who dies before reaching a hospital)
DOB	date of birth
DOD	date of death; Department of Defense
DOE	Department of Energy; depending/depends on experience
DP	data processing; dew point
DPM	doctor of podiatric medicine
DPT	diphtheria, pertussis, and tetanus (a mixed vaccine)
DPW	Department of Public Works
dram pers	[L *dramatis personae*] characters or actors in a drama
DST	daylight saving time
DTs, the	delirium tremens

DUI	driving under the influence
DVA	Department of Veterans Affairs
DVM	doctor of veterinary medicine (*see also* VMD)
DVS	doctor of veterinary surgery
DWEM	dead white European male
DWI	driving while intoxicated
Dx	diagnosis
EC	European Community
ECF	extended care facility
ECG, EKG	[G *elektrokardiogramm*] (for diagnosis of heart disease) electrocardiogram *or* cardiogram (the graphic record); electrocardiograph *or* cardiograph (the device)
EDA	Economic Development Administration
EDT	eastern daylight time
EEG	(for determining brain-wave activity) electroencephalogram (the graphic record); electroencephalograph (the instrument)
EENT	eye, ear, nose, and throat
EEOC	Equal Employment Opportunity Commission
EER	energy efficiency ratio
EFL	English as a foreign language

EFT, EFTS	electronic funds transfer (system)
EFTA	European Free Trade Association
e.g.	[L *exempli gratis*] for example; for the sake of example; such as
EIC	earned income credit
EMS	emergency medical service; European Monetary System
EMT	emergency medical technician
ENG	electronic news gathering
Eng	England; English
EO	executive order
EOE	equal opportunity employer
EOM	end of month
EOP	Executive Office of the President
EP	European plan; extended play
EPA	Environmental Protection Agency
EPCOT Center	experimental prototype community of tomorrow (at Walt Disney World's Magic Kingdom, near Orlando, Florida)
EPS	earnings per share
ER	emergency room
ERA	earned run average; Emergency Relief Administration; Equal Rights Amendment
ESL	English as a second language

ESOP	employee stock ownership plan
ESP	extrasensory perception
Esq, Esqr	esquire
EST	eastern standard time
ESV	earth satellite vehicle
ET	extraterrestrial
ETA	estimated time of arrival
et al	[L *et alibi*] and elsewhere; [L *et alii* (m pl), *et aliae* (f pl), or *et alia* (neut pl)] and others
ETC	earned income credit
etc	[L *et cetera*] and so forth
ETD	estimated time of departure
ETO	European theater of operations
ETV	educational television
F	(degrees) Fahrenheit; French
f	female; feminine
FAA	Federal Aviation Administration
FAO	Food and Agriculture Organization (of the United Nations)
fax	facsimile (by shortening and respelling); facsimile machine
FBI	Federal Bureau of Investigation

FCA	Farm Credit Administration
FCC	Federal Communications Commission
FD	fatal dose; fire department; focal distance
FDA	Food and Drug Administration
FDIC	Federal Deposit Insurance Corporation
FDR	Franklin Delano Roosevelt (32nd president of the United States)
Fed, FRS	Federal Reserve System
fem	female; feminine
FEMA	Federal Emergency Management Agency
FEPA	Fair Employment Practices Act
FEPC	Fair Employment Practices Commission
FERA	Federal Emergency Relief Administration
FF	fast forward
FFA	Future Farmers of America
FGT	federal gift tax
FHA	Federal Housing Administration
FHLMC	Federal Home Loan Mortgage Corporation (called "Freddie Mac")
FICA	Federal Insurance Contributions Act
fl oz	fluid ounce
FM	frequency modulation (of radio wave)

FNMA	Federal National Mortgage Association (pronounced "Fannie Mae")
FOB	free on board; freight on board; fresh off the boat
FOIA	Freedom of Information Act
FPO	fleet post office
Fr	France; French
FRB	Federal Reserve Board (policy-making body of the Federal Reserve System)
FRM	fixed rate mortgage
FS	filmstrip; food stamps; Foreign Service
FTC	Federal Trade Commission
FTZ	free-trade zone
FUO	fever of unknown origin
FWD	forward; four-wheel drive
FX	effects (special); foreign exchange
FY	fiscal year
FYI	for your information
G	(certification mark) used to certify that a motion picture is of such a nature that persons of all ages may be allowed admission; German; Gulf
GA	Gamblers Anonymous; General Assembly (UN)
GAAP	generally accepted accounting principles

GAO	General Accounting Office
GATT	General Agreement on Tariffs and Trade
GAW	guaranteed annual wage
GDP	gross domestic product
GED	General Educational Development (tests); general equivalency diploma (high school)
gen	gender; general; genitive; genus
Ger	German; Germany
GGPA	graduate grade point average
GI	galvanized iron; gastrointestinal; government issue; *informal* a member or former member of the U.S. armed forces, especially an enlisted man in the army
Gk	Greek
GM	general manager; grand master; guided missile
GNI	gross national income
GNMA	Government National Mortgage Association (pronounced "Ginnie Mae")
GNP	gross national product
GOP	Grand Old Party (Republican)
gov	government; governor
govt	government
GP	general practice; general practitioner
gp	group

GPA	grade point average
GPO	general post office; Government Printing Office
Gr	Greece; Greek
gr	grain(s); gram(s); gross
grad	graduate; graduated
GRAS	generally recognized as safe (by the FDA)
GSA	General Services Administration; Girl Scouts of America
GSL	Guaranteed Student Loan
GSUSA	Girl Scouts of the United States of America
GU	genitourinary (pertaining to both the reproductive organs and the urinary tract)
H-bomb	hydrogen bomb
HCL	high cost of living
HD	heavy-duty
HDL	high-density lipoprotein ("good" cholesterol—compare *LDL*)
HDTV	high-definition television
HEW	(Department of) Health, Education, and Welfare
hgwy, hwy	highway
HHS	(Department of) Health and Human Services

HI	head injury; high intensity; humidity index
HIV	human immunodeficiency virus (the pathogen that transmits AIDS)
HMO	health maintenance organization
HO	habitual offender
HOPE	Health Opportunity for People Everywhere
HP	high pressure; horsepower
HRS	Health and Rehabilitation Services
HS	high school
HST	Hawaii standard time (no daylight saving time in Hawaii)
HUD	(Department of) Housing and Urban Development
HZV	herpes zoster virus
ib, ibid	[L *ibidem*] in the same place, volume, or case
IBF	International Boxing Federation
IBW	ideal body weight
ICBM	intercontinental ballistic missile
ICC	International Control Commission; Interstate Commerce Commission
ICCAT	International Commission for the Conservation of Atlantic Tuna
ICD	intrauterine contraceptive device

ICU	intensive care unit
ID	identification; intelligence department
id	[L *idem*] the same; the same as has been mentioned
IDU	injection drug user
i.e.	[L *id est*] that is
ILO	International Labor Organization
IMF	International Monetary Fund
IMP	international match point
inc	income; incorporated
IND	investigational new drug
INS	Immigration and Naturalization Service
INTELSAT	International Telecommunications Satellite
Interpol	International Criminal Police Organization (also *ICPO*)
IOC	International Olympic Committee
IOU	I owe you
IP	inpatient
IQ	intelligence quotient
IR	infrared
IRA	individual retirement account; Irish Republican Army
IRS	Internal Revenue Service

It   Italian; Italy

IUD   intrauterine device

IV   intravenous; intravenous drip *or* injection

IVF   in vitro fertilization

JC   junior college (a two-year college that awards associate's degrees)

JCC   Jewish Community Center

JCS   joint chiefs of staff

JD   [NL *juris doctor*] doctor of jurisprudence, doctor of law; [NL *jurum doctor*] doctor of laws; justice department

JFK   John Fitzgerald Kennedy (35th president of the United States); John F. Kennedy International Airport (servicing the New York City area)

JP   jet propulsion; justice of the peace

JV   junior varsity

K   Kelvin; kindergarten; king (chess)

KGB   [Russ *Komitet Gosudárstvennoĭ Bezopasnosti*] (formerly Soviet) Committee for State Security

KIA   killed in action

KISS   keep it simple, stupid

KKK   Ku Klux Klan

km   kilometer

KO	knockout (boxing)
L	Latin
laser	light amplification by stimulated emission of radiation
LBO	leveraged buyout
LC	letter of credit; Library of Congress
LD	lethal dose; long distance (telephone call)
LDC	less developed country
LDL	low-density lipoprotein ("bad" cholesterol—compare *HDL*)
LE	leading edge; lupus erythematosus (skin disorder)
LEM	lunar excursion module (spacecraft)
LEP	limited English proficiency
LHD	[NL *litterarum humaniorum doctor*] doctor of humane letters; doctor of humanities
lib	liberation; library
lit	liter; literacy; literal; literature
LLB	[NL *legum baccalaureus*] bachelor of laws
LLD	[NL *legum doctor*] doctor of laws
LPN	licensed practical nurse
LSAT	Law School Admission Test
LSD	lysergic acid diethylamide (hallucinogenic drug)

ltd	limited
LWV	League of Women Voters
m	male; married; masculine; meter; mile
M&A	mergers and acquisitions
MA	[ML *magister artium*] master of arts; mental age; Middle Ages; military academy
MAD	mutual assured destruction
MADD	Mothers Against Drunk Driving
MAP	modified American plan
masc	masculine
MASH	mobile army surgical hospital
MBA	master of business administration
MBE	Multistate Bar Examination
MBS	Mutual Broadcasting System
MC	master/mistress of ceremonies; medical corps; member of Congress
MCAT	Medical College Admission Test
mcg	microgram (one millionth of a gram)
MCP	male chauvinist pig
MD	medical department; [NL *medicinae doctor*] doctor of medicine; muscular dystrophy
MDC	more developed country
MDT	mountain daylight time

ME	medical examiner
MEGO	my eyes glaze over
METO	Middle East Treaty Organization
mg	milligram (one thousandth of a gram)
MI	myocardial infarction (heart attack)
MIA	missing in action
MiG	a type of Russian fighter plane named for its designers, Artem Mikoyan and Mikhail Gurevich (*i* is the Russian word for *and*)
ML	Medieval Latin; Middle Latin
MLF	multilateral force
MLR	minimum lending rate
MMA	Metropolitan Museum of Art (New York)
MMPI	Minnesota Multiphasic Personality Inventory
MO	mail order; [NL *modus operandi*] a method of procedure; money order
MOL	manned orbiting laboratory
MoMA	Museum of Modern Art (New York)
MOR	middle of the road (radio music format)
MPAA	Motion Picture Association of America
mpg	miles per gallon
mph	miles per hour
MPX	multiplex

MRI	magnetic resonance imaging
MS	[L *manuscriptum*] manuscript; master of science; Medicaid Services; multiple sclerosis
MSG	monosodium glutamate
MSS	manuscripts
MST	mountain standard time
MTO	Mediterranean theater of operations
MTV	Music Television
MVP	most valuable player
MYOB	mind your own business
NAACP	National Association for the Advancement of Colored People
NAFTA	North American Free Trade Agreement
NARAL	National Abortion Rights Action League
NASA	National Aeronautics and Space Administration
NASDAQ	National Association of Securities Dealers Automated Quotations
NASL	North American Soccer League
NATO	North American Treaty Organization
NBA	National Basketball Association
NBC	National Broadcasting Company
NC	no charge

NCAA	National Collegiate Athletic Association
NC-17	(certification mark) used to certify that a motion picture is of such a nature that no one under the age of 17 can be admitted
NEA	National Education Association; National Endowment for the Arts
NEH	National Endowment for the Humanities
NET	National Education Television
neut	neuter
NFC	National Football Conference
NFL	National Football League
NIH	National Institutes of Health
NIMBY	not in my backyard
NIMH	National Institute of Mental Health
NL	National League; Neo-Latin; New Latin
NLRB	National Labor Relations Board
NMHA	National Mental Health Association
NMSQT	National Merit Scholarship Qualifying Test
NNP	net national product
NOAA	National Oceanic and Atmospheric Administration
non seq	[L *non sequitur*] it does not follow
NOW	National Organization for Women
NP	no protest; notary public

NPR	National Public Radio
NPT	nonproliferation treaty
NRA	National Rifle Association
NRC	Nuclear Regulatory Commission
NREM	nonrapid eye movement (sleep)
NSAIDS	nonsteroidal anti-inflammatory drugs
NSC	National Security Council
NSF	National Science Foundation; not sufficient funds
NSPCA	National Society for the Prevention of Cruelty to Animals
NYNEX	New York New England Exchange (a regional Bell telephone company)
NYSE	New York Stock Exchange
OAS	Organization of American States
OASDHI	Old Age, Survivors, Disability, and Health Insurance (Social Security)
OB-GYN	obstetrician-gynecologist
OC	oral contraceptives
OD	[L *oculus dexter,* right eye] doctor of optometry; on demand
OD'd	*street term* for death due to a drug overdose (especially an illegal drug); *colloquialism* overindulged in a pleasurable activity
OJT	on-the-job training

OMBE	Office of Minority Business Enterprise
OOB	off off Broadway
OP	observation post; operative procedure; out of print; outpatient
OPEC	Organization of Petroleum Exporting Countries
OSHA	Occupational Safety and Health Administration
OT	occupational therapy; overtime
OTB	offtrack betting
OTC	over-the-counter
OTEC	ocean thermal energy conversion (by solar power)
Oxfam	Oxford Committee for Famine Relief
PA	physician's assistant; power of attorney; press agent; public-address system
PAC	political action committee
PANDA	pregnant and addicted
PBJ	peanut butter and jelly (sandwich)
PBS	Public Broadcasting Service
PC	Peace Corps; personal computer; politically correct; professional corporation
PCB	polychlorinated biphenyl (toxic carcinogen)
pct	percent; percentage

PD	[ML *per diem*] by the day; police department; postal district; public domain
PDT	Pacific daylight time
P/E	price to earnings ratio
PEN	International Association of Poets, Playwrights, Editors, Essayists, and Novelists
PET	positron-emission tomography (scan to study blood circulation)
PETA	People for the Ethical Treatment of Animals
PFI	physical fitness index
PFP	Partnership for Peace
PG	(certification mark) used to certify that a motion picture is of such a nature that persons of all ages may be allowed admission but parental guidance is suggested
PGA	Professional Golfers' Association
PG-13	(certification mark) used to certify that a motion picture is of such a nature that persons of all ages may be admitted but parental guidance is suggested especially for children under 13
PGY	post graduate year
p&h	postage and handling
PhB	[NL *philosophiae baccalaureus*] bachelor of philosophy
PhD	[NL *philosophiae doctor*] doctor of philosophy

PHS	Public Health Service
PID	pelvic inflammatory disease
PIK	payment in kind
PIN	personal identification number
PINS	person in need of supervision
PIP	primary information person
pkwy	parkway
P/L	profit and loss
pl	plural
PLO	Palestine Liberation Organization
P.M.*	[L *post meridiem*] after noon
PMS	premenstrual syndrome
PMT	premenstrual tension
PO	parole officer; postal (money) order; post office; purchase order
POB	post office box
POC	port of call
POE	port of embarkation; port of entry
POP	point of purchase
POS	point of sale
POSSLQ	person of the opposite sex sharing living quarters (U.S. Census)

* Exception to *Webster's*.

POV	point of view
POW	prisoner of war
PP	parcel post; postpaid; prepaid
pp	pages
PPH	paid personal holidays
PPO	preferred provider organization
PPS	[NL *post postscriptum*] a second or additional postscript
PR	press release; public relations; Puerto Rico
PRC	People's Republic of China
pres	present; president
PRO	public relations officer
prof	professional; professor
pro tem	[L *pro tempore*] for the time being; temporary
PRT	personal rapid transit
PS	[NL *postscriptum*] postscript; power steering; power supply; public school
PSA	public service announcement
PSAT/ NMSQT	Preliminary Scholastic Aptitude Test/ National Merit Scholarship Qualifying Test
PSD	prevention of significant deterioration (EPA standard of measurement)
PST	Pacific standard time

PT	Pacific time; physical therapy; physical training
PTA	Parent-Teacher Association
PTSD	posttraumatic stress disorder
PTV	public television
PUD	planned unit development
PWA	person with AIDS
q	quart; quarterly; question
Q&A	*informal* question-and-answer (format)
QA	quality assurance
QC	quality control
QE2	*Queen Elizabeth 2* (ocean liner)
qq	questions
ques	question
R	(certification mark) used to certify that a motion picture is of such a nature that admission is restricted to persons over a specified age (as 17) unless accompanied by a parent or guardian
RA	rheumatoid arthritis
radar	radio detection and ranging
R&B	rhythm and blues
R&D	research and development

R&R	rest and recreation; rest and recuperation; rock and roll
RBI	run(s) batted in
RC	Red Cross
RD	rural delivery
RDD	random digit dialing (marketing)
RDS	respiratory distress syndrome
REIT	real estate investment trust
REM	rapid eye movement (during sleep)
Rep	Republican
rep	repair; report; representative; republic
RF	radio frequency
RH	relative humidity
RN	registered nurse
RNA	ribonucleic acid (genetics)
ROTC	Reserve Officers' Training Corps
rpm	revolutions per minute
rps	revolutions per second
RR	railroad; rural route
RRM	renegotiable rate mortgage
RRR	return receipt requested
RRT	rapid rail transit

RSFSR	[Russ *Rossiĭskaya Sovetskaya Federativnaya Sotsialisticheskaya Respublika*] Russian Soviet Federated Socialist Republic
RSVP	[F *répondez s'il vous plaît*] please reply
Russ	Russia; Russian
RV	recreational vehicle
Rx	prescription (pharmacy symbol for *prescription*, derived from [L] *recipe*)
SAC	Strategic Air Command
SAD	seasonal affective disorder
SADD	Students Against Drunk Driving
SAG	Screen Actors Guild
SALT	Strategic Arms Limitation Treaty (*SALT I*, 1972; *SALT II*, 1979)
s&h	shipping and handling
S&L	savings and loan (association)
SASE	self-addressed stamped envelope
SAT	Scholastic Assessment Tests
SB	[NL *scientiae baccalaureus*] bachelor of science; simultaneous broadcast
SBA	Small Business Administration
SC	Security Council (of the United Nations)
ScD	[L *scientiae doctor*] doctor of science

scuba	self-contained underwater breathing apparatus
SDI	Strategic Defense Initiative
SEC	Securities and Exchange Commission
secy	secretary
sen	senate; senator; senior
SETI	search for extraterrestrial intelligence
SF	science fiction
SG	surgeon general
SHF	superhigh frequency
SICU	surgical intensive care unit
SIDS	sudden infant death syndrome
SIECUS	Sex Information and Education Council of the United States
sitcom	situation comedy
S-M, S/M	sadomasochism; sadomasochistic
SM	[NL *scientiae magister*] master of science
SNG	synthetic natural gas (also called *synfuel*)
sonar	sound navigation and ranging
SOP	standard operating procedure
Sp	Spain; Spanish
SPCA	Society for the Prevention of Cruelty to Animals

SPCC	Society for the Prevention of Cruelty to Children
spec	special; specialist
specs	specifications
SPF	sun protection factor
SRO	single-room occupancy; standing room only
SS	same size; Social Security; steamship; sworn statement
SSA	Social Security Administration
SSI	supplemental security income
SSN	Social Security number
SST	supersonic transport
START	Strategic Arms Reduction Treaty (*START I*, 1991; *START II*, 1993)
stat	[L *statim*] immediately; statute
STD	sexually transmitted disease
SVS	still-camera video system
SWAK	sealed with a kiss
SWAT	Special Weapons and Tactics
TA	transit authority
TAT	Thematic Apperception Test
TB	thoroughbred; tubercle bacillus; tuberculosis
TBA	to be announced

temp	temperature; *informal* temporary employee
TGIF	thank God it's Friday
TGV	[F *train à grande vitesse*] high-speed train
THI	temperature-humidity index
TIN	taxpayer identification number
TKO	technical knockout
TLC	tender loving care
TM	trademark (™); transcendental meditation
TMJ	temporomandibular joint
TNT	trinitrotoluene
TO	telegraph office; turnover
TQM	total quality management
TSS	toxic shock syndrome
TVA	tax on value added; Tennessee Valley Authority
U	[*Union of Orthodox Hebrew Congregations*] kosher certification—often enclosed in a circle; university; unsatisfactory
UC	under construction; undercover
UCR	Uniform Crime Report
UDAG	Urban Development Action Grant
UFO	unidentified flying object

UHF	ultrahigh frequency
UI	unemployment insurance
UK	United Kingdom
UN	United Nations
UNCF	United Negro College Fund
UNCTAD	United Nations Conference on Trade and Development
UNEF	United Nations Emergency Force
UNESCO	United Nations Educational, Scientific, and Cultural Organization
UNICEF	United Nations Children's Fund (formerly *United Nations International Children's Emergency Fund*)
univ	universal; university
UPC	Universal Product Code
UPI	United Press International
U.S.*	United States
U.S.A.*	United States Army; United States of America
USAF	United States Air Force
USCG	United States Coast Guard
USECC	United States Employees' Compensation Commission
USES	United States Employment Service

* Exception to *Webster's*.

USGA	United States Golf Association
USMC	United States Marine Corps
USN	United States Navy
USO	United Service Organizations
USP	United States Pharmacopeia
USPS	United States Postal Service
USS	United States Senate; United States ship
USSR	Union of Soviet Socialist Republics
USTA	United States Tennis Association
UV	ultraviolet
v	verse; versus; voltage; volume
VA	Veterans Administration
VAT	value-added tax
VC	venture capital; Vietcong
VCR	videocassette recorder
VD	venereal disease
VF	video frequency; visual field
VFD	volunteer fire department
VFW	Veterans of Foreign Wars
VHF	very high frequency
VIP	*informal* very important person

VISTA	Volunteers in Service to America
viz	[L *videlicet*] that is to say; namely
VJ	veejay; video jockey
VLF	very low frequency
VMD	[NL *veterinariae medicinae doctor*] doctor of veterinary medicine
VNA	Visiting Nurse Association
VO	voice-over
VOA	Voice of America
VP	vice president
VRM	variable rate mortgage
vs	verse; versus
VTOL	vertical takeoff and landing
VTR	videotape recorder; videotape recording
WAC	Women's Army Corps (founded in 1943 and integrated into the U.S. Army in 1978)
WASP	white Anglo-Saxon Protestant
WATS	Wide Area Telecommunications Service (special networks offered by AT&T)
WAVES	Women Accepted for Volunteer Emergency Service (founded in 1942 and established permanently in 1948 as the Women's Reserve of the U.S. Naval Reserve)
WBA	World Boxing Association

WBC	World Boxing Council
WHO	World Health Organization
WIA	wounded in action
WOC	without compensation
WP	word processing
WPI	wholesale price index
wpm	words per minute
X	(certification mark) used before the adoption of *NC-17* to certify that a motion picture was of such a nature that persons under a specified age (usually 17) were denied admission
XL	extra large; extra long
XS	extra small
YA	young adult
YB	yearbook
YMCA	Young Men's Christian Association
YMHA	Young Men's Hebrew Association
YOB	year of birth
yr	year; younger; your
yrbk	yearbook
yuppie	young urban professional (from the late 1980s and often derogatory)

| YWCA | Young Women's Christian Association |
| YWHA | Young Women's Hebrew Association |

ZBB	zero-based budgeting
ZEG	zero economic growth
ZIP (Code)	Zone Improvement Program
ZPG	zero population growth

STATE NAMES

State or Possession	Prose Abbreviation	Postal Code
Alabama	Ala.	AL
Alaska	*none*	AK
American Samoa	Amer. Samoa	AS
Arizona	Ariz.	AZ
Arkansas	Ark.	AR
California	Calif.	CA
Canal Zone	C.Z.	CZ
Colorado	Colo.	CO
Connecticut	Conn.	CT
Delaware	Del.	DE
District of Columbia	D.C.	DC
Florida	Fla.	FL
Georgia	Ga.	GA
Guam	*none*	GU
Hawaii	*none*	HI
Idaho	*none*	ID
Illinois	Ill.	IL
Indiana	Ind.	IN
Iowa	*none*	IA
Kansas	Kans.	KS
Kentucky	Ky.	KY
Louisiana	La.	LA
Maine	*none*	ME
Maryland	Md.	MD
Massachusetts	Mass.	MA

State or Possession	Prose Abbreviation	Postal Code
Michigan	Mich.	MI
Minnesota	Minn.	MN
Mississippi	Miss.	MS
Missouri	Mo.	MO
Montana	Mont.	MT
Nebraska	Nebr.	NE
Nevada	Nev.	NV
New Hampshire	N.H.	NH
New Jersey	N.J.	NJ
New Mexico	N.Mex.	NM
New York	N.Y.	NY
North Carolina	N.C.	NC
North Dakota	N.Dak.	ND
Ohio	*none*	OH
Oklahoma	Okla.	OK
Oregon	Oreg.	OR
Pennsylvania	Pa.	PA
Puerto Rico	P.R.	PR
Rhode Island	R.I.	RI
South Carolina	S.C.	SC
South Dakota	S.Dak.	SD
Tennessee	Tenn.	TN
Texas	Tex.	TX
Utah	*none*	UT
Vermont	Vt.	VT
Virginia	Va.	VA
Virgin Islands	V.I.	VI
Washington	Wash.	WA
West Virginia	W.Va.	WV
Wisconsin	Wis.	WI
Wyoming	Wyo.	WY

NOTE: Where an abbreviation does not exist, use the full name of state or possession.

CLASSIFIEDS DEMYSTIFIED

Real Estate Ads

AC	air conditioning	BR	bedroom
blc	balcony	bth	bathroom

C/AC	central air-conditioning	gar	garage
cl	closet	HWDFL	hardwood floors
DM	doorman	kit	kitchen
DR	dining room	mbl	marble
DW	dishwasher	SF	square feet
EIK	eat-in kitchen	SL	split level
FDR	formal dining room	ter	terrace
fpl	fireplace	VU	view
FR	family room	VWS	views
		WBF	wood-burning fireplace

Personal Ads

Sample Abbreviations:

A Asian	F female	NS nonsmoking
B black	G gay	S single
Bi bisexual	H Hispanic	W white
C Christian	J Jewish	WW widowed
D divorced	M male	
DDF drug and disease free	NR nonreligious	

BF	black female
BiF	bisexual female
BiM	bisexual male
BM	black male
DDFWF	drug and disease free white female
DJF	divorced Jewish female
DJM	divorced Jewish male
DWF	divorced white female

DWJF	divorced white Jewish female
DWJM	divorced white Jewish male
DWM	divorced white male
GBF	gay black female
GBM	gay black male
GWF	gay white female
GWM	gay white male
JF	Jewish female
JF/NR	Jewish female/nonreligious
JM	Jewish male
NSWM	nonsmoking white male
SAF	single Asian female
SAM	single Asian male
SBF	single black female
SBM	single black male
S/DA/WF	single or divorced Asian or white female
S/DB/WM	single or divorced black or white male
S/DF	single or divorced female
S/DJF	single or divorced Jewish female
S/DJM	single or divorced Jewish male
S/DM	single or divorced male
S/DWF	single or divorced white female

S/DWJF	single or divorced white Jewish female
S/DWM	single or divorced white male
SF	single female
SHF	single Hispanic female
SHM	single Hispanic male
SM	single male
SWCF	single white Christian female
SWCM	single white Christian male
SWF	single white female
SWM	single white male
WWF	widowed female
WWM	widowed male
WWWCF	widowed white Christian female

9

Compound Words & Phrases

A *compound* is a word composed of two or more components that are also words or word bases.

Some compounds are written as one, two, or more separate words: *bridesmaid, housetop, blood pressure, high school, air traffic controller, beast of burden.* Other compounds are joined by a hyphen (a short line, less than half as long as the en dash): *cross-examine, almond-eyed, one-liner, bird's-eye view, bed-and-breakfast, devil-may-care.*

When a *compound modifier*—two or more words that express a single concept—*precedes* a noun, use hyphens to join *all* words in the compound *with the exception of* the adverb *very* and all adverbs that end in *ly: a part-time job, reddish-brown hair, a prisoner-of-war trial, an easily remembered rule.*

Some combinations that are hyphenated before a noun are not hyphenated when they *follow* a noun: *He works only part time. Her hair is reddish brown. He was a prisoner of war.*

However, where a noun *follows* a form of the verb *to be*, the hyphen is usually retained to avoid confusion. *The student is serious-minded. The woman is soft-spoken. The child is well-behaved.*

The hyphen is also used to separate noninclusive numbers, such as telephone and Social Security numbers: (1-617) 227-9659, 1-617 227-9659, *or* 1-617-227-9659; SSN: 123-45-6789.

To hyphenate or not to hyphenate is one of the most perplexing problems a writer faces in the proper usage of contemporary English. The intricacies of hyphenation are akin to those of accent marks in French, but, unlike French, English keeps changing. In recent years, there has been a trend toward making compound words and phrases more compact, perhaps thought to speed up the reading and comprehension processes, by (1) eliminating hyphens and closing up words or (2) hyphenating two words previously written separately.

Adding further confusion is the disagreement as to form found in today's major dictionaries—not only with their competition, but also within their own pages. For example, one dictionary makes two words of *access road*, but one word for *accessway*. Another dictionary presents the adjectival and adverbial forms of the word meaning "not using boxing gloves" *bare-knuckle* or *bare-knuckled*, while spelling the word meaning "on the bare back of a horse" *bareback* or *barebacked*. Another dictionary eliminates hyphens altogether in words beginning with *bare*.

A phrase used for nearly a century recently appeared in a highly respected educational publication as one word—*lifeform*. Upon looking it up in four different leading dictionaries, the following versions were found: (1) *life-form*, (2) *life form*, and (3) *life-form* or *life form*. The fourth source, a major unabridged dictionary, does not list it at all.

In addition, there are numerous rules and exceptions to the rules for compounds, including those governing two-thought compounds (*agro-industrial* but *socioeconomic*) and compound proper nouns and adjectives designating dual heritage (*Italian-American* but *Latin American*).

The following "minidictionary" of compound words contains a wide range of up-to-date examples—in many cases their hyphenation (or not) is determined by their usage or **part of speech**. Of the eight parts of speech, six are referred to in this section.

PARTS OF SPEECH

Noun *(n)* identifies anything that can be named, from people and places to ideas and emotions (*actor, theater, love*).

Adjective *(adj)* modifies a noun *(good, bad, large)*.

Verb *(v)* expresses an action, state, or relation between two things *(looked, is, could)*.

Adverb *(adv)* modifies a verb, adjective, or another adverb *(well, badly, largely)*.

Preposition *(prep)* forms phrases that modify verbs, nouns, or adjectives *(by, in, beneath)*.

Interjection *(interj)* expresses emotion, but is not considered part of the sentence structure *(Hey!, No!, Encore!)*.

The other two parts of speech are: **pronoun** *(pron)*, which replaces or substitutes for a noun or noun phrase *(I, you, who)* and **conjunction** *(conj)*, which connects words, phrases, clauses, or sentences *(and, but, if)*. An additional abbreviation used in the following list is *n pl* (noun plural).

For the sake of brevity in the following list—which contains formal, informal, *and* slang expressions—compound modifiers are designated as *adjectives*, noun phrases as *nouns*, and verb phrases as *verbs*. For the sake of clarity in compounds with two forms, unhyphenated or one-word forms precede those with hyphens or that are comprised of two or more unconnected words.

A battery *n*
able-bodied *adj*
about-face *n* or *v*
aboveboard *adj* or *adv*
aboveground *adj*
absentminded *adj*
academic year *n*
accessway *n*
accident-prone *adj*
achievement-oriented *adj*
acid-fast *adj*
acid-forming *adj*
acid rain *n*
acid rock *n*

acid-tongued *adj*
acid-washed *adj*
across-the-board *adj*
activewear *n*
acute-care *adj*
add-on *adj* or *n*
ad-lib *adj, n* or *v*
ad lib *adv*
adman *n*
A-frame *n*
Afro-pop *n*
aftereffect *n*
after-hours *adj*
afterimage *n*

afterlife *n*
aftermath *n*
afternoon *adj* or *n*
afternoons *adv*
aftershave *n*
aftershock *n*
aftertaste *n*
after-tax *adj*
age group *n*
agelong *adj*
age-old *adj*
agreed-upon *adj*
AIDS-awareness *n*
AIDS-related *adj*
AIDS-tainted *adj*
air bag *n*
airborne *adj*
airbrush *n* or *v*
air-condition *v*
air-conditioned *adj*
air conditioner *n*
air-conditioning *adj*
air conditioning *n*
air-dry *adj* or *v*
airfare *n*
airfield *n*
airline *n*
airliner *n*
airmail *adj, adv, n* or *v*
airman *n*
air-minded *adj*
airplane *adj* or *n*
air pocket *n*
airsick *adj*
air strike *n*
airstrip *n*
airtight *adj*
airtime *n*
air-to-air *adj* or *adv*
air-to-ground *adj* or *adv*
airwaves *n pl*
airway *n*
all-American *adj* or *n*

all-around *adj*
all clear *n*
all-day *adj*
all-expenses-paid *adj*
all in *adj*
all-inclusive *adj*
all-night *adj*
all-nighter *n*
all-or-nothing *adj*
all-out *adj*
allover *adj* or *n*
all over *adv*
all-purpose *adj*
all right *adv*
all-star *adj* or *n*
all-time *adj*
all told *adv*
almond-eyed *adj*
alpha dog *n*
also-ran *n*
amidships *adj* or *adv*
angel dust *n*
  (phencyclidine)
angelfish *n*
angel food cake *n*
angel-hair pasta *n*
angina pectoris *n*
anorexia nervosa *n*
antacid *adj* or *n*
antedate *n* or *v*
antioxidant *adj* or *n*
antismog *adj*
antismoking *adj*
A-OK *adj* or *adv*
applecart *n*
apple-pie *adj*
apple pie *n*
apple-polish *v*
applesauce *n*
appliance garage *n* (in
  kitchens)
après-ski *adj* or *n*
armchair *adj* or *n*

armrest *n*
arm-twist *v*
arm-twisting *n*
arm-wrestle *v*
arm wrestling *n*
around-the-clock *adj*
art deco *n*
art film *n*
art form *n*
art rock *n*
arts and crafts *n*
artwork *n*
assault and battery *n*
assembly line *n*
atom-bomb *v*
atom bomb *n*
atomic-energy *adj*
atomic energy *n*
atom smasher *n*
attention-getting *adj*
audience-proof *adj*
audience share *n*
audiocassette *n*
audiovisual *adj* or *n*
autoeroticism *n*
autoimmunity *n*
awestruck *adj*

baby boomer *n*
baby-sit *v*
baby-sitter *n*
baby talk *n*
backache *n*
back-and-forth *adj* or *n*
back and forth *adv*
backbite *n* or *v*
backbone *n*
backbreaking *adj*
backdrop *n* or *v*
backfire *n* or *v*
backhand *adj, adv, n* or *v*
backhanded *adj*
backlash *n*

backlist *adj, n* or *v*
backlog *n* or *v*
back-order *v*
back order *n*
backpack *n* or *v*
backroom *adj*
back room *adj* or *n*
backseat *adj* or *n*
backside *n*
backslide *n* or *v*
backstage *adj, adv* or *n*
backstroke *n* or *v*
back-talk *v*
back talk *n*
back-to-basics *adj*
backtrack *v*
backup *adj* or *n*
back up *v*
backyard *n*
bad-mouth *v*
bag lady *n*
bagman *n*
bailout *adj* or *n*
bail out *v*
bake sale *n*
ballet master *n*
ballet mistress *n*
ball game *n*
ballot box *n*
ballpark *adj* or *n*
ballplayer *n*
ballpoint *adj* or *n*
ballroom *adj* or *n*
bar code *n*
bareback *adj* or *adv*
bareknuckle *adj* or *adv*
barelegged *adj* or *adv*
barn dance *n*
barnstorm *v*
barnyard *adj* or *n*
barroom *adj* or *n*
bass clef *n* (F clef)
bathhouse *n*

bathing suit *n*
bath mat *n*
bathrobe *n*
bathroom *n*
bathtub *n*
battle-ax *n*
battle fatigue *n*
battlefield *n*
battleground *n*
battle plan *n*
battleship *n*
battle station *n*
bay window *n*
beach ball *n*
beachboy *n*
beach buggy *n*
beachcomber *n*
beachfront *adj* or *n*
beachgoer *n*
beachwear *n*
beanbag *n*
bean curd *n* (tofu)
bear-hug *v*
bear hug *n*
beat-up *adj* or *n*
beat up *v*
bed-and-breakfast *n*
bed board *n*
bedbug *n*
bedfellow *n*
bedmate *n*
bedsheet *n*
bedside *adj* or *n*
bed table *n*
bedtime story *n*
beefcake *adj* or *n*
beef cattle *n*
beefed-up *adj*
beefsteak *n*
beehive *n*
beekeeper *n*
behind-the-scenes *adj*
bell-bottom *adj*

bell-bottoms *n pl*
bellyache *n* or *v*
belly-up *adj*
belly up *v*
belowdecks *adv*
belowground *adj*
belt-tightening *n*
bench-press *v*
bench press *n*
benchwarmer *n*
bench warrant *n*
best-case *adj*
best in show *n*
best man *n*
bestseller *n*
best-selling *adj*
beta-blocker *n*
better-off *adj*
big bang theory *n*
big bucks *n*
big-business *adj*
big business *n*
big-city *adj*
big deal *interj* or *n*
bighead *n*
bighearted *adj*
big-league *adj*
big league *n*
big-name *adj*
big name *n*
big-ticket *adj*
big-time *adj*
big time *n*
big wheel *n*
bigwig *n*
bilateral *adj* or *n*
bi-level *adj* or *n*
bipartisan *adj*
birdcall *n*
bird-dog *v*
bird dog *n*
birdhouse *n*
bird-of-paradise *n* (plant)

bird of paradise *n* (bird)
bird of prey *n*
birdsong *n*
bird-watch *v*
bird-watcher *n*
birthday *adj* or *n*
birth defect *n*
birthmark *n*
birthplace *n*
birthright *n*
birthstone *n*
bitch goddess *n*
bitewing *adj* or *n*
bitter end *n*
bittersweet *adj* or *n*
black-and-blue *adj*
black-and-white *adj*
black and white *n*
blackball *n* or *v*
black book *n*
black comedy *n*
black eye *n*
black-flag *v*
black flag *n*
black gold *n*
blackhead *n*
black hole *n*
blackjack *n* or *v*
blacklist *n* or *v*
black-market *v*
black market *n*
blackout *n*
black out *v*
black sheep *n*
black-tie *adj*
black tie *n*
blacktop *adj, n* or *v*
blastoff *n*
blast off *v*
blind alley *n*
blind date *n*
blindfold *adj, n* or *v*
blockbuster *n*

block party *n*
blood-and-guts *adj*
blood bank *n*
bloodcurdling *adj*
blood doping *n*
bloodhound *n*
bloodline *n*
bloodmobile *n*
blood money *n*
bloodred *adj*
bloodshed *n*
bloodshot *adj*
bloodstained *adj*
bloodstream *adj* or *n*
bloodthirsty *adj*
blood-typing *n*
blood vessel *n*
blow-by-blow *adj* or *n*
blow-dry *n* or *v*
blow-dryer *n*
blowhole *n*
blown-up *adj*
blowout *n*
blow out *v*
blow over *v*
blowup *n*
blue blood *n*
blue-blooded *adj*
blue book *n*
bluebottle *n*
blue-chip *adj*
blue chip *n*
blue jeans *n*
blush-on *n*
bobsled *n*
body bag *n*
bodybuilder *n*
body count *n*
body English *n*
bodyguard *n*
body language *n*
body-mike *v*
body mike *n*

body politic *n*
body shirt *n*
body shop *n*
body stocking *n*
bodysuit *n*
bone-dry *adj*
bookcase *n*
book club *adj* or *n*
bookend *n*
booking office *n*
bookkeeper *n*
bookmaker *n*
bookmobile *n*
bookplate *n*
bookseller *n*
bookshelf *n*
bookshop *n*
bookstore *n*
book value *n*
bookworm *n*
bottom-line *adj*
bottom line *n*
bottom-of-the-line *adj*
bowlegged *adj*
brainstorm *n* or *v*
brainstorming *adj* or *n*
brain trust *n*
brainwashing *adj* or *n*
brand-new *adj*
breakdown *adj* or *n*
break down *v*
breakeven *n*
break-even *adj*
break-in *adj* or *n*
break in *v*
breakout *n*
break out *v*
breakthrough *n*
break through *v*
breakup *n*
break up *v*
breathtaking *adj*
bred-in-the-bone *adj*

bric-a-brac *n*
broadcast *adj*, *n* or *v*
brokenhearted *adj*
brown bagging *n*
brownout *n*
bubble wrap *n* or *v*
buck passer *n*
buck-passing *n*
buddy-buddy *adj*
bulimia nervosa *n*
bullfighting *n*
bullpen *n*
busywork *n*
butterfat *n*
butterfingered *adj*
butterfingers *n pl*
butterfly *adj*, *n* or *v*
button-down *adj*
buzz saw *n*
buzzword *n*
by-and-by *n*
by and by *adv*
by and large *adv*
byline *n* or *v*
bypass *adj*, *n* or *v*
byplay *n*
by-product *n*
bystander *n*
byword *n*

cabdriver *n*
cabin cruiser *n*
cabinetmaker *n*
cabin fever *n*
cable car *n*
cablegram *n*
cable-TV *n*
caffeine-free *adj*
callback *adj* or *n*
call box *n*
caller ID *n*
call-in *adj* or *n*
call in *v*

call-up *n*
call up *v*
camcorder *n*
campfire *n*
campsite *n*
candid-camera *adj*
candid camera *n*
candleholder *n*
can-do *adj*
candy-striped *adj*
candy striper *n*
cannonball *adj* or *n*
cannot *v*
capital gain *n*
capital-intensive *adj*
cardboard *adj* or *n*
card-carrying *adj*
card catalog *n*
cardholder *n*
carfare *n*
carjacking *n*
carload *n*
carpool *n* or *v*
carport *n*
carryall *n*
carry-in *adj* or *n*
carry-on *adj* or *n*
carry on *v*
carry-out *adj* or *n*
carry out *v*
carry-over *n*
carry over *v*
carry through *v*
car seat *n*
carsick *adj*
car wash *n*
casebook *n*
case history *n*
caseload *n*
case study *n*
casework *n*
cash-advance *adj*
cash advance *n*

cash-and-carry *adj* or *n*
cash bar *n*
cashbook *n*
cash cow *n*
cash-in *n*
cash in *v*
cast-iron *adj*
cast iron *n*
cast-off *adj* or *n*
catchall *n*
catchphrase *n*
catch-up *adj* or *n*
catch up *v*
catchword *n*
cats and dogs *adv*
cattle call *n*
cattleman *n*
cause-and-effect *adj*
cave-in *adj* or *n*
cave in *v*
caveman *n*
cease-fire *n*
cease fire *v*
cellblock *n*
cellmate *n*
cha-cha *n* or *v*
chain-smoker *n*
chairlift *n*
chairperson *n*
charge-off *n*
checkbook *n*
checkmate *n* or *v*
checkoff *n*
check off *v*
checkup *n*
check up *v*
chicken-fried *adj*
chickenpox *n*
chin-up *n*
choir loft *n*
choirmaster *n*
chow-chow *n* (preserve or relish)

chow chow n (breed of
dog)
city hall n
cityscape n
city-state n
citywide adj or adv
civic-minded adj
civil-rights adj
civil rights n
classroom n
classwork n
clean-cut adj
clean-living adj
cleanup adj or n
clean up v
clear-cut adj or n
clear-eyed adj
clearheaded adj
cliff dweller n
cliff-hang v
cliff-hanger n
cloak-and-dagger adj
close-cropped adj
closed-caption adj
closed-door adj
closed-shop adj
closed shop n
closefisted adj
close-in adj
close in v
close-knit adj
close-out adj or n
close-up adj or n
close up v
clotheshorse n
club chair n
clubhouse n
coastline n
coast-to-coast adj or adv
code blue n
code-name v
coffeemaker n
coffee-table book n

cold-blooded adj
color-blind adj
color blindness n
color-coded adj
comeback n
come back v
comedy drama n
come-hither adj
company-paid adj
concertgoer n
concert grand n
concertmaster n
consumer-products adj
continentwide adj or adv
copyright n or v
cost-cutting adj
cost-effective adj
cost-of-living adj
cost of living n
cost-plus adj
cost-push inflation n
counterintelligence n
countryside n
countrywide adj or adv
countywide adj or adv
courtroom n
coverall n
cover-all adj
cover-up adj or n
cover up v
crackdown n
crack down v
crack-up n
crack up v
crash-land v
crawlspace n
credit-card adj
credit card n
crime-fighter n
crisscross v
cross-addicted adj
cross-country adj or n
cross-cultural adj

cross-dress *v*
cross-examination *n*
cross-examine *v*
cross-eye *n*
cross-eyed *adj*
cross fire *n*
cross-index *v*
cross index *n*
crossover *adj* or *n*
cross over *v*
cross-ownership *n*
cross-section *v*
cross section *n*
crosstown *adj, adv* or *n*
cross-train *v*
crowd-pleasing *adj*
curtain raiser *n*
custom-made *adj*
custom-order *v*
cut-and-dried *adj*
cutback *n*
cut back *v*
cut-in *adj* or *n*
cut in *v*
cutoff *adj* or *n*
cut off *v*
cutthroat *adj* or *n*
cutting-edge *adj*
cutting edge *n*

damage-control *adj*
damage control *n*
daredevil *adj* or *n*
dark horse *n*
darkroom *n*
dartboard *n*
dashboard *n*
data bank *n*
database *n*
data processing *adj* or *n*
datebook *n*
date rape *n*
daybreak *n*

day-care *adj*
day care *n*
daydream *n* or *v*
day letter *n*
daylong *adj*
day nursery *n*
day student *n*
daytime *adj* or *n*
daytimes *adv*
day-to-day *adj*
deadbeat *adj* or *n*
dead bolt *n*
dead center *adv*
dead-end *adj* or *v*
dead end *n*
deadhead *n*
dead heat *n*
deadline *n*
deadlock *n* or *v*
dead-on *adj*
deadpan *adj, adv, n* or *v*
dean's list *n*
deathbed *adj* or *n*
death-row *adj*
death row *n*
deathtrap *n*
decision-making *adj*
decision making *n*
deep-fry *v*
deep fryer *n*
deep-rooted *adj*
deep-sea *adj*
deep-seated *adj*
deep-set *adj*
deficit-cutting *adj*
deficit-reduction *adj*
degree-day *n*
demand-pull inflation *n*
demand-side *adj*
demigod *n*
demigoddess *n*
desktop *adj* or *n*
devilfish *n*

devil-may-care *adj*
dewdrop *n*
dewlap *n*
dew point *n*
dewy-eyed *adj*
diehard *adj* or *n*
dingdong *adj, n* or *v*
dining car *n*
dining room *n*
dinner theater *n*
dinnertime *n*
dipstick *n*
direct-examination *n*
direct-examine *v*
direct-mail *adj*
direct mail *n*
direct-mailer *n*
dirt bike *n*
dirt-cheap *adj* or *adv*
dirty linen *n*
dirty-minded *adj*
dirty pool *n*
dirty-tricks *adj*
dirty tricks *n*
disc jockey *n*
dishcloth *n*
dishtowel *n*
dishwasher *n*
dishwater *n*
diving board *n*
doe-eyed *adj*
doeskin *adj* or *n*
dog and pony show *n*
dog biscuit *n*
dog collar *n*
dog days *n*
dog-eared *adj*
dog-eat-dog *adj*
doggy bag *n*
doghouse *n*
dogleg *adj, n* or *v*
dognap *v*
do-good *adj*

do-gooder *n*
dog-paddle *v*
dog paddle *n*
dog show *n*
dogsled *n* or *v*
dog tag *n*
do-it-yourselfer *n*
dollars-and-cents *adj*
dome light *n*
do-nothing *adj* or *n*
doomsday *adj* or *n*
doorbell *n*
door chain *n*
do-or-die *adj*
doorknob *n*
doorman *n*
door prize *n*
door-to-door *adj* or *adv*
double-bill *v*
double bill *n*
double-blind *adj*
double boiler *n*
double-book *v*
double-breasted *adj*
double-check *v*
double check *n*
double-cross *v*
double cross *n*
double-date *v*
double date *n*
double-dealing *adj* or *n*
double-decker *adj* or *n*
double-digit *adj*
double-dip *v*
double-duty *adj*
double-edged *adj*
double-entry *adj*
double entry *n*
double feature *n*
doubleheader *n*
double helix *n*
double-occupancy *adj*
double occupancy *n*

double-park *v*
double play *n*
double-ring *adj*
double-sided *adj*
double-space *v*
doublespeak *n*
double spread *n*
double standard *n*
doughboy *n*
down-and-dirty *adj*
down-and-out *adj*
downhill *adj, adv* or *n*
down-home *adj*
down-in-the-mouth *adj*
downlink *adj* or *n*
down-market *adj*
downplay *v*
downscale *adj* or *v*
downside *adj*
downsize *v*
downstate *adj* or *adv*
down-the-line *adj*
down-to-earth *adj*
down-to-the-wire *adj*
downtown *adj* or *adv*
drawn-out *adj*
draw poker *n*
drawstring *n*
dreadlocks *n*
dreamland *n*
dreamworld *n*
dress code *n*
dressmaker *adj* or *n*
dress rehearsal *n*
dress shirt *n*
dress-up *adj* or *n*
dried-up *adj*
drive-by *adj* or *n*
drive-in *adj* or *n*
drive-through *adj* or *n*
drive time *n*
driveway *n*
drop cloth *n*

drop-dead *adj* or *adv*
drop-in *adj* or *n*
drop-off *adj* or *n*
drop off *v*
dropout *n*
drop out *v*
drop-ship *v*
drop shipment *n*
drug abuse *n*
drugged-out *adj*
drugstore *n*
drum major *n*
drum majorette *n*
drumroll *n*
drumstick *n*
dry-clean *v*
dry cleaner *n*
dumbbell *n*
dumbfound *v*
duty-free *adj* or *adv*

earache *n*
ear clip *n*
eardrum *n*
earlobe *n*
earmark *n* or *v*
earphone *n*
earring *n*
earsplitting *adj*
earthbound *adj*
earthquake *n*
earthshaking *adj*
earth-shattering *adj*
earthworm *n*
eastbound *adj*
easy-care *adj*
easygoing *adj*
easy listening *n*
easy-to-use *adj*
ebb tide *n*
eggbeater *n*
egghead *n*
eggnog *n*

egg roll *n*
egg-shaped *adj*
eggshell *adj* or *n*
egg white *n*
ego-trip *v*
ego trip *n*
eightball *n*
800 number *n*
eight-track tape *n*
either-or *adj* or *n*
elbowroom *n*
electro-optics *n*
e-mail *n*
empty calorie *n*
empty-handed *adj*
empty-headed *adj*
empty nester *n*
end-consumer *n*
endgame *n* (chess)
energy audit *n*
energy-efficient *adj*
entry-level *adj*
entryway *n*
even-steven *adj*
even-tempered *adj*
everyday *adj* or *n*
every day *adv*
everyplace *adv*
everything *n* or *pron*
everywhere *adv*
every which way *adv*
evildoer *n*
evil-minded *adj*
extra-dry *adj*
extra-large *adj*
extralegal *adj*
extramarital *adj*
extra-mild *adj*
eyeball *adj*, *n* or *v*
eye bank *n*
eyebrow *n*
eye-catcher *n*
eye-catching *adj*

eye chart *n*
eye contact *n*
eyecup *n*
eyedropper *n*
eyeglass *n*
eyelash *n*
eye lens *n*
eyeliner *n*
eye-opener *n*
eye-opening *adj*
eye shadow *n*
eyesight *n*
eye socket *n*
eyes-only *adj*
eyesore *n*
eyestrain *n*
eye-to-eye *adj*
eye to eye *adv*
eyewash *n*
eyewear *n*
eyewitness *n* or *v*

facecloth *n*
facedown *adv* or *n*
face-lift *n* or *v*
face-off *n*
face-saver *n*
face time *n*
face-to-face *adj* or *adv*
face towel *n*
faceup *adv*
face up *v*
fact-finding *adj* or *n*
fadeaway *n*
fade away *v*
fade-in *n*
fade in *v*
fade-out *n*
fade out *v*
fail-safe *adj*, *n* or *v*
fairground *n*
fair-haired *adj*
fair-minded *adj*

fair play *n*
fair shake *n*
fair-trade *adj or v*
fair trade *n*
fairway *n*
fair-weather *adj*
fairyland *n*
fairy-tale *adj*
fairy tale *n*
fallout *n*
fall out *v*
fancy-free *adj*
fan mail *n*
fanny pack *n*
far and away *adv*
far and wide *adv*
faraway *adj*
fare-beater *n*
far-fetched *adj*
far-flung *adj*
far-gone *adj*
far-off *adj*
far-out *adj*
far-ranging *adj*
far-reaching *adj*
farsighted *adj*
fast and loose *adv*
fast-food *adj*
fast food *n*
fast-forward *v*
fast forward *n*
fast-lane *adj*
fast-talk *v*
fast-track *adj or v*
fast track *n*
feedback *n*
fee-for-service *adj*
feel-good *adj*
fee splitting *n*
feetfirst *adv*
felt-tip pen *n*
fender bender *n*
fever pitch *n*

fiberoptic *adj*
fiber optics *n*
field-test *v*
field test *n*
field trip *n*
fieldwork *n*
fifty-fifty *adj or adv*
figurehead *n*
figure skating *n*
fill-in *n*
fill in *v*
fill-up *n*
fill up *v*
filmcard *n*
film clip *n*
filmgoer *n*
filmmaker *n*
filmstrip *n*
fine art *n*
fine print *n*
fine-tune *v*
fingernail *n*
finger-pointing *n*
fingerprint *n or v*
fingertip *adj or n*
firearm *n*
firebomb *n or v*
fire chief *n*
fire escape *n*
fire extinguisher *n*
firefighter *n*
fireman *n*
fireplug *n*
fireproof *adj or v*
fire-retardant *adj*
fireside *adj or n*
fire station *n*
firetrap *n*
fire truck *n*
firstborn *adj or n*
first-class *adj or adv*
first class *n*
first-degree *adj*

firsthand *adj* or *adv*
first-name *adj*
firstnighter *n*
first-quarter *adj*
first quarter *n*
first-rate *adj* or *adv*
first-run *adj*
first run *n*
first-string *adj*
fishbowl *n*
fish cake *n*
fish fry *n*
fishhook *n*
fish story *n*
fistfight *n*
five-and-dime *adj* or *n*
five-and-ten *adj* or *n*
five-star *adj*
fixed-income *adj*
fixed-point *adj*
fixed-rate *adj*
fixer-upper *n*
fix-it *adj*
flagpole *n*
flagship *adj* or *n*
flag-waver *n*
flameproof *adj* or *v*
flame-retardant *adj* or *n*
flapjack *n*
flare-up *n*
flare up *v*
flashback *n*
flash back *v*
flashbulb *n*
flash card *n*
flashcube *n*
flash flood *n* or *v*
flash-forward *n*
flash in the pan *n*
flash point *n*
flatfooted *adj* or *adv*
flat-out *adj*
fleabite *n*

flea-bitten *adj*
flea market *n*
flesh and blood *n*
fleshpot *n*
flimflam *n* or *v*
flip chart *n*
flip-flop *n* or *v*
flip side *n*
flip-up *adj* or *n*
flip up *v*
floodlight *n* or *v*
floodwater *n*
floor-length *adj*
floor-manage *v*
floor manager *n*
floor-through *adj* or *n*
flowchart *n*
fly-by-night *adj* or *n*
flyleaf *n*
fly rod *n*
foghorn *n*
foil-lined *adj*
foldaway *adj* or *n*
foldout *adj* or *n*
folk hero *n*
folklore *n*
folk singer *n*
folk song *n*
follow-through *n*
follow through *v*
follow-up *adj* or *n*
follow up *v*
foolhardy *adj*
foolproof *adj*
footlights *n*
footlocker *n*
footnote *n* or *v*
footprint *n*
force-feed *v*
forearm *n* or *v*
foreboding *adj* or *n*
forecast *n* or *v*
forehand *adj, adv* or *n*

foreign-born *adj*
fork-tender *adj*
formalwear *n*
formfitting *adj*
form letter *n*
forthcoming *adj or n*
forthright *adj or adv*
fortune cookie *n*
fortune hunter *n*
fortune-teller *n*
foulmouthed *adj*
foul-up *n*
foul up *v*
four-footed *adj*
four-letter *adj*
four-poster *n*
foursome *n*
four-star *adj*
foxhound *n*
fox terrier *n*
fox-trot *n or v*
frame-up *n*
free and easy *adj or adv*
free-fall *adj, n or v*
free-fire zone *n*
free-floating *adj*
free-form *adj or adv*
free form *n*
freestanding *adj*
freeway *n*
freeze-dried *adj*
freeze-dry *v*
freeze-frame *n*
freshwater *adj or n*
front-end *adj*
front end *n*
front-page *adj or v*
front page *n*
front-runner *n*
fuel-efficient *adj*
full-scale *adj*
full-service *adj*
full-size *adj*

full-term *adj*
full-time *adj*
fun and games *n pl*
fund-raise *v*
fund-raiser *n*
fund-raising *adj or n*

gallbladder *n*
gallerygoer *n*
gallstone *n*
game bird *n*
gamekeeper *n*
game show *n*
gang-rape *v*
gang rape *n*
garden-variety *adj*
gas-guzzler *n*
gas station *n*
gate-crasher *n*
gatekeeper *n*
gay-oriented *adj*
gearshift *n*
gear up *v*
gemstone *n*
gender bender *n*
gender-bending *adj*
gender-biased *adj*
gender-neutral *adj*
gender-specific *adj*
gene pool *n*
general-purpose *adj*
gene-splicing *n*
germfree *adj*
germproof *adj*
getaway *adj or n*
get-out *n*
get out *v*
get-together *n*
get together *v*
get-up-and-go *n*
get-well *adj*
ghost town *n*
ghostwriter *n*

giftware *n*
gift wrap *n* or *v*
ginger ale *n*
gingerbread *n*
give-and-take *n*
giveback *n*
give back *v*
glad-hand *v*
glad hand *n*
glassy-eyed *adj*
global village *n*
globe-trotter *n*
go-ahead *adj* or *n*
goal line *n*
goalpost *n*
go-around *n*
go around *v*
go-between *n*
god-awful *adj*
godchild *n*
godfather *n*
God-fearing *adj*
godforsaken *adj*
godmother *n*
godsend *n*
go-getter *n*
go-go *adj*
going-over *n*
goings-on *n*
golden-ager *n*
golden oldie *n*
gold-filled *adj*
goldfish *n*
go-no-go *adj*
good-faith *adj*
good faith *n*
good-for-nothing *adj* or *n*
good-hearted *adj*
good-looking *adj*
good-neighbor *adj*
good old boy *n*
goodwill *n*
goof-off *n*

goof off *v*
go-round *n*
grandchild *n*
grandfather *n* or *v*
grandmother *n*
grand-slam *adj*
grand slam *n*
grassroots *adj*
grass roots *n*
greasepaint *n*
great-aunt *n*
great-nephew *n*
great-niece *n*
great-uncle *n*
greenback *n*
greenbelt *n*
green card *n*
green-eyed *adj*
greengrocer *n*
greenhouse *adj* or *n*
green light *n*
greenroom *n*
green thumb *n*
greyhound *n*
gridiron *n* or *v*
gridlock *n*
grief-stricken *adj*
grillwork *n*
groundbreaking *adj* or *n*
ground floor *n*
ground zero *n*
grownup *n*
grown-up *adj*
G-string *n*
G-suit *n*
guardrail *n*
guest-shot *n*
guidebook *n*
guide dog *n*
guilt-free *adj*
gumdrop *n*
gun buyback *n*
gun control *n*

gunfighter *n*
gung-ho *adj* or *adv*
gunpoint *n*
gun-shy *adj*
gut-wrenching *adj*

habit-forming *adj*
hairbrush *n*
haircoloring *n*
haircut *n*
hairline *adj* or *n*
hair-raiser *n*
hair-raising *adj*
hairstylist *n*
half-and-half *adj, adv* or *n*
half-baked *adj*
half brother *n*
half-cocked *adj*
half-dollar *n*
halfhearted *adj*
half-hour *adj* or *n*
half-hourly *adj* or *adv*
half-moon *n*
half sister *n*
halftime *adj* or *n*
halftone *adj* or *n*
half-truth *n*
halfway *adj* or *adv*
hallmark *n* or *v*
handbag *n*
handbook *n*
hand-feed *v*
handgun *n*
handheld *adj*
hand in hand *adv*
handmade *adj*
hand-me-down *adj* or *n*
handout *n*
hand out *v*
hand over *v*
handpick *v*
hands-down *adj*
hands down *adv*

handsfree *adj*
hands-off *adj*
hands-on *adj*
hand-to-hand *adj*
hand to hand *adv*
hand-to-mouth *adj*
handwork *n*
hand-wringing *n*
handwriting *n*
handwrought *adj*
hangdog *adj* or *n*
hang gliding *n*
hangnail *n*
hangout *n*
hang out *v*
hangover *n*
hangtag *n*
hang-up *n*
hang up *v*
hanky-panky *n*
happy-go-lucky *adj*
happy hour *n*
happy talk *n*
hard-and-fast *adj*
hardback *adj* or *n*
hardball *adj* or *n*
hard-bitten *adj*
hard-boil *v*
hard-boiled *adj*
hard-copy *adj*
hard copy *n*
hard-core *adj*
hard core *n*
hardcover *adj* or *n*
hard-edged *adj*
hard hat *n*
hardheaded *adj*
hardhearted *adj*
hard-hitting *adj*
hard-liner *n*
hard-nosed *adj*
hard-of-hearing *adj*
hard-pressed *adj*

hard-put *adj*
hard-rock *adj*
hard rock *n*
hard-sell *adj* or *v*
hard sell *n*
hard up *adj*
hard-won *adj*
has-been *n*
hatchet job *n*
hatchet man *n*
have-nots *n pl*
hay fever *n*
hayloft *n*
haystack *n*
headache *n*
head and shoulders *adv*
headboard *n*
headfirst *adv*
headhunter *n*
headlight *n*
headlong *adj* or *adv*
headmaster *n*
headmistress *n*
head-on *adj* or *adv*
head over heels *adv*
headstrong *adj*
head-to-head *adj* or *adv*
headwaiter *n*
healthcare *or* health-care
    adj
healthcare *or* health care *n*
hearing dog *n*
hearsay *adj* or *n*
heartache *n*
heart attack *n*
heartbeat *n*
heartbreak *n*
heartfelt *adj*
heartrending *adj*
heartsick *adj*
heartthrob *n*
heart-to-heart *adj* or *n*
heat-seal *v*

heatstroke *n*
heave-ho *n*
heaven-sent *adj*
heavy-duty *adj*
heavy-handed *adj*
heavy-metal *adj*
heavy metal *n*
heavyweight *adj* or *n*
hell-raiser *n*
helter-skelter *adv* or *n*
hero-worship *v*
hero worship *n*
heyday *n*
hide-and-seek *n*
hideaway *adj* or *n*
hi-fi *adj* or *n*
high and dry *adj*
high and low *adv*
high-and-mighty *adj*
highbrow *adj* or *n*
high-class *adj*
high concept *n*
high-end *adj*
high-energy *adj*
higher-up *n*
high-fiber *adj*
high-income *adj*
high-interest *adj*
high-level *adj*
high-pressure *adj* or *v*
high-profile *adj*
high profile *n*
high-profit *adj*
high-quality *adj*
high-resolution *adj*
high-rise *adj* or *n*
high-speed *adj*
high spot *n*
high-strength *adj*
high-strung *adj*
high-tech *adj* or *n*
high-tension *adj*
high-ticket *adj*

high-value-added *adj*
hip-hop *adj* or *n*
hit-and-miss *adj*
hit-and-run *adj*, *n* or *v*
hit-or-miss *adj*
hit or miss *adv*
hocus-pocus *n* or *v*
hodgepodge *n*
hog-wild *adj*
holdout *n*
hold out *v*
holdover *n*
hold over *v*
holdup *n*
hold up *v*
holier-than-thou *adj*
homebuyer *n*
home-care *adj*
home center *n*
homecoming *n*
homegrown *adj*
home invasion *n*
homeland *n*
homeroom *n*
home rule *n*
home screen *n*
home-shopping *adj*
home video *n*
homework *n*
honky-tonk *adj* or *n*
honor roll *n*
horn-rims *n*
horror-struck *adj*
horseman *n*
horse opera *n*
horse race *n*
horse show *n*
horsewoman *n*
hot-blooded *adj*
hotheaded *adj*
hot line *n*
hot-wire *v*
hour-long *adj*

houseguest *n*
housekeeper *n*
housemother *n*
houseparent *n*
houseperson *n*
house-sit *v*
house-sitter *n*
house-sitting *n*
house-to-house *adj*
housewarming *n*
hovercraft *n*
how-to *adj* or *n*
hubcap *n*
hungover *adj*
hung-up *adj*
hunter-gatherer *n*
hush-hush *adj*

ice bag *n*
iceberg *n*
ice-cold *adj*
ice-cream *adj*
ice cream *n*
ice hockey *n*
ice-skate *v*
ice skate *n*
ill-advised *adj*
ill at ease *adj*
ill-bred *adj*
ill-fated *adj*
ill humor *n*
ill-humored *adj*
ill-mannered *adj*
imagemaker *n*
in-between *adj* or *n*
in between *adv* or *prep*
indoor *adj*
indoors *adv*
industrial-strength *adj*
infectious-disease *adj*
infopreneur *n*
in-group *n*
in-house *adj* or *adv*

in-joke *n*

in-kind *adj*

in-law *n*

inner-city *adj*

inner city *n*

inner-directed *adj*

innersole *n*

innerspring *adj*

inner tube *n*

innkeeper *n*

in-print *adj*

in-residence *adj*

in-service *adj*

instant replay *n*

in-store *adj*

interest-bearing *adj*

in-your-face *adj*

ironclad *adj*

ironfisted *adj*

iron hand *n*

iron-handed *adj*

iron-on *adj* or *n*

iron-pumper *n*

island-hop *v*

ivory tower *n*

ivory-towered *adj*

jack-o'-lantern *n*

jackpot *n*

jailbreak *n*

jam-pack *v*

jam-packed *adj*

jam-up *n*

jawbreaker *n*

jazzman *n*

jazz-rock *n*

jellybean *n*

jellyfish *n*

jelly roll *n*

jet-black *adj*

jet lag *n*

jet-lagged *adj*

jetliner *n*

jet plane *n*

jet-propelled *adj*

jet set *n*

jet-setter *n*

jet stream *n*

jitterbug *n* or *v*

jobholder *n*

job-hopping *n*

job-hunter *n*

joint return *n*

jukebox *n*

jump-start *n* or *v*

junk art *n*

junk bond *n*

junk food *n*

junk mail *n*

keepsake *n*

kettledrum *n*

keyboard *n* or *v*

keyhole *adj* or *n*

keynote *adj*, *n* or *v*

keystone *n*

kickback *n*

kick back *v*

kickboard *n*

kickoff *n*

kick off *v*

kindhearted *adj*

kingmaker *n*

king-size *adj*

kiss-and-tell *adj*

knapsack *n*

knee bend *n*

kneecap *n* or *v*

knee-deep *adj*

knee-high *adj* or *n*

knee-jerk *adj*

knee jerk *n*

kneeling bus *n*

knee-slapper *n*

kneesocks *n pl*

knickknack *n*

knifepoint *n*
knockabout *adj* or *n*
knockdown *adj* or *n*
knock-down-drag-out *adj* or *n*
knock-kneed *adj*
knockoff *n*
knock off *v*
knockout *adj* or *n*
knock out *v*
knothole *n*
know-how *n*
know-it-all *adj* or *n*
know-nothing *adj* or *n*

labor-intensive *adj*
labor of love *n*
labor relations *n*
labor-saving *adj*
ladyfinger *n*
lady-killer *n*
laid-back *adj*
lamb's wool *n*
lamppost *n*
landfall *n*
landfill *n* or *v*
landlord *n*
landmark *n* or *v*
land-poor *adj*
landscaper *n*
laptop *adj* or *n*
large-print *adj*
larger-than-life *adj*
large-scale *adj*
last-ditch *adj*
late-breaking *adj*
late charge *n*
late-night *adj*
law-abiding *adj*
lawbreaker *n*
law-enforcement *adj*
law enforcement *n*
lawgiver *n*

lawmaker *n*
layaway *n*
lay away *v*
layoff *n*
lay off *v*
layout *n*
lay out *v*
layover *n*
lay over *v*
layperson *n*
lead-free *adj*
lean-to *adj* or *n*
lease-purchase *n*
left-hand *adj*
left hand *n*
left-handed *adj*
left-of-center *adj*
leftover *adj* or *n*
left-wing *adj*
left-winger *n*
legroom *n*
leg warmers *n*
legwork *n*
lengthwise *adj* or *adv*
letdown *n*
let down *v*
letter carrier *n*
letterhead *n*
letterman *n*
letter-perfect *adj*
letter-size *adj*
letup *n*
let up *v*
levelheaded *adj*
lie-detector *adj*
lie detector *n*
life-and-death *adj*
life belt *n*
lifeblood *n*
lifeboat *n*
life-care *adj*
life cycle *n*
life-form *n*

life-giving *adj*
lifeguard *n*
lifelike *adj*
lifelong *adj*
life-or-death *adj*
life raft *n*
lifesaving *adj or n*
life-size *adj*
life-support *adj*
life support *n*
life-threatening *adj*
lifetime *adj or n*
lifework *n*
liftoff *n*
light-duty *adj*
lighter-than-air *adj*
light-fingered *adj*
light-footed *adj*
light-handed *adj*
lightheaded *adj*
lighthearted *adj*
lighthouse *n*
light show *n*
lightweight *adj or n*
light-year *n*
lily-white *adj or n*
limelight *n or v*
line-item *adj*
line item *n*
line of credit *n*
liner notes *n*
lineup *n*
line up *v*
linkup *n*
link up *v*
lip-read *or* lipread *v*
lip-synch *or* lip-sync *n or v*
liquid-filled *adj*
little-known *adj*
littleneck *n*
little theater *n*
lived-in *adj*
live-in *adj or n*

livelong *adj*
livestock *n*
live wire *n*
living bank *n*
living room *n*
living will *n*
loan sharking *n*
locked-in *adj*
locker-room *adj*
locker room *n*
lockout *n*
lock out *v*
locksmith *n*
lockup *n*
lock up *v*
lonely-hearts *adj*
long-acting *adj*
long-distance *adj or adv*
longhaired *adj*
longhand *adj or n*
long-lash *adj*
long-lasting *adj*
long play *n*
long-playing *adj*
long-range *adj*
long-run *adj*
long run *n*
long shot *n*
longstanding *adj*
long-stemmed *adj*
long-term *adj*
longtime *adj*
long-winded *adj*
look-alike *adj or n*
lookout *n*
look out *v*
look-over *n*
look over *v*
look-see *n*
lookup *n*
look up *v*
loophole *n or v*
loose-jointed *adj*

loose-leaf *adj*
lopsided *adj*
lose-lose *adj*
loudspeaker *n*
lounge car *n*
loungewear *n*
lovebird *n*
lovebug *n*
love child *n*
love-in *n*
lovemaking *n*
lovey-dovey *adj*
loving-kindness *n*
low-budget *adj*
low-cal *adj*
low-cost *adj*
lowdown *adj* or *n*
low-end *adj*
lower-class *adj*
lower class *n*
low-grade *adj*
low-income *adj*
low-interest *adj*
low-key *adj* or *v*
low-level *adj*
lowlife *n*
low-lying *adj*
low-pressure *adj*
low-profile *adj*
low profile *n*
low-profit *adj*
low-rate *v*
low-rent *adj*
low-rise *adj* or *n*
low-tech *adj*
low-tension *adj*
low-ticket *adj*
lunchroom *n*
lunchtime *n*

machine-gun *v*
machine gun *n*
made-up *adj*

mailbox *n*
mail carrier *n*
mail-in *adj* or *n*
mail in *v*
mail-order *adj*
mail order *n*
mainline *adj* or *v*
main line *n*
mainliner *n*
mainspring *n*
mainstream *adj, n* or *v*
major-medical *adj*
make-ahead *adj*
make-believe *adj* or *n*
make-or-break *adj*
makeover *n*
make over *v*
makeshift *adj* or *n*
makeup *n*
make up *v*
male bonding *n*
man-child *n*
man-for-man *adj*
man-hour *n*
manhunt *n*
manic-depressive *adj* or *n*
manpower *n*
man-sized *adj*
manslaughter *n*
man-tailored *adj*
man-to-man *adj*
man-year *n*
manyfold *adv*
many-sided *adj*
markdown *n*
mark down *v*
marketplace *n*
market price *n*
market-research *v*
market research *n*
market share *n*
markup *n*
mark up *v*

masscult *n*

mass-market *adj*

mass marketing *n*

mass merchandising *n*

mass-produce *v*

mass production *n*

master class *n*

masterpiece *n*

master-plan *v*

master plan *n*

masthead *adj* or *n*

match-up *n*

match up *v*

mate-guarding *n*

meadowland *n*

meals-on-wheels *n*

mean-spirited *adj*

meantime *adv* or *n*

meanwhile *adv* or *n*

meatball *n*

meat loaf *n*

meltdown *n*

melting-pot *adj*

melting pot *n*

me-too *adj*

microwave-safe *adj*

middle age *n*

middle-aged *adj*

middle-class *adj*

middle class *n*

middle-level *adj*

middle-of-the-road *adj* or *n*

middle school *n*

middleweight *adj* or *n*

midlife *n*

mid-life *adj*

mind-bending *adj*

mind-blowing *adj*

mind-boggling *adj*

mind-expanding *adj*

mind reader *n*

mind-set *n*

minipark *n*

miniseries *n*

misty-eyed *adj*

mixed-media *adj*

mixed media *n*

mixed-up *adj*

model-perfect *adj*

mom-and-pop *adj* or *n*

money-back *adj*

moneyman *n*

money-market *adj*

money market *n*

moonlight *adj*, *n* or *v*

moonrock *n*

moonstruck *adj*

mop-up *n*

mop up *v*

mortarboard *n*

most-favored-nation *adj*

mothball *n* or *v*

moth-eaten *adj*

motherland *n*

mother lode *n*

mother-of-pearl *adj* or *n*

motorboat *n* or *v*

motorbus *n*

motorcycle *n* or *v*

motor home *n*

motor scooter *n*

mousetrap *n* or *v*

mouth-to-mouth *adj*

mouthwash *n*

mouthwatering *adj*

moviegoer *n*

much-needed *adj*

mudslinger *n*

multimedia *adj* or *n*

multiplex *adj*, *n* or *v*

muscle-bound *or*
    musclebound *adj*

museumgoer *n*

museum piece *n*

music-video *adj*

must-see *adj* or *n*

nail-biter *n*
name-brand *adj* or *n*
name-calling *n*
name-dropping *n*
nameplate *n*
narrow-minded *adj*
near miss *n*
nearsighted *adj*
near-term *adj*
nerve-racking *adj*
nest egg *n*
networking *adj* or *n*
newborn *adj* or *n*
new-fashioned *adj*
newfound *adj*
newlywed *n*
news agency *n*
newsbreak *n*
newscast *n*
news conference *n*
newsletter *n*
newsmagazine *n*
news media *n*
newspaper *n*
newspeak *n*
newsperson *n*
newsstand *n*
news story *n*
newsweekly *n*
newsworthy *adj*
new-wave *adj*
new wave *n*
next-door *adj* or *adv*
nickel-and-dime *adj* or *v*
night and day *adv*
nightclub *n* or *v*
night court *n*
nightgown *n*
night-light *n*
nightlong *adj* or *adv*
nightmare *n*
night person *n*
nighttime *adj* or *n*

nip and tuck *adj* or *adv*
nitpick *adj*, *n* or *v*
no-fault *adj* or *n*
no-fly zone *n*
no-frills *adj*
no-go *adj*
no-good *adj* or *n*
no-holds-barred *adj*
no-host *adj*
noisemaker *n*
noise pollution *n*
no-knock *adj*
no-minimum *adj*
no-no *n*
noontime *n*
nosebleed *n*
nose cone *n*
nose job *n*
no-show *adj* or *n*
notepad *n*
notepaper *n*
noteworthy *adj*
not-for-profit *adj*
no-win *adj*
nurse-midwife *n*
nurse-practitioner *n*
nursery rhyme *n*
nursery school *n*
nursing home *n*
nut-brown *adj*
nutcracker *n*
nuts-and-bolts *adj*
nuts and bolts *n*

obsessive-compulsive *adj*
  or *n*
odd-job *v*
odd man out *n*
odds and ends *n*
off and on *adv*
offbeat *adj* or *n*
off-brand *adj* or *n*
off-Broadway *adj* or *adv*

off Broadway *n*
off-camera *adj* or *adv*
off-campus *adj*
off-color *adj*
offhand *adj* or *adv*
off-hour *adj* or *n*
officeholder *n*
off-key *adj* or *adv*
off-limits *adj*
off-mike *adj*
off-off-Broadway *adj* or *adv*
off off Broadway *n*
off-peak *adj*
off-ramp *n*
offscreen *adj* or *adv*
off-season *adj, adv* or *n*
offset *adj, n* or *v*
offshoot *n*
offshore *adj, adv* or *prep*
off-site *adj* or *adv*
offspring *n*
offstage *adj* or *adv*
off-the-books *adj*
off-the-job *adj*
off-the-record *adj*
off-the-wall *adj*
offtrack *adj* or *adv*
off-white *adj* or *n*
oilman *n*
oil spill *n*
oil well *n*
old-boy network *n*
old-fashioned *adj*
old fashioned *n*
old-girl network *n*
old-time *adj*
old-timer *n*
old-world *adj*
on-again, off-again *adj*
on-and-off *adj*
on and off *adv*
onboard *adj*

on-camera *adj* or *adv*
one-dimensional *adj*
one-liner *n*
one-man *adj*
one-nighter *n*
one-night stand *n*
one-on-one *adj, adv* or *n*
one-piece *adj* or *n*
one-sided *adj*
one-stop *adj*
onetime *adj*
one-to-one *adj*
one-track *adj*
one-up *v*
one-upmanship *n*
one-way *adj*
one-woman *adj*
ongoing *adj*
on-limits *adj*
on line *adj*
onlooker *n*
on-peak *adj*
on-ramp *n*
on-screen *adj* or *adv*
on-season *adj, adv* or *n*
on-site *adj* or *adv*
onstage *adj* or *adv*
on-the-job *adj*
on-the-record *adj*
on-the-scene *adj*
on-the-spot *adj*
open-air *adj*
open air *n*
open-and-shut *adj*
open bar *n*
open classroom *n*
open-door *adj*
open-end *adj*
open-ended *adj*
open enrollment *n*
open-eyed *adj*
open-faced *adj*
openhanded *adj*

open-hearted *adj*
open-heart surgery *n*
open housing *n*
open-line *adj*
open marriage *n*
open-minded *adj*
openmouthed *adj*
open season *n*
operagoer *n*
opera house *n*
out-and-out *adj*
outdated *adj*
outdistance *v*
outer space *n*
out-front *adj*
outlaw *adj, n* or *v*
outmoded *adj*
out-of-body *adj*
out-of-bounds *adj*
out of bounds *adv*
out-of-court *adj*
out-of-date *adj*
out-of-pocket *adj*
out-of-sight *adj*
out-of-the-way *adj*
outpatient *n*
outplacement *n*
outsmart *v*
outward-bound *adj*
overall *adj* or *n*
overcommit *v*
overdose *n* or *v*
overdub *n* or *v*
overeat *v*
overexposure *n*
overextend *v*
overkill *n*
overstructured *adj*
over-the-counter *adj*
ozone layer *n*

pack animal *n*
pack date *n*

packhorse *n*
pack rat *n*
painkiller *n*
paintbrush *n*
pan-broil *v*
pancake *n* or *v*
pantsuit *n*
pantyhose *n*
paperback *adj* or *n*
paper-clip *v*
paper clip *n*
paper-thin *adj*
paper trail *n*
paper-train *v*
paperweight *n*
paperwork *n*
parent-child *adj*
part and parcel *n*
parti-colored *adj*
part-time *adj*
part time *n*
passageway *n*
passalong *adj* or *n*
pass along *v*
passbook *n*
pass-fail *adj* or *n*
pass-through *adj* or *n*
pass through *v*
passive-aggressive *adj*
passive smoking *n*
patchwork *adj, n* or *v*
pat-down *n*
pathbreaking *adj*
pathfinder *n*
pay-as-you-go *adj* or *n*
payback *n*
pay back *v*
pay cable *n*
paycheck *n*
payday *n*
pay dirt *n*
payoff *adj* or *n*
pay off *v*

payout *n*

pay out *v*

pay-per-view *adj or n*

pay phone *n*

payroll *n or v*

pay-TV *n*

peacekeeping *adj or n*

peacetime *adj or n*

pen name *n*

penny-ante *adj*

penny pincher *n*

penny-pinching *adj*

pepper-and-salt *adj or n*

person-day *n*

person-to-person *adj or adv*

person-year *n*

phasedown *n*

phase down *v*

phaseout *n*

phase out *v*

phone-in *n*

photocopy *n or v*

photo-essay *or* photo essay *n*

photo finish *n*

picker-upper *n*

pick-me-up *n*

pickpocket *n or v*

pickproof *adj*

pickup *adj or n*

pick up *v*

picture-book *adj*

picture book *n*

picture-perfect *adj*

picture-postcard *adj*

picture tube *n*

piece by piece *adv*

piece goods *n*

pie chart *n*

piecemeal *adj or adv*

pigeonhole *n or v*

pigeon-toed *adj*

piggyback *adv, n or v*

pig-out *n*

pig out *v*

pigpen *n*

pigskin *n*

pileup *n*

pillowcase *n*

pillow talk *n*

pinch-hit *v*

pinch hit *n*

pinhole *n*

pink-collar *adj*

pinkeye *n*

pink-slip *v*

pink slip *n*

pin money *n*

pinpoint *adj, n or v*

pinstripe *n*

pinstriped *adj*

pint-size *adj*

pinup *adj or n*

pipe dream *n*

pipeline *n or v*

pipe-rack *adj*

pipe rack *n*

pistol-whip *v*

pitch-black *adj*

pitch-dark *adj*

pitchfork *n or v*

pitch in *v*

pitch pipe *n*

pit stop *n*

pitter-patter *adj, adv or n*

placeholder *n*

place mat *n*

plainclothes *adj*

plainclothesman *n*

plain sailing *n*

plainspoken *adj*

plain-wrap *adj*

planeload *n*

playact *v*

playacting *n*

playback *n*

play back v
playbill n
play-by-play adj or n
play date n
playgoer n
playhouse n
playing card n
play-off n
play off v
playpen n
playroom n
playwright n
playwriting n
plea-bargain n or v
plugged-in adj
plug-in adj or n
plug in v
pocket park n
pocket-size adj
point-blank adj or adv
poison-pen adj
police force n
policeman n
police officer n
policeperson n
police station n
policewoman n
policymaker n
policy-setting adj
political-action adj
political correctness n
politically correct adj
pooh-pooh v
pooper-scooper n
pop-top adj or n
pop-up adj or n
porthole n
postage-stamp adj
postage stamp n
postmark n
post office n
postseason adj
potholder n

pothole n
pot roast n
potshot n or v
poverty-level adj
poverty level n
poverty-stricken adj
power base n
powerbroker n
powerhouse n
power play n
practice-teach v
practice teacher n
praiseworthy adj
preeminent adj
preschool adj or n
preschooler n
price-cutter n
price-fixing n
price index n
primary-care adj
primary care n
prime rate n
prime-time adj
prime time n
prizefight n
prizewinner n
pro-choice adj
pro-choicer n
product line n
profit and loss n
profitsharing adj
profit sharing n
pro-life adj
pro-lifer n
proof-of-purchase n
protest vote n
public speaking n
public-spirited adj
pull date n
pullover adj or n
pull over v
pull-tab adj or n
pull-up n

punch-drunk *adj*
purebred *adj* or *n*
push-button *adj*
push button *n*
push-in *adj*
push in *v*
pushover *n*
pushpin *n*
push-up *adj* or *n*
put-down *n*
put down *v*
put-on *adj* or *n*
put on *v*
put-upon *adj*

quarter-hour *n*
quartermaster *n*
queen-size *adj*
quick fix *n*
quick-freeze *v*
quicksand *n*
quick study *n*
quick-tempered *adj*
quick-witted *adj*

rabbit ears *n*
racehorse *n*
racetrack *n*
race-walk *v*
race walking *n*
radiobroadcast *n* or *v*
ragtime *n*
ragweed *n*
rainout *n*
rain out *v*
rainwear *n*
rainy-day *adj*
rainy day *n*
rake-off *n*
rake off *v*
rank-and-file *adj*
rank and file *n*
rapid-fire *adj*

rapid fire *n*
rattletrap *adj* or *n*
raw bar *n*
read-through *n*
read through *v*
readymade *n*
ready-mix *adj* or *n*
ready-to-wear *adj* or *n*
real-estate *adj*
real estate *n*
real-life *adj*
real-world *adj*
real world *n*
rear-end *v*
rear end *n*
recessionproof *adj*
redcap *n*
red-carpet *adj*
red carpet *n*
red-eye *adj* or *n*
red-handed *adj*
redhead *n*
redheaded *adj*
red-hot *adj* or *n*
rent control *n*
rent-controlled *adj*
rent-stabilization *n*
rent-stabilized *adj*
rest stop *n*
revolving-door *adj*
right-hand *adj*
right hand *n*
right-handed *adj* or *adv*
right-of-center *adj*
right-of-way *n*
right-on *adj*
rightsize *v*
right-to-die *adj*
right-to-know *adj*
right-to-work *adj*
right-wing *adj*
ring binder *n*
ringleader *n*

ringmaster *n*
ringworm *n*
rinky-dink *adj* or *n*
riot act *n*
ripoff *n*
rip off *v*
rip-roaring *adj*
riptide *n*
risk management *n*
riverbank *n*
riverboat *n*
riverside *adj* or *n*
roadblock *n* or *v*
road hog *n*
roadhouse *n*
road map *n*
road-test *v*
road test *n*
rock-bottom *adj*
rock bottom *n*
rock climbing *n*
rocket scientist *n*
rock-'n'-roll *adj, n* or *v*
role model *n*
role-play *v*
roll-around *adj*
roll around *v*
rollaway *adj* or *n*
rollback *n*
roll back *v*
roll call *n*
roller-coaster *adj* or *v*
roller coaster *n*
roller-skate *v*
roller skate *n*
roll-on *adj* or *n*
roll on *v*
rollout *n*
roll out *v*
rollover *n*
roll over *v*
roll-up *n*
roll up *v*

root beer *n*
root canal *n*
rough-and-ready *adj*
rough-and-tumble *adj* or *n*
rough-cut *adj*
rough cut *n*
roughneck *n* or *v*
roundabout *adj* or *n*
round-shouldered *adj*
roundtable *n*
round-table *adj*
round-the-clock *adj*
round-trip *adj*
round trip *n*
roundup *n*
round up *v*
roustabout *n*
rubber band *n*
rubber cement *n*
rubberneck *n* or *v*
rubber-stamp *adj* or *v*
rubber stamp *n*
rub in *v*
rub off *v*
rubout *n*
rub out *v*
rule-breaking *adj*
runaround *n*
run around *v*
runaway *adj* or *n*
run away *v*
rundown *n*
run-down *adj*
run down *v*
run-in *adj* or *n*
run in *v*
running mate *n*
run-on *adj* or *n*
run-through *adj* or *n*
run through *v*
rush-hour *adj*
rush hour *n*

sacred cow *n*
saddlebag *n*
saddle blanket *n*
safe-conduct *n*
safecracker *n*
safe-deposit *adj*
safeguard *n* or *v*
safekeeping *n*
safe-sex *adj*
safe sex *n*
safety belt *n*
safety-deposit *adj*
safety glass *n*
sailboarding *n*
sailboat *n*
sailfish *n*
salad bar *n*
salad dressing *n*
salesman *n*
salesmanship *n*
salesperson *n*
sales slip *n*
sales tax *n*
saleswoman *n*
salt-and-pepper *adj*
saltshaker *n*
saltwater *adj*
salt water *n*
sandbag *n* or *v*
sandbox *n*
sandcastle *n*
sand dollar *n*
sandhog *n*
sandlot *adj* or *n*
sand trap *n*
sauceboat *n*
saucepan *n*
sawed-off *adj*
sawhorse *n*
scale-down *n*
scale down *v*
scale-up *n*
scale up *v*

scatter pin *n*
scattershot *adj*
scene-stealer *n*
school-age *adj*
school age *n*
schoolbag *n*
schoolboy *adj* or *n*
school break *n*
school bus *n*
schoolchild *n*
school district *n*
schoolgirl *n*
schoolhouse *n*
schoolkid *n*
schoolmaster *n*
schoolmate *n*
schoolmistress *n*
schoolroom *n*
schoolteacher *n*
schoolwork *n*
school year *n*
sci-fi *adj* or *n*
scot-free *adj*
screenplay *n*
screen-test *v*
screen test *n*
screenwriter *n*
screw around *v*
screwball *adj* or *n*
screw-on *adj*
screw on *v*
screw-top *adj* or *n*
screw-up *n*
screw up *v*
scriptwriter *n*
S-curve *n*
scuttlebutt *n*
seabed *n*
sea breeze *n*
seacoast *n*
seafood *n*
seagoing *adj*
seajack *n* or *v*

sea legs *n*
sea level *n*
seaplane *n*
seaport *n*
sea power *n*
searchlight *n*
search warrant *n*
seascape *n*
seashell *n*
seashore *n*
seasick *adj*
seaside *adj* or *n*
seat belt *n*
seat-of-the-pants *adj*
seawater *n*
seaweed *n*
seaworthy *adj*
second-class *adj* or *adv*
second class *n*
second fiddle *n*
second-generation *adj*
second-guess *v*
secondhand *adj* or *adv*
second hand *n*
secondhand smoke *n*
second home *n*
second-rate *adj*
secret-service *adj*
secret service *n*
Seeing Eye dog *n*
see-through *adj* or *n*
self-correcting *adj*
self-destruct *v*
self-employed *adj*
self-image *n*
self-inflicted *adj*
self-mailer *n*
self-replicating *adj*
sell-back *n*
sell date *n*
sellout *n*
sell out *v*
semiabstract *adj*

semiannual *adj*
semiautomatic *adj* or *n*
semicircle *n*
semidetached *adj*
semifinalist *n*
semi-independent *adj*
send-off *n*
send off *v*
send-up *n*
send up *v*
serious-minded *adj*
service center *n*
serviceman *n*
serviceperson *n*
servicewoman *n*
set by *v*
set down *v*
set-in *adj*
setoff *n*
set off *v*
set on *v*
set-piece *adj*
set piece *n*
set-to *n*
set to *v*
set-up *n*
sex appeal *n*
sexed-up *adj*
sex hormone *n*
sex kitten *n*
sex-linkage *n*
sex-linked *adj*
sex object *n*
sexploitation *n*
sexpot *n*
sex shop *n*
sex symbol *n*
sexual abuse *n*
shakedown *n*
shake down *v*
shakeout *n*
shake out *v*
shake-up *n*

shake up *v*

shape-up *n*

shape up *v*

shareholder *n*

sharp-cut *adj*

sharpshooter *n*

sharp-tongued *adj*

sharp-witted *adj*

shatterproof *adj*

sheepdog *n*

sheepskin *adj or n*

sheet music *n*

shelf life *n*

shellfish *n*

shell game *n*

shell shock *n*

shipboard *adj or n*

shipbuilder *n*

shipshape *adj or adv*

shipwreck *n or v*

shirtsleeve *n*

shock-resistant *adj*

shock-test *v*

shock wave *n*

shoehorn *n*

shoestring *adj or n*

shoo-in *n*

shoo in *v*

shoot-'em-up *n*

shoot-out *n*

shoot out *v*

shoot-up *n*

shoot up *v*

shopkeeper *n*

shoplifter *n*

shorefront *adj or n*

shoreline *n*

shortchange *v*

short-circuit *v*

short circuit *n*

shortcoming *n*

shortcut *adj or n*

short-cut *v*

shorthanded *adj*

short-haul *adj*

short-lived *adj*

short-order *adj*

short-range *adj*

short-run *adj*

shortsighted *adj*

short-tempered *adj*

short-term *adj*

shortwave *adj, n or v*

short-winded *adj*

shotgun *adj or n*

shoulder-length *adj*

show business *n*

showcase *n or v*

showdown *n*

showgirl *n*

showman *n*

show-me *adj*

show-off *n*

show off *v*

showpiece *n*

showplace *n*

showstopper *n*

show tune *n*

shrink-wrap *n or v*

shutdown *n*

shut down *v*

shut-in *adj or n*

shut in *v*

shutoff *n*

shut off *v*

shutout *n*

shut out *v*

sick and tired *adj*

sickbed *n*

sick day *n*

sick leave *n*

sick pay *n*

sickroom *n*

sidebar *n*

side-by-side *adj*

side by side *adv*

sidecar *n*
side dish *n*
side effect *n*
side-glance *n*
sidekick *n*
sidelight *n*
sideline *n* or *v*
sidelong *adj* or *adv*
sideman *n*
side road *n*
sideshow *n*
sidesplitting *adj*
sidestep *v*
side step *n*
sideswipe *n* or *v*
sight-read *v*
sightsee *v*
sight-seeing *adj* or *n*
sign-in *n*
sign in *v*
sign-off *n*
sign off *v*
sign-on *n*
sign on *v*
sign-out *n*
sign out *v*
sign-up *n*
sign up *v*
silkscreen *adj, n* or *v*
silver screen *n*
silver-tongued *adj*
sing-along *n*
sing along *v*
single-breasted *adj*
single-family *adj*
single file *adj* or *adv*
single-handed *adj* or *adv*
single-minded *adj*
single-occupancy *adj*
single occupancy *n*
single-sex *adj*
single-space *v*
singsong *adj* or *n*

sinkhole *n*
sit-down *adj* or *n*
site-specific *adj*
sit-in *n*
sit-up *n*
six-shooter *n*
skateboard *n* or *v*
sketchbook *n*
ski jump *n*
ski lift *n*
skin-deep *adj* or *adv*
skin-dive *v*
skin diving *n*
skin flick *n*
skinhead *n*
skinny-dip *n* or *v*
skin-search *v*
skin search *n*
skintight *adj*
skybox *n*
skybridge *n*
skycap *n*
sky cover *n*
skydiving *n*
sky-high *adj* or *adv*
skyjack *v*
skylight *n*
skyline *n* or *v*
skyrocket *n* or *v*
skywalk *n*
sleep-away *adj*
sleep-in *adj* or *n*
sleep in *v*
sleeping pill *n*
sleep sofa *n*
slice-of-life *adj*
sling-back *adj* or *n*
sling chair *n*
slipcase *n*
slipcover *n* or *v*
slippery slope *n*
slipshod *adj*
slip-up *n*

slip up *v*
slow-motion *adj*
slow motion *n*
slumlord *n*
small-claims court *n*
small-minded *adj*
small-scale *adj*
small-time *adj*
smart money *n*
smash hit *n*
smash-up *n*
smear-sheet *n*
smoke detector *n*
smokeout *n*
snail-paced *adj*
snail's pace *n*
snakebite *n*
snake pit *n*
snapback *n*
snap back *v*
snap-off *adj*
snap-on *adj*
snob appeal *n*
snowbird *n*
snowbound *adj*
snowcapped *adj*
snowfall *n*
snow-white *adj*
soapbox *adj* or *n*
soap opera *n*
so-called *adj*
social climber *n*
social-minded *adj*
softback *adj* or *n*
soft-boiled *adj*
soft-pedal *v*
soft pedal *n*
soft-sell *adj* or *v*
soft sell *n*
soft-shell *adj* or *n*
soft-shoe *adj*
soft-spoken *adj*
sole-source *adj*

solid-state *adj*
songwriter *n*
sonic boom *n*
so-so *adj* or *adv*
soul-searching *n*
soundalike *n*
sound bite *n*
soundstage *n*
soundtrack *n*
space-age *adj*
spaceborne *adj*
space cadet *n*
spacecraft *n*
spaced-out *adj*
space-saving *adj*
spacewalk *n* or *v*
spearhead *n* or *v*
special effects *n pl*
special-interest *adj*
special-order *v*
special order *n*
speechwriter *n*
speed bump *n*
speed dial *n*
speed limit *n*
speed-read *v*
spellbound *adj*
spin control *n*
spin doctor *n*
spine-chilling *adj*
spin-off *n*
spin-out *n*
split-level *adj* or *n*
sports car *n*
sportscast *n*
sports-watching *n*
sportswriter *n*
spot-check *v*
spotlight *n* or *v*
spray-painted *adj*
spur-of-the-moment *adj*
square-shouldered *adj*
squeaky-clean *adj*

squeeze bottle *n*
stagecraft *n*
stage director *n*
stage fright *n*
stagehand *n*
stage left *n*
stage-manage *v*
stage right *n*
stagestruck *adj*
standard-bearer *n*
standby *adj or n*
stand by *v*
stand-in *n*
stand in *v*
standoff *adj or n*
stand off *v*
stand-up *adj or n*
stand up *v*
starboard *adj or n*
star-crossed *adj*
stargaze *v*
starry-eyed *adj*
starstruck *adj*
star-studded *adj*
start-up *adj or n*
start up *v*
statehouse *n*
state-of-the-art *adj*
state of the art *n*
stateroom *n*
stateside *adj or adv*
station break *n*
station house *n*
stationmaster *n*
station-to-station *adj or adv*
station wagon *n*
steadfast *adj*
steam iron *n*
steamship *n*
steel-trap *adj*
steel trap *n*
steelworker *n*

stepbrother *n*
step-by-step *adj*
stepchild *n*
stepdaughter *n*
stepfamily *n*
stepfather *n*
stepladder *n*
stepmother *n*
stepped-up *adj*
steppingstone *n*
stick-to-itiveness *n*
stir-crazy *adj*
stockbroker *n*
stockholder *n*
stock market *n*
stockroom *n*
stone-cold *adv*
stone-faced *adj*
stone-ground *adj*
stonewall *adj or v*
stone wall *n*
stonewashed *adj*
stop-and-go *adj*
stopgap *adj or n*
stoplight *n*
stopover *n*
store-bought *adj*
storefront *adj or n*
storyline *n*
storyteller *n*
straight-ahead *adj*
street people *n pl*
street-smart *adj*
street smarts *n pl*
streetwise *adj*
stressed-out *adj*
stress-test *v*
stress test *n*
strife-torn *adj*
strikebreaker *n*
stripped-down *adj*
strip-search *v*
strip search *n*

strong-arm *adj* or *v*
strongbox *n*
strong-minded *adj*
stun gun *n*
success story *n*
sugar-free *adj*
sum-up *n*
sum up *v*
sunblock *n*
sunburn *n* or *v*
sunstroke *n*
superhighway *n*
supper club *n*
suppertime *n*
supply-side *adj*
sustained-release *adj*
swearing-in *n*
swearword *n*
sweaterdress *n*
sweater-vest *n*
sweatpants *n*
sweat suit *n*
sweet-and-sour *adj*
sweet-talk *v*
sweet talk *n*
sweet tooth *n*
swimsuit *n*
switchblade *n*

tab key *n*
tablecloth *n*
table-hop *v*
tabletop *adj* or *n*
tailgate *adj, n* or *v*
taillight *n*
tailor-made *adj* or *n*
take-along *adj* or *n*
take-charge *adj*
take-home pay *n*
takeoff *n*
take off *v*
takeout *adj* or *n*
take out *v*

takeover *n*
take over *v*
talking head *n*
talking-to *n*
talk radio *n*
talk-show *adj*
talk show *n*
tank top *n*
tap-dance *v*
tap dance *n*
tap dancer *n*
tape deck *n*
tape-record *v*
tape recorder *n*
target date *n*
tastemaker *n*
tax-deductible *adj*
tax-exempt *adj* or *n*
tax-free *adj*
taxicab *n*
tax-increase *adj*
tax increase *n*
taxpayer *n*
tea bag *n*
teach-in *n*
teamwork *n*
tea party *n*
teapot *n*
teardrop *n*
tear gas *n*
tearjerker *n*
tear sheet *n*
technobandit *n*
technopop *n*
techno-thriller *n*
tenderfoot *n*
tenderhearted *adj*
tension-filled *adj*
ten-speed *adj* or *n*
tenth-rate *adj*
tenure-track *adj*
terror-stricken *adj*
test-drive *v*

test-fly *v*
test-market *v*
test pattern *n*
test-tube *adj*
test tube *n*
textbook *adj* or *n*
thank-you *adj* or *n*
theater-in-the-round *n*
theme-park *adj*
theme park *n*
theme song *n*
thick and thin *n*
thickset *adj*
thick-skinned *adj*
thing-in-itself *n*
think tank *n*
thin-skinned *adj*
third-class *adj* or *adv*
third class *n*
third-degree *adj* or *v*
third degree *n*
third dimension *n*
thirdhand *adj* or *adv*
third-rate *adj*
thoroughfare *n*
thoroughgoing *adj*
thought-out *adj*
thought-provoking *adj*
threadbare *adj*
three-decker *n*
three-dimensional *adj*
three-handed *adj*
three-piece *adj* or *n*
thriftshop *n*
throwaway *adj* or *n*
throw away *v*
throwback *n*
throw back *v*
throw-in *n*
throw in *v*
thumbnail *adj*, *n* or *v*
thumbprint *n*
thumbs-down *n*

thumbs-up *n*
thundercloud *n*
thunderstorm *n*
tick-borne *adj*
ticketholder *n*
tideland *n*
tidewater *n*
tiebreaker *n*
tie-dye *n* or *v*
tie-dyed *adj*
tie-in *adj* or *n*
tie in *v*
tiepin *n*
tie-up *n*
tie up *v*
tight-knit *adj*
time bind *n*
time bomb *n*
time-consuming *adj*
timed-release *adj*
time-honored *adj*
time-out *n*
time-share *n* or *v*
time-sharing *n*
timetable *n*
time-tested *adj*
time warp *n*
tip-off *n*
tiptop *adj*, *adv* or *n*
titleholder *n*
to-do *n*
toeshoe *n*
toe-to-toe *adj* or *adv*
tollbooth *n*
toll call *n*
toll-free *adj* or *adv*
tone-deaf *adj*
tongue-in-cheek *adj*
tongue-lash *v*
tongue-tie *n* or *v*
toothache *n*
toothbrush *n*
toothpaste *n*

tooth powder *n*
too-too *adj or adv*
top billing *n*
topcoat *n*
top dog *n*
top dollar *n*
top-drawer *adj*
top drawer *n*
top-heavy *adj*
top-level *adj*
topnotch *adj*
top-of-the-line *adj*
topside *adj, adv or n*
torchbearer *n*
toss-up *n*
tote bag *n*
touchdown *n*
touch down *v*
touch-tone *adj or n*
touch-up *n*
touch up *v*
touchy-feely *adj*
tough love *n*
tough-minded *adj*
town hall *n*
townhome *n*
town house *n*
track record *n*
trade-in *adj or n*
trade in *v*
trademark *n or v*
trade-name *v*
trade name *n*
trade-off *n*
trade off *v*
trail bike *n*
trash can *n*
treat-and-release *adj*
treble clef *n* (G clef)
tri-city *adj or n*
trickle-down *adj*
trick-or-treat *v*
trick or treat *n*

trigger-happy *adj*
triple-decker *adj or n*
triple-digit *adj*
true-blue *adj*
true blue *n*
true-life *adj*
trumped-up *adj*
tryout *n*
try out *v*
T-shirt *n*
tumbledry *v*
tuned-in *adj*
tuned in *v*
tune-up *n*
turnabout *n*
turnaround *n*
turn around *v*
turndown *adj or n*
turn down *v*
turned-on *adj*
turnoff *n*
turnon *n*
turnout *n*
turnover *adj or n*
turnpike *n*
turntable *n*
turtleneck *n*
21st-century *adj*
21st century *n*
two-by-four *adj or n*
two-dimensional *adj*
two-faced *adj*
two-family house *n*
two-piece *adj*
two-piecer *n*
two-ply *adj*
two-seater *n*
twosome *n*
two-step *n or v*
two-suiter *n*
two-time *v*
two-tone *adj*
two-way *adj*

two-wheeler *n*
typecast *v*

uh-huh *interj*
uh-oh *interj*
uh-uh *interj*
underarm *adj* or *adv*
undercover *adj*
underdog *n*
underprivileged *adj*
under-the-counter *adj*
under-the-table *adj*
unit pricing *n*
unmade-up *adj*
up-and-coming *adj*
up-and-down *adj*
up and down *adv*
up-and-up *n*
update *n* or *v*
upend *v*
up-front *adj* or *adv*
uphill *adj, adv* or *n*
upmarket *adj* or *adv*
upper-class *adj*
upper class *n*
upscale *adj, n* or *v*
upside-down *adj*
upside down *adv*
upstage *adj, adv* or *v*
up-to-date *adj*
up-to-the-minute *adj*
U-shaped *adj*
U-turn *n* or *v*

vacuum cleaner *n*
vacuum-packed *adj*
veto-proof *adj*
vice-chairman *n*
vice-chancellor *n*
vice-consul *n*
vice president *n*
vice-regent *n*
viceroy *n*

videocassette *n*
videocassette recorder *n*
video jockey *n*
videotape *n* or *v*
violoncello *n* (cello)
V-neck *adj* or *n*
voice-mail *adj*
voice mail *n*
voice-over *n*
voiceprint *n*
V-shaped *adj*
V sign *n*

wake-up *adj* or *n*
wake up *v*
walkie-talkie *n* (radio)
walk-in *adj* or *n*
walk-on *n*
walkout *adj* or *n*
walk-through *adj* or *n*
walk-up *adj* or *n*
wall-to-wall *adj*
warhead *n*
warlord *n*
warm-blooded *adj*
warm-down *n*
warmed-over *adj*
warmhearted *adj*
warm-up *adj* or *n*
warm up *v*
war power *n*
warts-and-all *adj*
war zone *n*
wash-and-wear *adj*
washcloth *n*
washed-out *adj*
washed-up *adj*
wastebasket *n*
wasteland *n*
watchband *n*
watchdog *adj, n* or *v*
waterbed *n*
watercolor *adj* or *n*

watercooler *n*
watered-down *adj*
waterfront *n*
waterpower *n*
water-repellent *adj*
watersaver *n*
watershed *adj* or *n*
water-ski *v*
water ski *n*
water-skier *n*
water softener *n*
water-soluble *adj*
watt-hour *n*
wavelength *n*
way-out *adj*
way out *n*
weak-kneed *adj*
weak-minded *adj*
weather-beaten *adj*
weathercaster *n*
weatherman *n*
weather map *n*
weatherperson *n*
weatherwoman *n*
weekday *adj* or *n*
weekdays *adv*
weekend *adj, n* or *v*
weekends *adv*
weeknight *adj* or *n*
weigh-in *n*
well-adjusted *adj*
well-advised *adj*
well-being *n*
wellborn *adj*
well-bred *adj*
well-done *adj*
well-dressed *adj*
well-informed *adj*
well-known *adj*
well-off *adj*
well-rounded *adj*
well-thought-of *adj*
well-to-do *adj*

well-wisher *n*
wet bar *n*
wet blanket *n*
wetlands *n pl*
wet-mop *v*
wet suit *n*
whacked-out *adj*
wheeler and dealer *n*
wheeler-dealer *n*
whirlwind *adj* or *n*
whistle-blower *n*
whistle-stop *n* or *v*
whitecap *n*
white-collar *adj*
white-faced *adj*
white-hot *adj*
whiteout *n*
white out *v*
white-tie *adj*
whitewash *n* or *v*
whitewater *adj*
white water *n*
whiz-bang *adj* or *n*
whodunit *n*
whole-wheat *adj*
wide-angle *adj*
wide-awake *adj*
widebody *n*
wide-eyed *adj*
widemouthed *adj*
wide-open *adj*
wide-ranging *adj*
wide-screen *adj*
widespread *adj*
wild-and-crazy *adj*
wild-and-woolly *adj*
wild-card *adj*
wild card *n*
wildcat *adj, n* or *v*
wild-goose chase *n*
willpower *n*
wimp out *v*
windchill factor *n*

wind-down *n*
windfall *adj* or *n*
window-shop *v*
windshield *n*
wine cellar *n*
wine cooler *n*
winegrower *n*
winetaster *n*
winner-take-all *adj*
wintertime *n*
win-win *adj*
wiped-out *adj*
wipeout *n*
wipe out *v*
wiretap *adj, n* or *v*
wire-transfer *v*
wire transfer *n*
wised-up *adj*
wishbone *n*
wish list *n*
wishy-washy *adj*
witchcraft *n*
witch doctor *n*
with-it *adj*
witness stand *n*
wolfhound *n*
wolf pack *n*
woman-chaser *n*
womanpower *n*
won-lost *adj*
woodsman *n*
woodwind *adj* or *n*
woodworking *adj* or *n*
word association *n*
word-for-word *adj*
word for word *adv*
word-of-mouth *adj*
word processing *adj* or *n*
workaholic *n*
workbench *n*
workday *adj* or *n*
worked-up *adj*
work ethic *n*

workforce *n*
working-class *adj*
working class *n*
work off *v*
workout *n*
work out *v*
work over *v*
workplace *n*
work-release *adj*
work rules *n pl*
worksheet *n*
workshop *n*
workspace *n*
workstation *n*
work-study program *n*
workup *n*
work up *v*
workweek *n*
worldbeater *n*
world-class *adj*
world-famous *adj*
worldly-wise *adj*
world-shaking *adj*
world-weary *adj*
worldwide *adj* or *adv*
worn-out *adj*
worrywart *n*
worst-case *adj*
would-be *adj* or *n*
wraparound *adj* or *n*
wrap-up *n*
wrap up *v*
write-in *adj* or *n*
write in *v*
write-off *n*
write off *v*
write-up *n*
write up *v*
wrongdoer *n*
wrongdoing *n*
wrongheaded *adj*
wrong number *n*

wrought iron *adj* or *n*
wrought-up *adj* or *n*

X chromosome *n*
X-linked *adj*
X-rated *adj*
x-ray *adj, n* or *v* (also
  x ray, X ray, X-ray)

Y chromosome *n*
year-around *adj*
yearbook *n*
year-end *adj* or *n*
yearlong *adj*
year-round *adj*
yes-man *n*
yes-no question *n*
you-all *pron*
young adult *n*
youngblood *adj*

young blood *n*
youth hostel *n*
youthquake *n*
yo-yo *adj, n* or *v*
yule log *n*
yuletide *adj* or *n*
yum-yum *interj*

zero-base *adj*
zero hour *n*
zero-sum *adj*
zigzag *adj, adv, n* or *v*
zip-code *v*
zip code *n*
zip gun *n*
zip-in *adj*
zip in *v*
zip-out *adj*
zip out *v*
zookeeper *n*

· 10 ·
Preferred Spelling

While there are often two and occasionally more ways to spell many words and phrases correctly, there is always one preferred way. The following list includes examples of preferred American usage over chiefly British variations (designated by an asterisk) and many foreign words and phrases with diacritical marks (such as accents in French and tildes in Spanish) commonly used in both American and British English.

For	*Use*
abridgement	abridgment
absinth	absinthe
a capella	a cappella
accessorise*	accessorize
acclimatise*	acclimatize
accouterment	accoutrement
acknowledgement*	acknowledgment
adaptor	adapter
addible	addable

For	*Use*
advertize*	advertise
advertizement*	advertisement
advisor	adviser
aetiology*	etiology
afficionado	aficionado
afterwards	afterward
aggrandise*	aggrandize
agonise*	agonize
a la	à la
a la carte	à la carte
a la mode	à la mode
alarum *archaic*	alarm
aline	align
alinement	alignment
alright	all right *adv* all-right *adj*
altho	although
amidst	amid
amongst	among
amuck	amok
anaesthesia	anesthesia

For	Use
analogue*	analog
analyse*	analyze
anglicise*	anglicize
anyways *nonstandard*	anyway
aphrodisiacal	aphrodisiac *adj*
apologise*	apologize
appetiser*	appetizer
appetising*	appetizing
archeology	archaeology
ardour*	ardor
argyll	argyle
armour*	armor
artsy	arty
ascendent	ascendant
ascetical	ascetic
askant	askance
astronautical	astronautic
astronomic	astronomical
atomiser*	atomizer
awestricken	awestruck
awless	aweless

For	Use
axe	ax
ay	aye
backhanded *adv*	backhand
backwards	backward
bailer	bailor
baloney	bologna
bandana	bandanna
bannister*	banister
baptise*	baptize
barbeque	barbecue
barcarolle	barcarole
barebacked	bareback
barefooted	barefoot
bare-knuckled	bare-knuckle
barkeeper	barkeep
bat mitzvah	bas mitzvah
baulk*	balk
beduin	bedouin
behaviour*	behavior
belabour*	belabor

For	*Use*
belle époque	belle epoque
bell lyre	belle-lyra
bespoken	bespoke
bicolor *adj*	bicolored
blear-eyed	bleary-eyed
blintz	blintze
blizzardly	blizzardy
bobtailed	bobtail
boffo	boff
bogie *or* bogy	bogey
bogyman	bogeyman
boney	bony
bonnie	bonny
boogy *or* boogey	boogie
bookmarker	bookmark
bosque	bosk
bougainvillaea	bougainvillea
bourguignon	bourguignonne
bowdlerise*	bowdlerize
Brahmin	Brahman
briquet	briquette

For	Use
broadcasted	broadcast
broncho	bronco
brontosaur	brontosaurus
brutalise*	brutalize
buckeroo	buckaroo
budgeter	budgeteer
bullrush	bulrush
bumkin	bumpkin
burnous	burnoose
bursted	burst
bust *v*	busted
busted *adj*	bust
by-by	bye-bye
bye-election*	by-election
byelaw*	bylaw
Caesarian/caesarian	Caesarean/caesarean
cafe	café
cagy	cagey
Cajan	Cajun
calibre*	caliber

For	Use
Canada lynx	Canadian lynx
Canadian goose	Canada goose
candour*	candor
cannibalise*	cannibalize
canvass *n*	canvas
capitalise*	capitalize
cardsharp	cardsharper
catalogue	catalog
caviare	caviar
centralise*	centralize
centre*	center
cesarian	cesarean
cesarian section	cesarean section
chammy *or* shammy	chamois
chanty	chantey
Chanukah	Hanukkah
chaperone	chaperon
cheque*	check
chequer*	checker
chickory	chicory
chile *or* chilli	chili

For	Use
chimaera	chimera
chockful	chock-full
chocolatey	chocolaty
choosey	choosy
chukka	chukker
chutzpa *or* hutzpah *or* hutzpa	chutzpah
cigaret	cigarette
cineaste *or* cinéaste	cineast
cire	ciré
cithern *or* cithren	cittern
civilisation*	civilization
civilise*	civilize
clamour*	clamor
cliche	cliché
cliquy	cliquey
cloisonne	cloisonné
coastguardman	coastguardsman
coastwards	coastward
cockamamie	cockamamy
collectable	collectible

For	Use
colour*	color
condemnor	condemner
conjuror	conjurer
conveyer	conveyor
cookery book*	cookbook
cooky	cookie
copesetic *or* copasetic	copacetic
cosmical	cosmic
cosy, cozey, *or* cozie	cozy
counselling*	counseling
counsellor*	counselor
creme	crème
crème fraiche	crème fraîche
crêpe	crepe
crêpe de chine	crepe de chine
criticise*	criticize
crumby	crummy
crystallise*	crystallize
cullender	colander
curet	curette
curlycue	curlicue

For	*Use*
currie	curry
curtsey	curtsy
curvacious	curvaceous
daylight savings time	daylight saving time
début	debut
décor	decor
découpage	decoupage
defence*	defense
deflater	deflator
demagog	demagogue
dependant	dependent
descendent	descendant
dextrous	dexterous
dialog	dialogue
dietician	dietitian
diluvian	diluvial
dognaper	dognapper
donut	doughnut
dopy	dopey
double-decked	double-deck

For	*Use*
draught*	draft
draught* beer	draft beer
drouth	drought
druggy *n*	druggie
duffel coat	duffle coat
duffle bag	duffel bag
earthwards	earthward
élite	elite
empiric	empirical
encyclopaedia	encyclopedia
endeavour*	endeavor
enquire	inquire
enquiry	inquiry
enrol	enroll
enthral	enthrall
epaulette	epaulet
equalise*	equalize
erotical	erotic
esthetic	aesthetic
etagere	étagère

For	*Use*
euclidian	euclidean
exhalent	exhalant
exorcize	exorcise
expresso (coffee)	espresso
extemporise*	extemporize
externe	extern
extravert	extrovert
fabulistic	fabulist
façade	facade
facetted	faceted
faïence	faience
familiarise*	familiarize
fantastical	fantastic
fantom	phantom
feminise*	feminize
fête	fete
fetich	fetish
fettuccini *or* fettucine *or* fettucini	fettuccine
fibrefill	fiberfill
fibreglass	fiberglass

For	Use
finalise*	finalize
fiord	fjord
flautist	flutist
flavour*	flavor
fluidram	fluid dram
flukey	fluky
flutey	fluty
folksy	folksie
forwards *adv*	forward
frappe	frappé
freebee	freebie
frijol	frijole
frontwards	frontward
gamey	gamy
gerbille	gerbil
glamor	glamour
glamourize	glamorize
glamourous	glamorous
good-by	good-bye
gook	guck

For	Use
grey*	gray (but *greyhound*)
guerilla	guerrilla
habitue	habitué
halva	halvah
hamburg	hamburger
harbour*	harbor
hard-shelled	hard-shell
hari-kari	hara-kiri
haut	haute
hautboy (oboe)	hautbois
heroical	heroic
hiccough	hiccup
highflyer	highflier
high-muckety-muck	high-muck-a-muck
Hindoo	Hindu
Hindostani	Hindustani
hippy *n*	hippie
hokku	haiku
holloware	hollowware
honour*	honor

For	*Use*
honourable*	honorable
hookey	hooky
hoorah *or* hooray	hurrah
hopsacking	hopsack
hosannah	hosanna
hospitalise*	hospitalize
hound's-tooth check	houndstooth check
hula-hula	hula
Hunanese *adj*	Hunan
idealogy	ideology
idiotical	idiotic
idyl	idyll
immortalise*	immortalize
imposter	impostor
inclose	enclose
inclosure	enclosure
incorrupted	incorrupt
indictor	indicter
individualise*	individualize
indorse	endorse

For	*Use*
indorsement	endorsement
ingénue	ingenue
instal	install
instalment	installment
instil	instill
institutor	instituter
internalise*	internalize
interne	intern
intrench	entrench
inwards	inward
itemise*	itemize
jailor	jailer
jalapeno	jalapeño
jeweller*	jeweler
jewellery*	jewelry
jiujitsu *or* jiujutsu	jujitsu
Judaical	Judaic
judgement*	judgment
junky *n*	junkie
kaftan	caftan

For	*Use*
Kasbah	Casbah
Kashmir	Cashmere
kebab *or* kebob	kabob
Kelt, Keltic	Celt, Celtic
kerosine	kerosene
kibbitzer	kibitzer
kiddy	kiddie
kinfolks	kinfolk
king-sized	king-size
klatsch	klatch
kleig light	klieg light
kookie	kooky
labour*	labor
lacerated	lacerate
lacrimal	lachrymal
laic *adj*	laical
lambast	lambaste
laundrette	launderette
leapt	leaped
legitimise*	legitimize

For	*Use*
leitmotif	leitmotiv
lense	lens
leveller	leveler
libellous	libelous
liberalise*	liberalize
licence	license
life-sized	life-size
limey	limy
linguini	linguine
lionise*	lionize
liquify	liquefy
liquorice*	licorice
lissom	lissome
liveability	livability
liveable	livable
loadstar	lodestar
loadstone	lodestone
locater	locator
lollypop	lollipop
louvre	louver
loveable	lovable

For	*Use*
low-keyed	low-key
lubricous	lubricious
lustre	luster
lutanist	lutenist
lynchpin	linchpin
macintosh	mackintosh
macrame	macramé
Magna Charta	Magna Carta
mahjong	mah-jongg
maiolica	majolica
makeable	makable
malarky	malarkey
manilla	manila
mannikin	manikin
man-sized	man-size
marbleise*	marbleize
marvellous*	marvelous
matt	matte
maximise*	maximize
meagre*	meager

For	*Use*
meany	meanie
medallist	medalist
mediaeval	medieval
mêlée	melee
memorise*	memorize
merchandize	merchandise
mesmerise*	mesmerize
methodic	methodical
metier	métier
miaow	meow
microwaveable	microwavable
mineable	minable
miniscule	minuscule
moire	moiré
monicker	moniker
monolog	monologue
monopolise*	monopolize
Moslem	Muslim
motorise*	motorize
mould*	mold
moult*	molt

For	Use
mousey	mousy
moustache	mustache
moveable	movable
naïve	naive
naivete *or* naiveté	naïveté
namable	nameable
Neandertal	Neanderthal
negligé	negligee
neighbour*	neighbor
nickle	nickel
nicknack	knickknack
nite	night
nosey	nosy
novelise*	novelize
noways	noway
nowdays *not a word*	nowadays
nowheres *nonstandard*	nowhere
nymphette	nymphet
odour*	odor
oecumenical*	ecumenical

For	*Use*
oedema*	edema
oesophagus*	esophagus
offence	offense
ofttimes	oftentimes
okay	OK
omelet	omelette
optimise*	optimize
orangey	orangy
organdie	organdy
orthopaedic	orthopedic
outsized	outsize
outwards	outward
overscaled	overscale
oversea*	overseas
oversized	oversize
panelling*	paneling
pantys	panties
pareo	pareu
parlour*	parlor
parrakeet	parakeet

For	Use
Parsee	Parsi
parslied	parsleyed
parti-colored	parti-color
partizan	partisan
pasteurise*	pasteurize
pastromi	pastrami
pate	paté
pathologic	pathological
pâtisserie	patisserie
patronise*	patronize
pattie	patty
pavéed *or* pavéd *or* pave	pavé
pawnor	pawner
payor	payer
peck order	pecking order
pedagog	pedagogue
pedlar	peddler
Pekinese	Pekingese
penalise*	penalize
pencilling*	penciling
pendent *n*	pendant

For	Use
penlite	penlight
petalled	petaled
pharmacopeia	pharmacopoeia
phoney	phony
pilaff	pilaf
pinata	piñata
pint-sized	pint-size
pipet	pipette
pirogi	pierogi
pixillated	pixilated
pixy	pixie
pizazz	pizzazz
playwrighting	playwriting
plier	plyer
plough	plow
polarise*	polarize
pooh	pooh-pooh
popularise*	popularize
practise*	practice
pragmatical	pragmatic
premie	preemie

For	Use
premiere *adj* (top ranking)	premier *n*
première *n* (a first performance)	premiere
première *or* premier *v*	premiere
premiss	premise
preppie	preppy
pressurise*	pressurize
preteenager	preteen
pretence*	pretense
pretorian	praetorian
pricy	pricey
privatise*	privatize
processable	processible
programer	programmer
programing	programming
programme*	program
propellent	propellant
propellor	propeller
protestor	protester
psaltry	psaltery
psyche *v*	psych

For	*Use*
publicise*	publicize
pulverise*	pulverize
quadriphonic	quadraphonic
quahaug (clam)	quahog
quartette	quartet
queazy	queasy
quintette	quintet
Qur'an *or* Quran	Koran
radicalise*	radicalize
rajah	raja
ramequin	ramekin
rancour*	rancor
ranee	rani
rarified	rarefied
rarify	rarefy
rase*	raze
ratable	rateable
rationalise*	rationalize
rebeck	rebec
recognise*	recognize

For	*Use*
régime	regime
repellant	repellent
repp	rep
resume *or* resumé	résumé
reveller	reveler
revery	reverie
revitalise*	revitalize
rhumba	rumba
ricksha	rickshaw
ricrac	rickrack
right-angle *adj*	right-angled
romanticise*	romanticize
ropey	ropy
rouble	ruble
Roumanian *or* Rumanian	Romanian
rumour*	rumor
rustical	rustic
sabre	saber
saki	sake
saleable	salable

For	Use
sanserif	sans serif
sarabande	saraband
sarape	serape
saree	sari
satirise*	satirize
saute	sauté
savannah	savanna
saviour*	savior
savour*	savor
savoury*	savory
scaloppine	scallopini
schismatical	schismatic
schlep	schlepp
schlocky	schlock
schmalz	schmaltz
schmeer	schmear
schmoe	schmo
schrod	scrod
seawards	seaward
selvedge	selvage
semantical	semantic

For	*Use*
señor	senor
señora	senora
señorita	senorita
sensationalise*	sensationalize
sensitise*	sensitize
sepulcher	sepulchre
sequinned	sequined
Shakespearian *or* Shaksperean *or* Shaksperian	Shakespearean
shapeable	shapable
sharable	shareable
sharpy	sharpie
sheikh	sheik
sherbert	sherbet
sherd	shard
shiatzu	shiatsu
shillalah	shillelagh
shmooze	schmooze
shoppe	shop
shtick	schtick
sidewards	sideward

For	Use
signior	signor
sizeable	sizable
skilful*	skillful
skullduggery	skulduggery
slatey	slaty
slumbrous	slumberous
smidgeon *or* smidgin	smidgen
smoulder	smolder
socialise*	socialize
soignée	soigné
soirée	soiree
soliloquise*	soliloquize
sombre*	somber
sometimes	sometime
someways	someway
somewheres	somewhere
soreheaded *adj*	sorehead
soya bean	soybean
spacial	spatial
spacy	spacey
specialise*	specialize

For	*Use*
speciality*	specialty
specie *nonstandard*	species
spectre	specter
spic-and-span	spick-and-span
spikey	spiky
sports *adj*	sport
spryer	sprier
stedfast	steadfast
steely	steelie
stencilled*	stenciled
sternwards	sternward
stoney	stony
straightforwards	straightforward
straightjacket	straitjacket
straightlaced	straitlaced
stylise*	stylize
succour*	succor
suède	suede
sulphur	sulfur
summersault	somersault
sunwards	sunward

For	Use
swanky	swank
symbolise*	symbolize
sympathise*	sympathize
syphon	siphon
Szechwan *or* Sichuan	Szechuan
tabu	taboo
tantalise*	tantalize
tartare sauce	tartar sauce
teenaged	teenage
teepee	tepee
telecasted	telecast
tendonitis	tendinitis
terrorise*	terrorize
theatre	theater
thereabout	thereabouts
thoro *nonstandard*	thorough
thraldom*	thralldom
thru	through
tic-tac-toe	ticktacktoe
tiddlywinks	tiddledywinks

For	Use
tike	tyke
timber (sound quality)	timbre
time-release	timed-release
toffy	toffee
topfull	topful
tormenter	tormentor
tostado	tostada
towards	toward
towelling*	toweling
towny	townie
tranquility	tranquillity
tranquillize	tranquilize
tranquillizer	tranquilizer
transistorise*	transistorize
traumatise*	traumatize
travelled*	traveled
traveller*	traveler
travelling*	traveling
travelog	travelogue
trivialise*	trivialize
trolly	trolley

For	*Use*
tsar	czar
turquois	turquoise
twirp	twerp
ukelele	ukulele
upwards	upward
urbanise*	urbanize
useable	usable
utilise*	utilize
Valentine Day	Valentine's Day
valour*	valor
vaporise*	vaporize
vapour*	vapor
varicosed	varicose
vegie	veggie
veldt	veld
velours	velour
vendable	vendible
verandah	veranda
vermillion	vermilion
vice* (device)	vise

For	*Use*
vicuna	vicuña
videodisk	videodisc
videotext	videotex
vigour*	vigor
vitalise*	vitalize
vizor	visor
vocalise*	vocalize
wainscotting	wainscoting
weasely	weaselly
weensy	weeny
weiner	wiener
Welch	Welsh
Welsh rarebit	Welsh rabbit
westernise*	westernize
whacky	wacky
whereabout	whereabouts
whimsey	whimsy
whirr	whir
whizz	whiz
whizzbang	whizbang

For	*Use*
whodunnit	whodunit
wholistic	holistic
wilful	willful
winey	winy
winterise*	winterize
wintery	wintry
woful	woeful
womanise*	womanize
womaniser*	womanizer
woman's rights	women's rights
womenswear	women's wear
wonderstruck	wonderstricken
woodman	woodsman
woolled	wooled
woollen	woolen
wooly	woolly
wordlore	word-lore
workhour *or* working hour	work-hour
worksheet	work sheet
Xmas	Christmas

For	*Use*
yack (talk)	yak
yaup	yawp
yeshivah	yeshiva
yoghurt	yogurt
yogin	yogi
zed* (the letter *z*)	zee
zero-base *adj*	zero-based
zombi	zombie
Zuñi	Zuni

11

Frequently
Misspelled Words

A prerequisite to making a good impression in written or printed material is the avoidance of glaring and embarrassing spelling errors. They not only disrupt the reader's train of thought, but also reflect negatively on the writer's attention to detail and level of knowledge. Such errors in letters, memos, reports, or proposals from an organization also cast the organization in a bad light. Misspellings on résumés can ruin chances for getting a job.

Read your document over *thoroughly* before running it through the computer spell-checker. After spell-checking, do not pop the material into an envelope and put it in the mail, thinking it is perfect. At least 20 to 30 percent of spelling and usage errors do *not* get picked up by computer spell-checkers. You must read the copy carefully *at least* once more to catch a variety of errors, including those of layout and form. Additional read-throughs also give you the opportunity for fine-tuning. (If you have a grammar-checker, be sure to use it—but do not rely on it 100 percent either.)

Even worse than a misspelled word is a misspelled *name*. When in doubt about the spelling of a *famous person's name* and there is no available reference material, call your local library's reference department for the information. When in doubt about the spelling of a *key person's name and full title*, call the company—even if it means making a long-distance call.

Occasionally there is more than one correct spelling of

a word. It is better to use the preferred spelling (listed *first* in most dictionaries and illustrated in Chapter 10 of this book), but if you prefer the secondary spelling, use it. Be *consistent* in your spelling—do not use both forms interchangeably.

To stop making the same blunders repeatedly and because we frequently question the spelling of the same words, get into the habit of recording words you look up, creating your "personal dictionary."

While good spelling comes easier to some people than to others, learning to spell is an exercise of memory and determination, as well as mastery of the rules and exceptions. If you fed your mind as frequently as you feed your body—and learn to spell and use at least three new words a day—your vocabulary would increase by 1,095 words in one year (1,098 in leap years); 5,475 words in five years; 10,950 words in 10 years; and 21,900 words in 20 years!

Even if spelling does not come easily to you, it is *essential* to master the vocabulary of your chosen field. Not to do so courts disaster and jeopardizes future success.

To help meet the challenge of flawless spelling, I chose to present the following words *without* syllable-division or accent marks to make each word easier to read and, therefore, easier to remember.

aardvark
abacus
abandonment
abashed
abdominal
aberration
abeyance
abhorrent
ablution
aborigine
abrogate
abscess
abscond
absence
absinthe

absorption
abstemious
abstinence
abstruse
abundance
abut
abysmal
abyss
academe
accelerate
acceptance
accessible
accidentally
accolade
accommodation

accompaniment
accreditation
accrue
accumulate
accustom
achievable
acoustic
acquiesce
acquittance
acrimonious
acrobatics
acropolis
acrylic
acumen
adamant
additive
adequate
adherence
adjudicate
administrator
admissible
adolescence
adroit
advantageous
advisable
advisory
aerobic
aesthetic
affable
affidavit
Afghan
afoul
aggrandizement
aggravate
aggressor
aggrieved
aghast
aging
agrarian
aisle
alabaster
albacore
Albuquerque

alfalfa
alfresco
allegiance
allegorical
allergen
alliteration
alpaca
altercation
altruistic
amalgamation
amaryllis
amateur
ambidextrous
ameliorate
amenity
amethyst
amorphous
amortizement
ampersand
amphetamine
amphibian
amphitheater
amusedly
anabolic
anachronism
analgesic
analogous
analysis
anarchist
anathema
ancillary
androgynous
anecdotal
anemic
anemone
anglicize
angst
anguish
animus
annals
annihilate
annotate
anoint

anomaly
anonymous
antebellum
antecedent
antechamber
antedate
antediluvian
antelope
anthropoid
anthropomorphic
anvil
anxiety
aorta
apartheid
apathetic
aperitif
aperture
apex
aphorism
aplomb
apologize
apoplexy
apothecary
apparatus
apparel
apparent
apparition
appellate
appendage
appendectomy
appertain
appetite
appreciable
apprentice
appurtenance
apropos
aqueduct
aquiline
arachnid
arboreal
arboretum
arcane
archaic

archetype
archipelago
archivist
arduous
arguable
armored
arouse
arraignment
arrhythmia
artesian
arthritis
articulate
artifact
artisan
asbestos
ascendancy
ascertainment
asinine
askew
asparagus
aspersion
asphalt
asphyxiate
assemblage
assessment
assiduous
assonance
assuage
asterisk
asthma
astigmatism
asylum
asymmetry
atavistic
athlete
atomization
atonement
atrocious
atrocity
atrophy
attaché
attendance
attenuate

attest
attributable
attrition
atypical
audacious
audible
augmentation
austerity
authenticity
authoritarian
autistic
autonomous
autopsy
autumnal
auxiliary
avalanche
avaricious
avocado
awry
axiomatic
azalea

baboon
babushka
baccalaureate
bachelor
backgammon
badminton
bagel
Baghdad
baguette
bailiff
bailiwick
balance
balderdash
baleful
balky
balletomane
balustrade
bamboozle
banal
bankruptcy
baptism

barbarous
barbiturate
baron
baroness
baronet
baroque
barracuda
barrette
barrister
bassoon
bastardize
bastion
batik
baton
battalion
bauxite
bayou
bazooka
beanie
beauteous
beautician
bedazzle
befuddle
beget
beggar
beguiling
behavioral
behoove
beige
Beijing (formerly Peking,
    China)
beleaguered
belfry
believable
bellicose
belligerent
beluga
benefactor
beneficence
beneficiary
benevolent
benign
bequeath

bereavement
berserk
besiege
bestiality
bestiary
betrothal
bevel
beverage
bewilderment
biased
biathlon
bicuspid
bicycle
bifocal
bifurcated
bigamous
bigot
bikini
bilge
bilk
billiards
binaural
binocular
biodegradable
biofeedback
biographical
biopsy
biosphere
birdie
biscuit
bivouac
blamable
blandishment
blasphemous
blithe
blitzkrieg
blizzard
blouson
bludgeon
blurb
blurry
bodacious
bodice

boggle
bogus
bohemian
boisterous
bologna
bonanza
bonsai
bookkeeping
boomerang
bordello
botanical
boudoir
boundaries
bourbon
bourgeoisie
boutique
bowdlerize
boycott
boysenberry
brackish
braggadocio
braggart
braille (often cap)
braise
brandish
bravado
bravura
brawny
brazen
breadth
breathable
breathe
brethren
brewery
brief
brigadier
brilliant
broccoli
brochette
brochure
brokerage
bronchial
brothel

brougham
brouhaha
brusque
brutish
buccaneer
Buddhism
buffoonery
bugaboo
bulbous
bulletin
bulwark
bumptious
buoyancy
bureaucracy
burgeon
burglary
burlesque
bursar
bursitis
business
buttress
bystander

cabal
cacophony
cadaver
cafeteria
caffeine
caftan
cairn
cajole
calisthenics
calligrapher
calliope
calumny
calypso
camaraderie
camouflage
campaign
candescent
candor
canoeing
cantaloupe

cantankerous
capacious
cappuccino
capricious
capsulize
captor
carburetor
carcass
carcinogen
careen
career
Caribbean
caribou
caricature
carotid
carousel
carriage
cartilage
casserole
catalyst
catamaran
cataract
catarrh
catastrophic
categorical
category
caterpillar
cathartic
catheter
causality
cautionary
caveat
ceiling
celebrator
celerity
celibacy
cellulite
cemetery
census
centaur
cerebellum
cerebral
cerulean

cesspool
chameleon
chandelier
changeable
chaos
chaparral
chargeable
charisma
chasm
chauffeur
chauvinist
cheapie
cheetah
Chesapeake Bay
chicanery
chief
Chihuahua
chivalrous
choir
cholera
choleric
cholesterol
chromosome
chrysanthemum
churlish
cinnamon
circuitous
circumcision
cirrhosis
cistern
civility
clairvoyant
clamminess
clamor
clandestine
claustrophobia
clavichord
cleanliness
cleanness
cleavage
cleaver
clemency
clientele

clothes
coalesce
coconut
cocoon
codeine
codicil
coercion
cognac
cognizance
cohort
coiffure
coitus
collaborative
collateral
colleague
collector
colloquial
colossus
column
combustible
comestible
commandeer
commemorate
commensurate
commission
commitment
compartmentalize
compatible
competence
competition
comprise
concede
conceit
conceivable
concerted
concomitance
concur
concurrence
condemnation
condescending
condolences
conferred
conformable

conglomerate
congratulate
conjectural
conjugal
connubial
consanguineous
conscientious
conscious
consensus
consequential
constituency
construe
consulate
consumable
consummate
contemporaneous
contemptible
contentious
contributor
controversy
convalescence
convertible
conveyance
coolly
copulate
copyright
coquetry
corduroy
cornucopia
corollary
corporeal
corpulent
corroboration
countenance
counterfeit
couplet
courageous
covenant
Covent Garden (London)
covetous
crapulous
credence
credential

crisis
criticism
crocus
crotchety
crustacean
cryptic
crystalline
culinary
culpable
culprit
cupola
curfew
curiosity
curlicue
cursive
curtailed
curvaceous
cushy
cutesy
cybernetics
cyclorama
cylinder
cynosure
cyst
czar
czarina
Czech
Czechoslovakia

dachshund
daffodil
dahlia
dandelion
debauched
debilitate
debtor
decadence
decathlon
deceive
decibel
deciduous
decisive
defeatist

defendant
deficit
definite
defoliate
degenerate
deign
deity
delectable
deleterious
demagogue
democratize
demonic
denunciation
departmentalize
dependability
dependent
depravity
derivative
descendant
desiccated
desirable
desperate
desultory
detente
deterioration
detoxification
devastation
devour
dewy
dexterity
dexterous
diabetes
diaphragm
diarrhea
dichotomy
different
diffident
dignitary
dilemma
dilettante
diligence
diminutive
dinosaur

diphtheria
diphthong
dirigible
disappear
disappoint
disastrous
discipline
discomfiture
disconsolate
discreditable
discrepancy
discretionary
discriminative
disdainful
disease
disheveled
dismissal
dispassionate
dispensary
disproportionate
disreputable
dissatisfaction
disseminate
dissident
dissipate
dissociate
dissonance
distinguished
distraught
distributor
diuretic
diurnal
divergent
diversified
divestiture
divine
doggedness
dogmatic
doldrums
dolorous
domicile
dormitory
dosage

dossier
douse
draconian
droll
dross
drought
drowned
drowsy
drudge
druid
drunkenness
dubious
duchess
duke
dullard
duly
dumbbell
dungeon
duplicity
dynamism
dysfunctional
dyspeptic

easily
ecclesiastical
echelon
eclectic
eclipse
ecstasy
ecstatic
ecumenical
edible
edification
Edinburgh (Scotland)
educator
eerie
effeminate
effervescence
efficacious
efficacy
efficiency
effrontery
egalitarian

egregious
eighth
either
ejector
electrician
eleemosynary
elephant
elicitor
eligibility
elitism
elixir
eloquence
emanation
embarrassing
embellishment
embezzler
emblazon
embodiment
emeritus
emissary
emollient
empirical
employee
encouraging
encumbrance
encyclopedia
endorphin
endurance
energetic
enervate
enforceable
enigmatic
enthusiastic
enticement
entourage
entrepreneurial
enviable
envoy
enzyme
ephemeral
epicenter
epidemiology
epilepsy

epilogue
equator
equilibrium
equine
equinox
equitable
equivalence
equivocate
eradicator
erroneous
erudition
escalator
escrow
esoteric
especially
espionage
espresso
essential
esteemed
estimable
ethereal
etiquette
eucalyptus
eunuch
euphemism
evangelical
exacerbate
exaggerate
exceed
excel
exclamatory
excruciating
executor
exegesis
exemplary
exemplify
exercise
exhaustive
exhibition
exhilarating
exhortation
exigency
existence

existentialism
exorcise
exorcism
expediter
expeditious
expel
experience
experiment
expletive
expurgate
exquisite
extemporaneous
extinguish
extol
extortion
extraneous
extricate
exuberant
exude

facetious
facilities
factious
factual
faculty
fallacious
familiar
fanaticism
fanciful
fantasy
fascinate
fastidious
fatigability
fatigue
feasible
febrile
fecundity
feigned
felicitous
felonious
feral
ferrous
fervent

fetal
fettuccine
fetus
feudal
fibrillation
fickle
fictitious
fiduciary
fiend
filibuster
Filipino
filmdom
financier
firmament
fiscal
fission
fjord
flaccid
flaky
flatulence
fledgling
flirtatious
flotsam
fluctuate
fluorescent
fluoridate
flurry
foliage
follicle
forage
forceps
forcible
forehead
foreign
forfeit
forfeiture
forsythia
forty
fossilize
fourteen
fracas
fractious
fragmentary

fragrant
franchiser
frankfurter
fraudulent
frenzied
fricassee
friend
frigidity
frivolous
fuchsia
fulminate
fungicide
funnel
furniture
furtive
fuselage
fusillade

gabardine
gadgetry
gaiety
gallivant
galoshes
gargantuan
gargoyle
garish
garrulous
gauche
gaudiness
gauge
gauze
gazebo
gazelle
genealogy
genial
genie
genitalia
genitourinary
genteel
geodesic
geometric
geriatric
germicidal

gesundheit
ghetto
gigolo
gingivitis
giraffe
glamour
glasnost
glaucoma
gnash
gnome
gonorrhea
gossamer
graffiti
grammarian
grandeur
grandiose
grateful
gratuitous
gregarious
greyhound
grievance
grievous
grotesque
grovel
gruesome
grungy
guarantee
guarantor
gubernatorial
guerrilla
guffaw
guidance
gypsum
gyration

habitual
habituate
haggard
hallelujah
Halloween
handkerchief
haphazard
harangue

harass
harassment
harlequin
hassle
haunch
Hawaiian
hazard
heckle
heifer
height
heinous
heirloom
heist
hemisphere
hemorrhage
hemorrhoid
hepatitis
herbaceous
herbage
hereditary
heredity
heresy
hermit
hexagonal
hibiscus
hierarchy
hijack
histamine
hoarse
hoary
homicide
honorary
hooky
horrendous
horrid
horticulture
hovel
humanitarianism
humiliating
humorous
hundredth
hurriedly
hyacinth

hybrid
hygiene
hypnotism
hypochondriac
hypocrisy
hypothesis
hysterectomy
hysteria

icicle
idiomatic
idiosyncrasy
illegal
illiterate
imaginary
imbalance
imbecile
immaturity
immediately
immolate
impeachment
imperceptive
impermeable
implausible
implement
impostor
impresario
impromptu
inalienable
inauguration
incarcerate
incestuous
incident
incision
incongruous
inconvenience
incorruptible
incredible
incumbent
incur
incurable
indefatigable
indelible

independent
indicia
indictment
indomitable
inebriate
inert
inertia
infantile
inferred
infidelity
infirmary
infirmity
inflatable
influential
initiate
initiative
innocent
innocuous
innuendo
innumerable
inoculate
inquire
inquiry
inscrutable
insensibility
insignia
insinuation
insipid
installation
instantaneous
instinctual
insufficiency
intercede
intermittent
intimadator
introspective
innuendo
inveigle
inveterate
irascible
iridescence
irreconcilable
irrelevant

irresistible
irreverent
irrevocable
isometric
isthmus
itinerant

jacquard
jaguar
Jamaican
jambalaya
jargon
jaundice
jaunty
javelin
jealous
jeopardize
jigsaw
jinx
jodhpur
Johns Hopkins University
  (Baltimore)
jonquil
journalistic
jowl
jubilant
jubilee
Judaism
judgment
jugular
Juilliard School, The
  (New York)
junta
juror
justifiable
juvenile
juxtapose

kabob
kaleidoscope
kangaroo
karakul
karate

kennel
khaki
kibbutz
kibitzer
kielbasa
kiln
kimono
kindergarten
kindle
kinetic
kinky
kiosk
kleptomaniac
knavery
knish
knockwurst
knowledgeable
kosher
kowtow
kumquat
Kuwait

laboratory
laborious
labyrinth
laceration
lackadaisical
lacquer
lacrosse
lager
lagniappe
lagoon
laic
lamentable
languid
languor
languorous
larceny
larva
laryngitis
larynx
lasagna
lascivious

latitude
lattice
laudatory
laureate
lavender
lecherous
lectern
leery
legislative
legislature
legitimacy
legitimize
leisure
length
leopard
leotard
lesbianism
lethargic
leukemia
leverage
leviathan
levitate
liable
liaison
libertine
libidinous
library
licentious
lieutenant
likable
likelihood
limousine
linear
lingerie
linguine
liquefy
liqueur
liquidate
liquidity
literature
lithe
lithesome
litigious

litmus
liturgical
livable
livelihood
liverwurst
loathe
loathsome
lobbyist
lobotomy
locust
logarithmic
loggia
loneliness
longevity
longitude
loquacious
lovable
lozenge
lubricant
luge
luminary
luminescence
luscious
lymph

macabre
macadamia
Machiavellian
machismo
mackerel
magnanimity
maintenance
maladroit
malady
malevolent
malfeasance
manageable
maneuver
marigold
marital
marriageable
marsupial
martial

masseur
masseuse
mastectomy
matrimonial
maturation
maudlin
mausoleum
mayonnaise
meager
medallion
medicinal
medieval
Mediterranean
megalomaniac
melancholy
mellifluous
membrane
memento
menagerie
mendacious
mercurial
meretricious
meringue
meritorious
mesmerize
messianic
metallurgy
metamorphosis
metaphor
methodology
microcosm
mien
migraine
mileage
millennium
miniature
minuscule
miscellaneous
mischief
mischievous
mishap
misogynist
misspelling

mistletoe
mnemonic
moccasin
mocha
modality
modicum
Mohammedanism
moisturizing
molar
molasses
molecule
mollusk
mongrel
monitor
monogamy
mononucleosis
monotheism
monotonous
monsignor
monstrosity
mortgage
mosaic
mosque
motility
mouton
movability
multitudinous
murmur
musculature
mustache
mutinous
mutual
myopic
myriad
myrrh
mysterious
mysticism
mystique
mythical
mythological

nadir
naive

naphtha
narcissistic
nativity
naturally
nautilus
navigable
necessary
necessity
nefarious
negativism
negligee
negligible
negotiable
neighbor
neither
nemesis
neuralgia
neurotic
neutrality
neutron
niacin
niche
nickel
niece
nightingale
nonchalant
noncommittal
nondescript
nonpareil
nonplussed
nostril
notable
notarization
noticeable
notoriety
nubile
nucleus
numismatic
nuptial
nutrient
nutriment
nuzzle
nymphomania

oafish
oasis
obdurate
obedience
obeisance
obese
obesity
obfuscate
obligatory
oblige
oblique
oblivious
obnoxious
oboe
obscene
obscenity
obscure
obsequious
observant
obsolescent
obstetrical
obstinacy
obstreperous
occasionally
occult
occur
occurrence
octagonal
odyssey
oedipal
offense
official
omission
omnipotent
omnipresent
omniscient
omnivorous
onerous
onyx
opacity
opalescence
opaque
opinion

opossum
opportune
optimistic
optimum
opulence
orchestral
ordinarily
orgiastic
origin
orthodoxy
orthopedist
oscillate
ostentatious
osteopathy
osteoporosis
ostrich
otolaryngology
outrageous
ovarian
oxidation

pachyderm
paean
pageant
palindrome
pallor
pamphlet
pandemonium
panorama
paradise
paraffin
paragon
parakeet
parallel
paramecium
parameter
paramount
paranoid
paraphernalia
parasite
parishioner
parliamentary
parlor

paroxysmal
particularly
pasteurize
pastime
pavilion
peaceable
peasant
peculiarity
pecuniary
peddler
pedophilia
peignoir
pejorative
pekoe
pelican
pendulous
penicillin
penurious
perceive
percolate
peremptory
performance
perfunctory
peril
peripatetic
permissible
perpendicular
perseverance
persistent
persona
personnel
perspicacious
persuasive
perverse
pessimist
petal
phantom
pharmaceutical
pharmacological
philanthropy
philately
phlegmatic
phosphorus

picnicking
pigeon
pillar
pinochle
piteous
Pittsburgh (Pennsylvania)
pituitary
plagiarism
plaited
plateau
playwright
plebeian
plenteous
plethora
pneumonia
podium
poinsettia
poised
poliomyelitis
politicking
pollster
posse
possessiveness
potentiality
potpourri
practicable
practitioner
pragmatism
precede
precipitous
precocious
predecessor
pretentious
prevaricate
primogeniture
prism
privilege
procedure
proceed
proclivity
prodigy
proffer
profligate

projectile
proliferation
promiscuity
promontory
propellant
propeller
propensity
prosaic
protégé(e)
protester
prototype
protuberance
pseudonymous
psychosis
psychosomatic
ptomaine
pugilistic
pungent
puppeteer
purloin
pursuant
pygmy

quackery
quadrant
quadruped
quagmire
quandary
quarrelsome
quell
querulous
query
questionnaire
quibble
quiescence
quixotic
quizzical
quorum
quotable
quotient

raccoon
raconteur

raffish
ragout
rancid
rancor
rapport
raptor
rapture
rarefied
rationale
raucous
reagent
recede
receivable
receptacle
receptor
reciprocity
recognize
recommend
reconnaissance
reconnoiter
recruitment
recumbent
recyclable
referable
referential
reflector
reforestation
refract
refute
regalia
regatta
regime
regimen
registrar
regrettable
rehabilitation
reign
reimbursement
reindeer
reinforce
relegate
relevance
reliable

relieve
remembrance
reminiscent
remiss
remittance
remnant
remuneration
renaissance
renascence
rendezvous
renege
renown
renowned
renunciation
repetitive
replaceable
replicate
reprehensible
repudiate
requiem
requisition
resalable
rescind
rescission
reservoir
residue
resiliency
resistible
resonance
respiratory
responsibility
restaurant
restaurateur
restraint
resuscitator
reticence
retina
retinue
retrieval
retriever
reveille
reverberate
reverential

revocable
rhapsodic
rhetoric
rheumatic
rhyme
rhythm
riant
riboflavin
rickety
riddance
ridicule
righteousness
rivet
Riviera
rococo
roentgen
romaine
Romania
roommate
rostrum
rotisserie
rotund
rotunda
roughage
rubella (German measles)
rudimentary
rueful
ruminant
ruminate
rummage

sable
saccharin
sacrifice
sacrilegious
safari
safflower
salacious
salamander
salary
salient
salmonella
sanctimonious

sandwich
sanguine
sapphire
satellite
satirical
saturated
saturnine
saucy
scaffold
scalpel
scarcity
scavenger
scenery
schism
schizophrenia
scholastic
sciatica
scintillating
scissors
scoundrel
scrounge
scruple
scrutinize
sculptor
scurrilous
secede
secretive
secular
sedative
sedentary
seditious
seismograph
seizure
selectee
semantic
semblance
Semitic
senile
sensate
sensibility
sensuality
sententious
sentinel

separate
sepulchral
sequencer
sequin
serendipity
sergeant
serrated
serviceable
sesquicentennial
severance
shakable
sheik
shellac
shepherd
sheriff
shrewd
siege
silhouette
simian
similar
simile
simulator
simulcast
simultaneous
sizable
skeletal
skiing
skillful
slalom
sleigh
sleuth
slithered
sloe
sloth
slough
sludge
sluggard
sluice
smarmy
smelt
smolder
socially
society

solace
solder
solemn
solicitous
soliloquy
solstice
sophomore
sorority
souvenir
sovereign
spackle
spaghetti
spasm
spatial
specimen
spectrum
spelunking
spirochete
sponsor
spurious
squander
stalwart
statistician
statutory
stealth
steroid
stimulant
strength
striate
striation
strident
stupor
suave
subpoena
subservient
subtle
succeed
successor
succinct
suddenness
sufficient
sulfur
sumptuous

superintendent
supersede
surfeit
surprise
surreptitious
surveillance
susceptible
suspicion
sustenance
sycophant
symmetrical
symposium
symptomatic
synagogue
synapse
synchronization
synergy
synonym
syphilis
syphilitic
syringe

tableau
taboo
tactful
talisman
Talmud
talon
tandem
tangential
tangible
tariff
tartan
tassel
tattoo
tawdry
tedium
teetotaler
temblor
temperamental
tempestuous
tenant
tendency

tendinitis
tendon
tendril
tenet
tepee
tepid
tercentenary
terminus
terpsichorean
tertiary
testicular
tetanus
textual
theism
theologian
theorem
therapeutic
thesaurus
thespian
thievery
thoracic
thorax
thorough
thrall
threshold
thwart
thyme
thyroid
tiara
tidbit
tidiness
tinsel
titillate
toboggan
tolerable
tonsil
tonsillectomy
tonsillitis
torpor
torrential
totalitarian
tournament
tourniquet

toxicity
trachea
tractable
tragedy
traipse
traitor
trajectory
tranquil
tranquillity
transcendental
transference
transferring
transient
transistor
transom
trapeze
travelogue
treacherous
tread
treasonous
treatable
trek
tremulous
triage
triathlon
triglyceride
triplicate
triumphant
trivia
trough
trounce
truant
truculent
trudge
truly
tryst
tuberculosis
tumultuous
turbulence
tussle
tutorial
tutu
twelfth

twerp
twinge
tycoon
tyke
tyrannical

ubiquitous
ukulele
ultimatum
umbilical
unanimity
unconscionable
uncontrollable
uncouth
unctuous
undoubtedly
unison
unkempt
unmitigated
unnecessary
unpalatable
unwieldy
upholsterer
uranium
usually
usurious
usurp
utensil
uterus
utilize
utopian

vacancy
vaccination
vacillate
vacuum
vagary
vagrancy
vague
valor
valuable
vandalize

vanquish
varicosity
variegated
vasectomy
vector
vegetable
vehemence
veil
vendor
vengeance
ventilator
veracious
verbatim
verbiage
verbose
verdant
verdure
verifiable
verisimilitude
vermin
vernacular
vertebrate
vertiginous
vestibule
vestige
veterinarian
viable
vicarious
vicissitude
victor
vigilance
vignette
vilification
villainous
vinaigrette
vinyl
virile
visage
viscera
visible
vitamin
vitriolic

vituperative
vociferous
volatile
volition
voluble
voluminous
voracious
voyeur
vulgarity
vulnerable

wannabe
wantonness
warrant
wearisome
weasel
weevil
weighty
weimaraner
weird
wheedle
whimper
whimsy
wholly
whorl
wieldy
willful
witticism
wizened
woeful
wondrous
woozy
worsted
wrathful
wreak
wretched
writhe
writing
wrought

xenophobe
xylophone

yachtsman
yachtswoman
yearling
yellowy
yeoman
yeti
yielding
yodel
yoga
yogi
yogurt
yucca (plant)

zabaglione
zany
zealot
zealous
zenith
zephyr
zinc
zinnia
zircon
zodiac
zoological
zucchini

12

Frequently Misused Words

Clarity is perhaps the most important element of successful communication in all its forms, particularly where the written word is concerned. However, the complexities of the English language often create confusion in choosing the right words; and incorrect choices cannot only obscure the meaning, but can also make the writing laughable, a disastrous result (except for comedy writers).

Many of our most confusing words fall into categories described by other confusing words—homographs, homophones, and homonyms.

A *homograph* is a word that is *written the same* as another word but has a different origin and meaning, and sometimes a different pronunciation:

homer   a home run in baseball, a homing pigeon, or an ancient Hebrew unit of measure

steer   to control the course of or guide, a hint or tip, or a male bovine animal castrated before sexual maturity

chaser   one who chases (has a sexual connotation); a drink of water, beer, or other mild beverage taken after a drink of hard liquor; a skilled worker who produces ornamental chasing on metal; or a tool for cutting screw threads

bow   a word with two pronunciations and more than a dozen meanings including: to submit to; to bend the head, body, or knee in reverence, submission, or shame; the forward part of a ship; a weapon; a knot with decorative loops; a wooden rod with horsehairs stretched from end to end used in playing an instrument of the viol or violin family; and a style of necktie

A *homophone* is a word that is *pronounced the same* as another word but differs in spelling, meaning, or both:

carat   the weight of precious stones, especially diamonds

caret   a writer's and proofreader's wedge-shaped mark to indicate the place where something is to be inserted

karat   a unit of fineness for gold equal to 1/24 part of pure gold to an alloy

carrot   an orangy or yellowish spindle-shaped edible root

carrot   a reward or advantage offered, especially as an inducement

A *homonym* is a word that can be *either* a homograph *or* a homophone.

There are many other kinds of confusing words whose use has nothing to do with meaning but with *form*—as when to use *who's* or *whose:*

who's   the contraction of *who is* or *who has*

    Who's (*who is*) coming to dinner?

whose   the possessive form of *who* and *which* used with persons and things as the object of a verb or a preceding preposition

    Whose turn is it to serve?

When in doubt about the usage of a word, look it up—either in a dictionary or a book devoted to the subject of confusing words (see *Bibliography*).

The frequently misused words chosen for inclusion in this book represent a compilation since 1990 of errors that I (1) corrected while editing the writing of others; (2) read in published material (books, magazines, and newspapers); or (3) saw or heard on television—a constant source of incorrectly used English.

abridged	*adj* describing a book that has been shortened from a previous edition of the same book
unabridged	*adj* describing a book that has *not* been shortened from a previous edition of the same book
accept	*v* to willingly receive, take, adopt, or admit
except	*conj* or *prep* with the exclusion or exception of
actual	*adj* existing in fact or reality
virtual	*adj* having the effect but not the form
adverse	*adj* pertaining to unfavorable effects or events
averse	*adj* pertaining to persons feeling opposed or disinclined (usually followed by *to*)
advice	*n* recommendation regarding a decision or course of action
advise	*v* to give advice or information
advocate	*n* one who pleads the case of another *v* to plead in favor of
avocation	*n* vocation or hobby
affect	*n* occasionally used in psychology to describe an emotion (term best avoided in everyday language) *v* to influence or change

effect	*n* a result or consequence *v* to cause or bring about
aggravate	*v* to worsen an already troublesome or vexing situation or condition
irritate	*v* to vex, annoy, exasperate, chafe, or drive someone to anger
aggressive	*adj* marked by combative readiness or obtrusive energy
assertive	*adj* disposed to or characterized by bold or confident assertion
agnostic	*n* one who believes there is insufficient evidence to know if there is a God or gods
atheist	*n* one who rejects all religious beliefs and denies the existence of a supreme being or beings
à la carte	*adj* or *adv* [F, by the bill of fare] describing a meal in which each menu item is priced separately
table d'hôte	*n* [F, lit., host's table] describing a complete meal of several courses as listed on the menu and offered at a fixed price
allude	*v* to make an indirect reference to something without specifically mentioning it
elude	*v* to evade or escape from a pursuer
allusion	*n* an implied or indirect reference, especially in literature
illusion	*n* a deception or a false perception of reality
delusion	*n* a persistent false psychotic belief regarding oneself, other persons, or objects
altar	*n* a tablelike platform used in a house of worship
alter	*v* to change the appearance but not the use of

ambivalent	*adj* having conflicting emotional attitudes toward a goal, object, or person
ambiguous	*adj* a term applicable only to written or spoken statements that have two or more possible meanings

amend	*v* to improve or correct in a general and broad sense
emend	*v* to edit written materials

amiable	*adj* describing a person who is friendly, pleasing, or congenial
amicable	*adj* describing a relationship that exists in a peaceful state, exhibiting goodwill and a desire of the parties not to quarrel

animal	*n* any living organism other than a plant
mammal	*n* an animal which feeds milk to its young from female mammary glands

antique	*n* an object, frequently decorative and rare, created or produced in a former period, or, according to U.S. customs laws, at least 100 years before date of purchase
antiques	*adj* an antiques store, an antiques dealer
collectible	*n* any object collected by those who have a special liking for that kind of object
memorabilia	*n pl* objects that stir memories or are worthy of remembrance

anxious	*adj* having a sense of foreboding, worry, apprehension, or an uneasy feeling or state of mind
eager	*adj* enthusiastic; impatient; keen or ardent in desire or feeling

anybody	*pron* any person (less formal than *anyone*)
any body	*n phrase* any group

apiary	*n* a place where bees are kept, especially a collection of hives or colonies of bees kept for their honey

aviary	*n* a large cage, house, or enclosure in which birds are kept
apprise	*v* to give notice to, inform, or tell
apprize	*v* to value, appreciate
arbitrator	*n* one who hears evidence from all parties in a dispute and makes a binding decision (in labor disputes, may also be nonbinding)
mediator	*n* one who hears evidence from all parties and tries by the exercise of reason or persuasion to bring them to an agreement
Arctic	*adj* pertaining to the region of the North Pole
Antarctic	*adj* pertaining to the region of the South Pole
ardor	*n* a great warmth of feeling or emotion
passion	*n* a deep, overpowering feeling or emotion
assassin	*n* a politically motivated killer
killer	*n* anyone who kills with a motive of any kind
murderer	*n* in law, one who kills another human being under specifically covered conditions—e.g., in the U.S., murder committed with malice aforethought
assent	*v* to agree to an opinion or a proposal
consent	*v* to grant or yield to a demand or request
assure	*v* to make another person sure of something
ensure	*v* to make certain or safe
insure	*v* to provide or obtain insurance to be paid in case of loss or damage
auger	*n* a tool or device for boring holes
augur	*n* one held to foretell events by omens
	v to predict the future, especially by omens

auspicious	*adj* describing a favorable omen that portends success before the start of something
propitious	*adj* describing a good omen for continuing favorable circumstances
avenge	*v* to right wrongs done to someone else
revenge	*n* an act or instance of retaliating in order to get even
	v to avenge wrongs done to oneself
vengeance	*n* violent revenge
bad	*adj* meaning unpleasant or spoiled—to follow such copulative verbs (verbs that connect subject and complement) as *look, smell, sound,* and *taste: I feel bad from overeating.* Should *not* be used as an adverb.
badly	*adj* referring to physical or emotional states (although *bad* is more common in formal writing): *She felt badly about her son's divorce.*
bazaar	*n* a marketplace; an event to sell miscellaneous contributed articles to benefit a cause
bizarre	*adj* markedly unusual, weird, or freakish; outrageously or whimsically strange
bear market	*n* a period of generally declining stock prices
bull market	*n* a period of generally increasing market prices
beast	*n* a large, four-footed animal; a vile person whose stupidity and brutality arouse contempt and loathing
brute	*n* a crude, cruel, dull person lacking in intelligence and human powers of reasoning
because	*conj* referring to the reason for something
since	*conj* referring to relation in time

beside	*prep* at the side of
besides	*conj* in addition to
better	*adj* of superior quality
bettor	*n* a person who bets
biannual	*adj* twice a year (synonym for *semiannual*)
biennial	*adj* every two years
bisect	*v* to divide something into two usually equal parts
dissect	*v* to separate into pieces, as an animal for scientific examination
blackout	*n* a total power failure over a large area
brownout	*n* a small, temporary voltage reduction
blatant	*adj* brazenly obvious, obtrusive, or offensively loud
flagrant	*adj* suggestive of an act so open or evident that it cannot be overlooked or ignored
boast	*v* to speak with excessive pride or vanity, especially about oneself, one's family, or one's community
brag	*v* to speak with exaggerated boasting (with little foundation) about oneself, one's family, or one's community
boat	*n* a watercraft of any size, but generally a small craft
ship	*n* a large, seagoing vessel propelled by power or sail
born	*adj* brought forth by birth
borne	*v* past participle of *bear,* used in all senses that do not refer to physical birth
brash	*adj* reckless, imprudent, or foolhardy
brassy	*adj* insolent, saucy, or forward
breach	*n* a fracture, violation, or rift
breech	*adj* or *n* pertaining to the back end of anything

bug	*n* a small concealed microphone or other device used for eavesdropping
tap	*n* a device attached to a telephone wire to pick up conversation on the line (also called *wiretap*)
bullion	*n* unminted precious metals of standards suitable for coining
bouillon	*n* a clear seasoned broth made usually from chicken or lean beef
bus	*n* a large motor vehicle
buss	*n* a kiss
bust	*n* a representation in any form of the head, shoulders, and upper torso of the human figure
statue	*n* a three-dimensional work of art representing the full figure of a person or animal
cannon	*n* a military weapon
canon	*n* a law or rule, particularly of a church; any comprehensive list of books within a field
canvas	*n* a heavy cloth of cotton, hemp, or linen
canvass	*n* or *v* pertaining to the solicitation of votes, subscriptions, or opinions
caucus	*n* in U.S. politics, a meeting of political party leaders to select candidates, elect convention delegates, or conduct other business
Caucasus, the	*n* a mountain range in Russia between the Black and Caspian seas (also called *Caucasus Mountains*)
cede	*v* to yield or formally surrender to another, as territory by treaty
secede	*v* to withdraw from an organization, as a political party or federation

celebrant   *n* a person conducting a religious rite
celebrator   *n* a person throwing a special party or
                 having an especially good time

Celsius   *adj* pertaining to a temperature scale that
                 is divided into 100 equal parts, in which
                 the freezing point of water is 0 degrees
                 and the boiling point is 100 degrees
                 (named after Anders Celsius [1701–44],
                 Swedish astronomer who devised the
                 scale, also called *centigrade*)
Fahrenheit   *adj* or *n* pertaining to a temperature scale
                 in which 32 degrees represents the
                 freezing point and 212 degrees the boiling
                 point (named after Gabriel Daniel
                 Fahrenheit [1686–1736], German physicist
                 who devised the scale and also introduced
                 the use of mercury in thermometers)

character   *n* the moral or ethical qualities of a person
reputation   *n* the estimation in which a person or thing
                 is regarded by the community or the
                 public in general

chiropodist   *n* a person qualified to diagnose and treat
                 disorders of the foot (also called
                 podiatrist)
chiropractor   *n* a practitioner of chiropractic, a
                 therapeutic system based primarily upon
                 the interactions of the spine and nervous
                 system

circuit   *n* a circular course or roundabout journey
conduit   *n* a pipe or tube for conveying water
conduct   *n* demeanor, deportment, or manners

college   *n* an institution of higher learning, often
                 part of a university, that grants a
                 bachelor's degree
university   *n* an institution of learning of the highest
                 level, comprised of colleges, having
                 research facilities, and granting bachelor's,
                 master's, and doctor's degrees

complacent	*adj* self-satisfied, unconcerned
complaisant	*adj* eager to please, amiable
compliant	*adj* obeying, obliging, or yielding, especially in a submissive way

complement	*n* or *v* pertaining to completeness or the process of supplementing something
compliment	*n* or *v* pertaining to praise or the expression of courtesy

compose	*v* to create or put together
comprise	*v* to contain, include all, or embrace

constant	*adj* pertaining to uniform or persistent occurrence or recurrence
incessant	*adj* pertaining to ceaseless or uninterrupted activity

contagious	*adj* communicable by contact with an infected person or object, usually in reference to a very easily transmitted disease such as influenza or the common cold
infectious	*adj* communicable by infection involving a microorganism that can be transmitted from one person to another only by a specific kind of contact, e.g., venereal diseases

continual	*adj* pertaining to a close, prolonged succession or recurrence
continuous	*adj* pertaining to an uninterrupted flow or spatial extension

contusion	*n* a bruise, a closed wound caused by the impact of a blunt object or a fall, which can produce "black and blue" marks
abrasion	*n* an injury caused by rubbing or scraping of the skin, as when one "skins" an elbow or knee or sustains other scuffing or friction injuries

co-op   *n* a shortened form of *cooperative,* as a dwelling, store, or program

coop   *n* a pen or cage, usually with bars or wire, for enclosing small animals

counselor   *n* in a legal sense, a person who conducts a case in court (usually, but not always, a lawyer)

counsel   *n* used collectively for a group of counselors

cum laude   *adj* or *adv* [L, with praise] with honors (used on college diplomas to grant the lowest of three special honors for grades above the average)

magna cum laude   *adj* or *adv* [L, with great praise] with high honors (the next-to-highest honor)

summa cum laude   *adj* or *adv* [L, with highest praise] with highest honors (the highest honor)

curriculum   *n* the courses of study offered by a school

syllabus   *n* the outline of a single course

damage   *n* destruction, injury, or harm as caused by a severe storm or accident

damages   *n* compensation for injury or loss that may be recovered in court

deliberate   *adj* pertaining to what is not done hastily but with full realization of one's actions

premeditated   *adj* pertaining to an act that has been planned in advance

desert   *n* a large arid, sandy region; the state or fact of deserving reward or punishment *v* to leave or run away from a person, place, or one's duty, and not return

dessert   *n* the final course of a meal, such as cake, pie, pudding, ice cream, or fruit

diagnosis   *n* determination of the nature of a cause of a disease

prognosis   *n* forecast of the probable course and outcome of a disorder

differ (from)	*v* to be unlike
differ (with)	*v* to disagree

discover — *v* to find something that had previously existed but been unknown until the moment of discovery

invent — *v* to make or create something new, especially something ingeniously devised

discreet — *adj* prudent, circumspect

discrete — *adj* separate, unconnected

disinterested — *adj* free from selfish motive or interest

uninterested — *adj* lacking interest

disown — *v* to refuse to acknowledge as one's own, repudiate, or renounce

disinherit — *v* to deprive a person who would otherwise inherit, such as an heir or next of kin

dissolute — *adj* marked by indulgence in things considered vices

resolute — *adj* marked by firm determination

distinct — *adj* pertaining to something perceived as being apart or different from others

separate — *adj* pertaining to a lack of connection or a difference in identity between two things

ecology — *n* the science or study of the relationship between organisms and their surroundings

environment — *n* the circumstances, objects, or conditions by which a person or a thing is surrounded (synonym for *surroundings*)

egoist — *n* a selfish, self-centered person

egotist — *n* a boastful person with an exaggerated and unrealistic concept of self-importance

el — *n* an elevated railroad (shortened form)

ell — *n* an extension, usually at right angles, to the end of a building

eminent	*adj* pertaining to a prominent or outstanding person or thing
imminent	*adj* pertaining to an act, usually of a threatening nature, about to take place
empathy	*n* imagining oneself being in and sensitive to another person's condition or predicament
sympathy	*n* a strong personal identification with another person's feelings
enjoin	*v* to charge, bid, require, or command
join	*v* to link, couple, or attach
ennui	*n* boredom or a feeling of weariness
etui	*n* [F, *étui*] a small ornamental case
ensue	*v* to follow, usually in immediate succession
sue	*v* to initiate legal proceedings or bring suit
entitled	*adj* having a right to do or have something
titled	*adj* referring to the name of a book or to members of a nation's nobility
royal	*adj* referring to the families of living and deceased sovereigns
envelop	*v* to hold, cover, or surround entirely
envelope	*n* a flat paper container for a letter or thin package
erotic	*adj* pertaining to the arousal of strong sexual desire, love, or physical pleasure
erotica	*n* works of literature or art that have an erotic theme or quality
exotic	*adj* pertaining to a person or thing from a foreign country or another culture that is strange, excitingly unusual, or intriguingly beautiful
eschew	*v* to abstain or keep away from
chew	*v* to crush or grind with the teeth

essence   *n* the basic nature of a thing; substance, spirit, or lifeblood

quintessence   *n* the pure and concentrated essence of a substance; the perfect embodiment of something

etiology   *n* the study of the causes of diseases

etymology   *n* the study of word derivation

ethnology   *n* a branch of anthropology that analyzes the origins and development of cultures

evoke   *v* to call up or to produce feelings or memories

invoke   *v* to call on a deity or Muse, as in prayer or supplication; to call forth or upon a spirit by incantation

exacerbate   *v* to intensify, aggravate, or worsen

exasperate   *v* to anger, vex, or infuriate

exceptionable   *adj* open to debate, question, or objection

exceptional   *adj* out of the ordinary; unusual or rare

face mask   *n* in sports, a protective device worn during play to prevent injury to the face

facial mask   *n* in skin care, a cosmetic preparation applied to the face and allowed to remain for a short time before being removed

farsighted   *adj* describing *hyperopia,* a condition in which the eyes can see distant objects but are unable to see close objects clearly

nearsighted   *adj* describing *myopia,* a condition in which the eyes can see close objects but are unable to see distant objects clearly

astigmatic   *adj* describing *astigmatism,* a condition that distorts or blurs vision for objects at any distance

presbyopic   *adj* describing *presbyopia* (aging eyes), a condition that occurs as people age, causing difficulty in focusing the eyes for reading and close work

farther	*adv* pertaining to physical distance or to a more advanced point
further	*adv* pertaining to an extension of time or degree; in addition
faze	*v* to embarrass or disturb
phase	*n* an aspect or stage
feather bed	*n* a mattress stuffed with feathers
featherbed	*v* to require an employer to hire more workers than needed to handle a job
felony	*n* a serious crime, such as murder, arson, or assault
misdemeanor	*n* a criminal offense defined as less serious than a felony
fewer	*n* a smaller amount pertaining to individual items
less	*n* a smaller amount pertaining to bulk or quantity
fiancé	*n* [F] a man engaged to be married
fiancée	*n* [F] a woman engaged to be married
fiscal	*adj* pertaining to the public treasury or revenues, or to financial matters in general
monetary	*adj* pertaining to money or to the mechanisms of its supply in the economy
flaunt	*v* to make an ostentatious or defiant display
flout	*v* to mock or show contempt for
forbear	*v* to avoid or shun
forebear	*n* an ancestor
fort	*n* a strong or fortified place occupied by troops; a permanent army post
forte	*n* a person's strong point
foul	*adj* offensive or out of line
fowl	*n* a bird, especially the larger domestic or wild birds used as food

freeze	*n* or *v* pertaining to the state of being frozen
frieze	*n* a sculptured or richly ornamental band used to decorate a building or piece of furniture
fulsome	*adj* disgusting, noisome, offensive
wholesome	*adj* promoting well-being; improving character
gaunt	*adj* excessively thin and angular
gauntlet	*n* a glove; a former military punishment
generous	*adj* indicative of the warm and sympathetic nature of the giver
charitable	*adj* indicative of both the goodness and kindness of the giver and the need of the recipient
gibe	*v* to taunt or smear
jibe	*v* to agree, conform, or fit; in sailing, to shift direction
gorilla	*n* a large ape of western equatorial Africa
guerrilla	*n* a member of a band of irregular soldiers and their tactics, including harassment and sabotage
gourmet	*n* one who likes fine food and is an excellent judge of food and drink
gourmand	*n* one who likes good food and tends to eat to excess; a glutton
gratuity	*n* a gift of money or a tip
gratify	*v* to delight, gladden, or give pleasure to
grill	*n* a cooking grate or surface
grille	*n* a metal grating that serves as a barrier or screen, especially an ornamental one, as at the front end of an automobile

grisly	*adj* horrifying, repugnant, or ghastly
grizzly	*adj* sprinkled or streaked with gray *n* shortened form for *grizzly bear,* a large brown bear of western North America
hangar	*n* a structure for housing and repairing aircraft
hanger	*n* a closet accessory for hanging a garment when not in use
harbor	*n* a sheltered body of water along a shore deep enough for a ship to anchor
port	*n* a city with a harbor; a haven, where ships may ride secure from storms
heterosexual	*adj* or *n* pertaining to someone who is sexually attracted to a person or persons of the opposite sex
homosexual	*adj* or *n* pertaining to someone who is sexually attracted to a person or persons of his or her own sex (also called *gay*)
bisexual	*adj* or *n* pertaining to someone who is sexually attracted to a person or persons of both sexes
unisexual	*adj* having only male or female organs in one individual, as an animal or flower
historic	*adj* pertaining to an outstanding event in history
historical	*adj* pertaining to any occurrence in the past
honesty	*n* denoting an uprightness and fairness impervious to deceit or fraud
integrity	*n* denoting a soundness of moral principle impervious to power or influence
hurricane	*n* a warm-core tropical cyclone that occurs east of the International Date Line (a theoretical line following approximately the 180th meridian)
typhoon	*n* a warm-core tropical cyclone that occurs west of the International Date Line

hypotension	*n* abnormally low blood pressure
hypertension	*n* persistently high blood pressure
ideal	*adj* pertaining to perfection, beauty, or the highest possible standard
idyllic	*adj* pertaining to a scene of charmingly simple rural or pastoral life
immigrant	*n* one who enters a country to take up permanent residence
emigrant	*n* one who leaves a country to take up residence elsewhere
immoral	*adj* contrary to established morals
amoral	*adj* indifferent to right or wrong
impassable	*adj* unpassable; unable to be surmounted
impassible	*adj* incapable of suffering pain or feeling emotion, impassive
impetus	*n* a starting, impelling, or driving force
impetuous	*adj* impulsive, rash, or eager
imply	*v* to assume or include
infer	*v* to deduce, guess, or reason
in	*prep* pertaining to location
into	*prep* pertaining to motion
incite	*v* to arouse, instigate, or spur
insight	*n* perception, apprehension, or self-knowledge
incredible	*adj* unbelievable
incredulous	*adj* skeptical
indict	*v* to charge with an offense or crime
arraign	*v* to call or bring before a court to answer to an indictment
indigent	*adj* poverty-stricken
indigenous	*adj* native to a particular region or environment

indiscreet	*adj* imprudent
indiscrete	*adj* not separated into distinct parts
indolent	*adj* habitually lazy, slow to heal
insolent	*adj* overbearing, impudent
redolent	*adj* exuding fragrance, odorous
insidious	*adj* corrupting, deceitful, or wily
invidious	*adj* hateful, injurious, offensively or unfairly discriminating
install	*v* to place in position or connect for service; to induct into an office, rank, or order
instill	*v* to cause to enter drop by drop, as a medication; to impart gradually
interplanetary	*adj* pertaining to a trip among the planets
interstellar	*adj* pertaining to a trip among the stars
interval	*n* a set of real numbers between two numbers, either including or excluding one or both
range	*n* a sequence, series, or scale between limits
its	*pron* the possessive form of *it*
it's	*contraction* of *it is* or *it has*
jail	*n* a place of detention of persons awaiting trial or arraignment, or convicted of minor offenses
penitentiary	*n* a maximum security institution maintained by state or federal authorities for serious offenders
prison	*n* a generic term for any place of confinement or involuntary restraint
jest	*n* a jeer or quip to be taken humorously; a prank
joke	*n* something said or done to provoke laughter

judge	*n* an appointed or elected officer with the power to make decisions in a court of law
magistrate	*n* a civil officer with limited judicial power, often a justice of the peace or judge of a police court
jurist	*n* one having thorough knowledge of the law, as a judge, lawyer, or scholar
juror	*n* a member of a jury
ketch	*n* a fore-and-aft rigged sailing vessel
kitsch	*n* something of tawdry design, often of poor quality, that appeals to popular or undiscriminating taste
kudo	*n* honor, glory, or acclaim
kudu	*n* a large African antelope
lama	*n* a priest of Lamaism, a religion of Tibet and Mongolia influenced by Buddhism
llama	*n* a South American pack animal distantly related to the camel
latitude	*n* the distance north or south of the equator, designated by parallels
longitude	*n* the distance east or west of Greenwich, England, designated by meridians
lay	*v* to put something down (past tense *laid*)
lie	*v* to recline (past tense *lay*)
levee	*n* an embankment designed to prevent the flooding of a river; a reception or assembly
levy	*n* an imposing or collecting, as of a tax, by authority or seizure
libel	*n* injury to a person's reputation through false and defamatory written or printed words or pictures, constituting a civil or criminal offense
slander	*n* injury to a person's reputation through false and defamatory spoken words or gestures, constituting a civil offense

libretto	*n* [It, little book] the words or text of an opera, oratorio, or musical play
librettist	*n* a person who writes a libretto
lyricist	*n* a person who writes the lyrics for songs
lightning	*n* the flashing of light produced by a discharge of atmospheric electricity
lightening	*n* the making of something less dark or heavy
like	*prep* used to compare nouns and pronouns
as	*conj* used to introduce clauses
linage	*n* the number of lines
lineage	*n* ancestry or descent
literally	*adv* word for word, factually, not imaginatively
figuratively	*adv* not in its usual or exact sense
locale	*n* the setting of a story, play, opera, or film
location	*n* a specific area; a place of activity or residence
lute	*n* a stringed musical instrument popular in the 16th and 17th centuries, having a long, fretted neck and a hollow pear-shaped body with a vaulted back
lyre	*n* a harplike stringed instrument of ancient Greece, generally consisting of a soundbox with two curved arms connected by a yoke from which strings are attached
luxuriant	*adj* lush, abundant, or flourishing
luxurious	*adj* rich, lavish, or extravagant
magnet	*n* something or someone that attracts
magnate	*n* a person of great importance or standing in a particular field
manner	*n* kind, custom, or style
manners	*n* deportment, behavior

| may | *auxiliary v* for expressing permission |
| can | *auxiliary v* for expressing ability |

| meantime | *n* the intervening time |
| meanwhile | *adv* pertaining to the intervening time or to two simultaneous events |

| medium | *adj* intermediate in size, degree, position, quantity, or quality |
| medial | *adj* mean, average, or being in the middle (synonym for *median*) |

| melody | *n* a succession of single musical notes |
| harmony | *n* any simultaneous combination of tones |

| midi | *n* a skirt, dress, or coat of mid-calf length |
| Midi | *n* the south of France |

| mileage | *n* the length, extent, or distance in miles |
| millage | *n* the tax rate, as for property, assessed in mills per dollar |

| milestone | *n* a stone used as a milepost; a significant event or stage in a person's life |
| millstone | *n* either of two circular stones used for grinding grain; a heavy burden |

| militate | *v* to operate or work against (usually used with *against*) |
| mitigate | *v* to make milder or less severe |

| missile | *n* an object or weapon for throwing, hurling, or shooting |
| missive | *n* a written message, letter |

| moiré | *n* a fabric such as silk or rayon with a watery, wavelike appearance |
| moray | *n* any of numerous, chiefly tropical eels (also called *moray eel*) |

| motif | *n* the main theme in a creative work, such as a book, musical score, or design |
| motive | *n* the inner drive or reason that causes a person's actions or manner |

Murphy's Law	*If something can go wrong, it will.* After a fictitious Murphy, allegedly the name of a bungling mechanic in the U.S. Navy educational cartoons of the 1950s
Peter Principle, the	*Each employee is promoted until he reaches his level of incompetence.* From the book by Canadian educator Laurence J. Peter, published by William Morrow in 1969
naive	*adj* lacking in worldly wisdom or informed judgment
artless	*adj* free from artificiality, guile, or craft; sincerely simple
naval	*adj* pertaining to a navy
navel	*n* a bellybutton (also used as an adjective in *navel orange,* so named for its small depression, like a navel, at its apex)
neutral	*adj* not engaged on either of two opposing sides; impartial; dispassionate
neural	*adj* of a nerve or the nervous system
new	*adj* pertaining to something that has not been long in existence
novel	*adj* pertaining to something new, unusual, and generally pleasing that has a strange, striking, or unexpected quality
noisy	*adj* clamorous, loud
noisome	*adj* offensive to the senses, especially to that of smell; noxious or harmful; highly obnoxious or objectionable
nourish	*v* to provide food or other nutriment necessary for promoting health and sustaining life
nurture	*v* to support and encourage; to rear, train, or educate
noxious	*adj* harmful, injurious, or corrupting
obnoxious	*adj* hateful, highly offensive, or objectionable

obscene	*adj* pertaining to something that is strongly offensive or objectionable to accepted standards of decency or morality
pornographic	*adj* pertaining to material of no artistic or scientific value designed to stimulate immoral thoughts and incite sexual desire
oculist	*n* an early term for someone who treats diseases and defects of the eye
optician	*n* a person who makes or sells eyeglasses and, usually, contact lenses
ophthal-mologist	*n* a doctor of medicine who specializes in treating diseases of the eye
optometrist	*n* a licensed professional who examines the eyes for defects in vision and eye disorders in order to prescribe corrective lenses or other treatment
official	*adj* authoritative, authorized
officious	*adj* interfering, meddling; aggressive in offering unsolicited services or advice
opera	*n* [It, work, opera, fr. L, work, pains] a lengthy drama, tragic or comic, usually entirely sung, accompanied by full orchestra and staged with scenery and costumes
operetta	*n* [It, dim. of *opera*] a short opera, usually of a light and amusing nature, in which there are some spoken parts (also called *light opera*)
opera buffa	*n* [It, lit., comic opera] an 18th-century farcical comic opera with dialogue in recitative (singing that sounds like speech)
ordnance	*n* military weapons and equipment
ordinance	*n* an authoritative rule or law; a decree, command, or order
ordonnance	*n* arrangement or disposition of parts, as of a play, picture, or literary work
ovine	*adj* pertaining to sheep
bovine	*adj* pertaining to cattle, buffalo, and kudus
porcine	*adj* pertaining to pigs

pain	*n* physical suffering of varying degrees of severity and length of time
ache	*n* a continuous, dull, prolonged pain
palate	*n* the roof of the mouth; a person's physical sense of taste
palette	*n* a thin oval or oblong board with a thumb hole on one end, on which an artist holds and mixes paints
pallet	*n* a small, hard bed; a portable platform used in warehouses
palling	*n* a fence of pales or spikes
appalling	*adj* inspiring horror, dismay, or disgust
pall-mall	*n* a 17th-century game in which a wooden ball was struck with a mallet in an attempt to drive it through a raised iron ring at the end of a playing alley; the alley in which the game was played
pell-mell	*adv* in headlong haste; in a recklessly disordered manner
paradigm	*n* an example serving as a model
paragon	*n* a model of perfection or excellence
pardon	*n* in law, an exemption or release of a person from any or further punishment for an offense, as by a governor
amnesty	*n* a general pardon granted to a group of persons for political offenses against a government
reprieve	*n* a delay of impending punishment, especially a death sentence, until a decision can be made regarding the possibility of pardon or reduction of sentence
parole	*n* the release from prison before a person's sentence (generally for a felony) is completed, on condition of good behavior
probation	*n* the suspension of sentence for a person convicted of but not yet imprisoned for a misdemeanor or less serious felony, on condition of good behavior

pedal	*v* to work or use the pedals of a musical instrument, as a piano or organ; to power various mechanisms, as a bicycle, with the feet
peddle	*v* to go from place to place with small articles, goods, and wares for retail sale
penal	*adj* pertaining to punishment for crimes and offenses
penile	*adj* pertaining to the male organ of urination and copulation
persecute	*v* to persistently harass or oppress someone because of race, religion, or beliefs
prosecute	*v* in law, to carry out a legal procedure against an accused person in a criminal or civil case
perspective	*n* point of view, vista, or a technique of depicting volumes and spatial relationships on a flat surface
prospective	*adj* pertaining to the future; potential, likely, or expected
prospectus	*n* a brochure describing the major features of a proposed project, business venture, or literary work, as a book or play, in sufficient detail for evaluation by prospective investors, participants, or buyers
pistol	*n* a small firearm meant to be held and fired with one hand (a handgun)
revolver	*n* a pistol in which the cartridges are held in a revolving cylinder behind the barrel
pore	*v* to gaze intently or steadily
pour	*v* to flow in a continuous stream
port	*n* the left-hand side of or direction from a vessel or aircraft when facing forward

starboard	*n* the right-hand side of or direction from a vessel or an aircraft when facing forward
poser	*n* a person who poses
poseur	*n* a person who pretends to be what he or she is not; an affected or insincere person
postulate	*v* to demand or require; to take for granted
stipulate	*v* in law, to include a requirement as part of a contract or agreement relating to a matter before the court, such as a divorce
premier	*n* a prime minister or leader of a provincial government
premiere	*n* a first public performance or showing of a creative work, as a play, opera, or film
pretense	*n* make-believe; an act intended to conceal personal feelings
pretext	*n* something put forward to conceal a true purpose; misleading appearance assumed intentionally
primeval	*adj* pertaining to the first age or ages of the world
primordial	*adj* pertaining to or existing at or from the very beginning
prehistoric	*adj* pertaining to the time before recorded history
principal	*adj* or *n* pertaining to someone or something first in rank, authority, importance, or degree
principle	*n* a fundamental truth, law, doctrine, or motivating force
profit	*n* a valuable return, net income, or advantage
prophet	*n* one who predicts future events
prophecy	*n* a prediction
prophesy	*v* to predict

prostate	*n* a gland surrounding the neck of the bladder and urethra in the human male and contributing a secretion to the semen
prostrate	*adj* stretched out with face on the ground in adoration or submission; prone or lying flat
prudent	*adj* sensible, sagacious, or thrifty
prudish	*adj* excessively proper or modest in speech, dress, or manner; reserved or coy
psychiatrist	*n* a doctor of medicine specializing in the study, treatment, and prevention of mental illness
psychologist	*n* a person trained in the science of the mind or of mental states and processes
psychoanalyst	*n* a person (in the U.S., usually a physician) trained to practice a method of diagnosis and treatment of mental and emotional disorders through ascertaining and analyzing the facts of the patient's mental life
analysand	*n* a person undergoing psychoanalysis
quark	*n* in physics, a hypothetical particle
quirk	*n* a peculiarity of action or behavior, eccentricity, or a sudden twist or turn
questioning	*n* the act of asking questions
questionable	*adj* open to doubt and inviting questioning
queue	*n* a braid of hair usually worn hanging at the back of the head; a waiting line of people or vehicles
cue	*n* a hint; a signal to a performer to begin a specific speech or action; in billiards and pool, a leather-tipped rod used for striking the cue ball
quietus	*n* anything that effectually ends or settles; removal from activity; death
quietude	*n* the quality or state of quiet and tranquillity

rabid	*adj* irrationally extreme in opinion or practice; mad; pertaining to rabies
avid	*adj* eager, enthusiastic, or ardent
rear	*v* to bring up a human
raise	*v* to bring up any living being, animal or human
rear-end	*v* to crash into the back of (as an automobile)
rear end	*n* the buttocks
rebut	*v* to argue to the contrary
refute	*v* to successfully contradict in an argument
recipe	*n* a formula or set of instructions for making something, especially food dishes
receipt	*n* a written acknowledgment of payment for something received, as money or goods
regardless	*adj* heedless, inattentive, or negligent
irregardless	*nonstandard English* because of double negative: *ir-* and *-less*. Use *regardless*.
reign	*n* the period a ruler is on the throne
rein	*n* the leather strap for controlling a horse
reluctant	*adj* unwilling to act
reticent	*adj* unwilling to speak
recalcitrant	*adj* unwilling to comply; resistant or rebellious
repertoire	*n* a list of performance pieces or productions
repertory	*n* a company that presents plays or operas
repress	*v* to curb, subdue, or exclude from consciousness
re-press	*v* to iron an article for the second time
reprise	*n* a musical repetition or a repeated performance
reprisal	*n* a retaliatory act or the regaining of something by recapture

resister	*n* one who opposes or withstands
resistor	*n* a device designed to introduce resistance into an electric circuit
review	*n* a written or oral evaluation; an examination or study
revue	*n* a musical show comprised of skits, songs, and dances
rifle	*v* to plunder, steal, or ransack and rob
riffle	*v* to leaf rapidly through a book or pile of papers
rigorous	*adj* severe, strict, or rigid
vigorous	*adj* strong, active, or energetic
rout	*n* a disorderly retreat, an overwhelming defeat
route	*n* a road, path, or course for passage or travel
ruthful	*adj* tender, woeful, or causing sorrow
ruthless	*adj* merciless, cruel
sadism	*n* a psychiatric condition in which sexual gratification is gained from inflicting physical or mental pain on others
masochism	*n* a psychiatric condition in which sexual gratification is gained from physical pain, humiliation, or domination; a taste for suffering
sado-masochism	*n* a psychiatric condition in which sexual gratification is gained from the infliction of physical or mental pain, either on others or on oneself
sapid	*adj* palatable; appealing to the taste or one's liking
vapid	*adj* having lost flavor or sharpness; lifeless, dull, or tedious

scheme	*n* a plan or program of action, especially an underhanded or crafty one
ploy	*n* a tactic to gain the advantage; ruse, gambit, or subterfuge
plot	*n* a secret plan for accomplishing some evil, hostile, unlawful, and often treasonable deed
Scot	*n* a native of Scotland
Scots	*n* the people of Scotland
Scottish	*adj* pertaining to Scotland, its people, or their language
Scotch	*adj* pertaining to things of Scottish origin, as *Scotch plaid* *n* a type of whiskey (spelled *whisky* when used with *Scotch*) distilled in Scotland from malted barley
scotch	*v* to stamp out, put an end to, or crush
scull	*n* an oar used to propel a small boat; a boat propelled by an oar or oars
skull	*n* the skeleton of the head of a human or other vertebrates (members of the animal kingdom having a spinal column: mammals, birds, reptiles, amphibians, and fishes)
seize	*v* to take hold of suddenly or forcibly, confiscate, or arrest
siege	*n* a military blockade of a city or fortified place to force its surrender
silicon	*n* a nonmetallic element occurring in a combined state in rocks and minerals, the most abundant element next to oxygen in the earth's crust
silicone	*n* any organic compound in which all or part of the carbon has been replaced by silicon
soupçon	*n* [F, a suspicion] a slight trace, as of a particular taste or flavor; dash, bit, or hint
soup du jour	*n* [F, *soupe du jour*, soup of the day] the soup featured by a restaurant on a particular day

stanch	*v* to stop the flow, as of blood
staunch	*adj* loyal, constant, or steadfast
startle	*v* to frighten or surprise someone suddenly, usually not seriously
stun	*v* to make senseless, dizzy, or groggy by a blow or as if by a blow
stationary	*adj* standing still, not moving
stationery	*n* writing paper and envelopes
steal	*n* the act or an instance of stealing; an exceptional bargain
stele	*n* an inscribed upright stone slab or pillar serving as a monument or marker
sterile	*adj* barren, not producing young; free from living germs or microorganisms (also called *aseptic*)
antiseptic	*adj* or *n* pertaining to a substance that inhibits the growth of pathogenic microorganisms but does not necessarily kill them
strategy	*n* the science or art of combining and employing the means of war in planning and directing massive military operations; skillful use of a stratagem
stratagem	*n* a plan, scheme, or trick for surprising or deceiving an enemy; a deception, maneuver, or contrivance
stringent	*adj* rigorously binding, strict, or powerful
astringent	*adj* sharp, harsh, or rigorous *n* a solution that cleans the skin and constricts the pores
suit	*n* a set of items to be used together, as clothing or cards; an instance of suing in a court of law
suite	*n* a number of things forming a series or set, as in music, rooms, or furniture

susceptible	*adj* especially liable or subject to some influence or agent, as to colds or flattery
vulnerable	*adj* capable of being physically wounded; open to attack or damage, physical or moral; in contract bridge, having won one of the games of a rubber
tacit	*adj* understood without being openly expressed; implied or unspoken
taciturn	*adj* silent, uncommunicative, or quiet
tamper	*v* to meddle or interfere in order to weaken or change for the worse
tinker	*v* to busy oneself in a project or try to make repairs in an unskilled manner
taro	*n* a stemless plant cultivated for its edible tuber (fleshy root)
tarot	*n* any of a set of 22 playing cards bearing allegorical representations, used for fortune-telling and as a trump card in tarok, a card game dating from the Renaissance
telephone	*n* or *v* pertaining to an instrument, system, or process for reproducing sounds at a distance, especially one in which sound is converted into electrical impulses for transmission by wire
phone	*n* or *v* shortened form of *telephone,* the longer form preferable in business or formal use
temerity	*n* reckless boldness, rashness, or audacity
timidity	*n* fearfulness or faintheartedness
tense	*adj* stretched tight, rigid, or made taut
terse	*adj* smoothly elegant, concise, or brusque
their	*pron* possessive form of *they*
there	*adv* referring to a place or expletive
they're	*contraction* of *they are*

tic	*n* an involuntary, compulsive, repetitive movement usually involving the face and shoulders
tick	*n* a bloodsucking, parasitic insect; a tapping or beat, as a clock pendulum
timber	*n* growing trees or their wood
timbre	*n* the musical quality of a sound or note
toothsome	*adj* pleasing to the taste; voluptuous or sexually desirable
toothy	*adj* having or displaying conspicuous teeth; savory; having a rough surface
toxin	*n* any poison produced by an organism (bacteria, plants, or animals)
tocsin	*n* a bell or bells used to sound an alarm
transsexual	*adj* or *n* pertaining to a person who suffers from a conflict over his or her sexual identification and who wishes to assume the physical characteristics and gender of the opposite sex
transvestite	*n* a person who derives sexual enjoyment from wearing clothes of the opposite sex (also called *cross-dresser*)
transverse	*adj* or *n* pertaining to lying or extending across or in a cross direction
traverse	*adj, n* or *v* pertaining to traveling across
troop	*n* a group of people or animals
troops	*n* several such groups, especially groups of soldiers
troupe	*n* an ensemble of theatrical performers
umbra	*n* shade, shadow, or spectral image
umbrage	*n* offense, annoyance, or displeasure
undergraduate	*adj* or *n* pertaining to a college or university student who has not received a first degree, especially a bachelor's

graduate	*n* a student who holds a bachelor's or first professional degree and is studying for an advanced degree; a person who has received a degree or diploma upon completing a course of study at a college, university, or school
collegian	*n* a student in or a graduate of a college
urban	*adj* pertaining to a city or town
urbane	*adj* suave, cosmopolitan, or sophisticated
usable	*adj* capable of being used; available or practicable for use
useful	*adj* capable of being put to use, especially for some advantageous end or purpose
use	*n* the act of using or employing
usage	*n* customary or habitual practice or established use, practices, or procedures
usual	*adj* pertaining to something to be expected by reason of previous experience
customary	*adj* pertaining to something in accordance with prevailing usage or individual practice
vacant	*adj* having no contents or occupant, empty, or not in use
vacuous	*adj* lacking intelligence or ideas, stupid, or idle
vain	*adj* egotistical, fruitless, or unimportant
vane	*n* a weather vane, a device for indicating wind direction
vein	*n* a blood vessel; body of ore; tone, touch, or hint
valedictorian	*n* the student ranking highest academically in a school graduating class, who delivers the valedictory address
salutatorian	*n* the student ranking second highest in the graduating class, who delivers the salutatory address

vamp	*n* or *v* pertaining to a seductive woman who uses her sensuality to exploit men (short for *vampire*)
vampire	*n* a supernatural being, usually male, commonly believed to be a reanimated corpse that sucks the blood of sleeping persons at night
vampire bat	*n* any of several kinds of mouse-sized New World bats that feed on small amounts of blood obtained from resting mammals and birds by means of a shallow cut made with specialized incisor teeth
venal	*adj* pertaining to whatever is available for a price; open to bribery
venial	*adj* pertaining to whatever is forgivable, pardonable, or excusable, as a sin (opposed to *mortal*)
venereal	*adj* pertaining to infectious diseases of a sexual nature
venerable	*adj* commanding respect because of great age or impressive dignity; interesting because of antique appearance; hallowed by lofty associations
vice	*n* an evil, wicked, or self-destructive habit
vise	*n* a heavy clasp with two jaws that are opened and closed by a lever or screw action
vicious	*adj* grossly immoral, depraved, or savage
viscous	*adj* pertaining to oily or syrupy liquids
viral	*adj* pertaining to or caused by a virus
virulent	*adj* highly infectious, actively poisonous, or spitefully hostile
voluptuary	*adj* pertaining to the preoccupation with luxury and sensual pleasure
voluptuous	*adj* sensuously pleasing or delightful

waive	*v* to give up a right or privilege
wave	*v* to motion with the hands; to move gently and freely back and forth, as by the breeze
water hole	*n* a natural source of drinking water, as a spring or well in the desert
watering hole	*n* a bar, nightclub, or other social gathering place where alcoholic drinks are served
weak	*adj* breakable, delicate, or not physically strong because of illness or extremes of age
feeble	*adj* pitiably physically weak; inferior
yahoo	*n* an uncultivated or boorish person, lout, or yokel
wahoo	*n* any of various American shrubs or small trees, as the winged elm or a linden; a large, swift mackerel (also called *peto*)
zeal	*n* intense enthusiasm or devotion in working for a cause or in pursuit of a goal
zest	*n* added flavor, a stimulating quality, or rich enjoyment

· 13 ·
The New Sensitivity Vocabulary

Welsh poet Dylan Thomas (1914–53) wrote in *Selected Letters* (1967) that: "There is always the one right word; use it, despite its foul or merely ludicrous associations." While contemporary novelists still have literary license, all other individuals who write face unprecedented challenges. Not only must they avoid dated expressions and keep up with constantly increasing vocabulary and changing usage, they also must develop a heightened sensitivity as to choice of words.

Many words that a generation ago were considered innocuous or even flattering have become unacceptable and are perceived as insulting, demeaning, or hurtful. It is essential to stay abreast of current usage and avoid inadvertently making a bad impression, or even a mortal enemy. It is now, as the French say, *de rigueur* not to offend *any* reader and to strive to be politically correct at all times.

Even the three words applied to children from birth through 12 months of age—*infant, baby,* and *babe*—can have negative connotations, the first two implying infantilism, the third possibly referring to a tough person or thing.

The words *boys* and *girls* are now confined to describing young people under the age of 12. *Girl,* however, is still a mainstay in the lyrics of contemporary popular music; *boy* has been taboo for some time. The words *boyfriend* and *girlfriend* used to signify a romantic attachment, but now frequently refer to a relationship that is platonic or one with a member of the same sex that is only one of camaraderie.

The words *ladies* and *gentlemen* are seldom used today and are no longer synonyms for *women* and *men*. *Lady* is now reserved primarily for use as a courtesy title for a member of the nobility or when a specific reference to fine manners is appropriate.

The pronouns *she* and *her* are no longer used when referring to a nation or ship, replaced by *it* and *its*. The same applies when weather forecasters assign a female or male name to a storm, as a hurricane or typhoon. Do not use *she, her,* or *hers* in pronoun reference—use *it* and *its*.

Avoid the use of *man* and *mankind* when referring to both men and women, and duplicated phrases such as *a man or a woman* or *mankind or womankind*. The list that follows this section contains several alternative expressions to cover both situations.

Use *spouse* instead of *wife* or *husband* when referring to attendees at a gathering that includes professional people—physicians and their spouses (*not* physicians and their wives *or* physicians and their husbands).

One should also generally try to avoid using words with feminine suffixes (*-enne, -ess, -ette,* or *-trix*). Many words of formerly masculine usage now apply to individuals of both sexes—including *actor, ambassador, artist, author, aviator, comedian, director, executor, heir, maestro, minister, poet, proprietor, sculptor, testator, usher,* and *virtuoso.* However, several words with feminine endings—*actress, executrix, heiress, hostess,* and *testatrix*—are still commonly used. To date, *waitress* has not acquired a generally accepted substitute.

The word *youth* also applies to both boys and girls from age 13 until their 18th birthdays. Use *young man* or *man* and *young woman* or *woman* for persons 18 and older, *young* until the word no longer seems appropriate.

References to any non-Caucasian group of people need to be approached with the utmost care, as preferred usages keep changing. The same applies in matters of sexuality and in describing physical and psychological impairments and in designations for what was formerly referred to as "the bad part of town."

While everyday speech is reeling from an overdose of profanity and obscene language, vulgar expressions should be avoided in written materials, especially references to body parts and bodily functions.

Tact has become an essential in writing today. Because aging is not an easily accepted fact of life in America, such words as *middle-aged, elderly,* and *senior citizen* should be used sparingly. Writers must also be careful to avoid sexist comments, racial and ethnic slurs, condescending phrases, demeaning stereotyping, and forms of contempt.

In business correspondence, there are new considerations regarding the wording of salutations and courtesy titles. (Some authorities now prefer not to use any form of courtesy title.) Depending upon a woman's marital status or personal choice, start the letter *Dear Mrs. Johnson,* or *Dear Ms. Johnson,* or *Dear Miss Johnson.* If the name of the person to whom you are writing is unknown and the letter is not a formal one, use a generic term in the salutation, such as *Dear Student, Dear Client,* or *Dear Homeowner.*

In formal correspondence when it is impossible to obtain the name of the person to whom you must write, use the salutation *Dear* followed by the name of the organization or department or the title of the person to whom you are writing. *Dear Sir* and *Gentlemen,* considered sexist by many, and *Dear Madam* are rarely used today, as is *To Whom It May Concern.*

The following lists contain word choices and grammatical constructions that will help guide careful and sensitive writers and speakers through the challenging maze of today's political correctness.

AVOIDING SEXISM & SEXUAL STEREOTYPING

For	*Use*
anchorman, anchorwoman	anchor, coanchor
average man, man in the street	average person, ordinary person
bachelor girl, old maid, spinster	unmarried woman

For	Use
bellboy, bellman	bellhop
boy (age 13 until his 18th birthday)	youth
businessman, businesswoman	specific terms, such as *advertising executive, retailer, stockbroker*
cameraman, camerawoman	camera operator, cinematographer (*cameraperson* declining in popularity)
chairman, chairwoman	chair (*chairperson* declining in popularity)
cleaning lady, cleaning woman	housecleaner, housekeeper, office cleaner
clergyman, clergywoman	member of the clergy *or* specific terms, such as *minister, priest, rabbi*
coed	college student
congressman, congresswoman	representative, member of Congress, congressional representative, congressional delegate, legislator
distaff side	women
divorcée	a divorced woman *or* a woman who is divorced
fair sex	women
fellow (academic sense)	scholar, recipient (of a fellowship)

For	*Use*
fellow, fella, feller	associate, partner, colleague, coworker, companion, comrade, counterpart, peer
fellow man	another human being, other people, citizens
female child (under the age of 12)	girl
female doctor	doctor, physician
female person (18 and older)	young woman *or* woman, depending upon general age
feminine	reword to avoid
fireman	firefighter
forefather	ancestor
girl (age 13 until her 18th birthday)	youth
girl athlete	athlete
houseboy	housekeeper
housewife	housekeeper
human	human being
insurance man	insurance agent
lady lawyer	lawyer, attorney
layman, laywoman	layperson, nonspecialist, nonprofessional
little woman, the	wife

For	*Use*
mailman, postman	letter carrier, mail carrier
male child (under the age of 12)	boy
male nurse	nurse
male person (18 and older)	young man *or* man, depending upon general age
male secretary	secretary
man	human being, human, person, individual
man and wife	husband and wife
mankind, man	human beings, humans, humankind, humanity, human race, human species, people, society, men and women
manly	reword to avoid
man-made	artificial, synthetic
married lady	married woman, wife
masculine	reword to avoid
men and girls	men and women, boys and girls
men and ladies	men and women, ladies and gentlemen
meter maid	meter reader, meter attendant

For	*Use*
patrolman, patrolwoman, policeman, policewoman	police officer, law enforcement officer
saleswoman, salesman	salesperson, sales representative
spokesman, spokeswoman	spokesperson, representative
stewardess, steward	flight attendant, cabin attendant
weatherman, weatherwoman	weather forecaster, weather reporter, weathercaster, meteorologist
womanly	reword to avoid
woman writer	writer *or* specific type, such as *novelist*
workingman, workingwoman, workman, workwoman	worker, wage earner

The pronoun *he,* as with the noun *man,* is no longer used to represent an individual of either sex. To circumvent the third person singular masculine pronoun, restructure the sentence so that the substituting pronoun does not specify sex *or* includes both masculine and feminine forms; otherwise rephrase the sentence to avoid any pronoun.

All picnickers should bring their own lunch.
As captain of the team, one has a great responsibility.
If a student is late, send him or her (*or* her or him) to the principal's office.
Everyone brought presents.

To balance *he/him/his* and *she/her/hers* in lengthy prose, some professional writers use only masculine pronoun forms throughout one paragraph or chapter, alternately using only feminine forms in the following paragraph or chapter.

DESCRIBING PHYSICAL & MENTAL CONDITIONS

For	*Use*
arthritic	an arthritic condition *or* a person with arthritis
blind	only as an adjective for a person with total vision loss; *visually challenged* or *visually impaired* for a person with partial vision loss
crippled, disabled, handicapped	physically challenged *or* a person with a disability
a person with mental problems that can be treated on an outpatient basis	emotionally disturbed
a person with mental problems so severe as to require institutionalization	mentally ill
a mentally ill person who is violent	mentally disturbed
deaf	only as an adjective for a person with total hearing loss; *hearing impaired* for a person with partial hearing loss

For	*Use*
deaf and dumb *(Do not use.)*	hearing and speech impaired *or* a person who cannot hear or speak
deaf-mute *(Do not use. A mute person may or may not be deaf.)*	
diabetic	a diabetic condition *or* a person with diabetes
harelip	cleft palate
infantile paralysis	polio
mentally retarded	developmentally disabled
mute	a person who cannot speak
obese	severely overweight
reformed alcoholic	recovering alcoholic

REFERRING TO RACIAL & ETHNIC BACKGROUND

For	*Use*
Africa or any of its people or languages	African
an American of African heritage	African-American
Asia or any of its people or languages	Asian
an American of Asian heritage	Asian-American

For	Use
light-skinned peoples	Caucasian *or* White
a person of European and Asian descent	Eurasian
a Spanish-speaking country south of the United States	Latin American nation
a Spanish-speaking person of Latin American descent	Latina, Latino
an American Indian	Native American (A *native American* refers to *any* native-born American.)
a person whose parentage is a mixture of:	a person of mixed ancestry
European and Hindu European and Muslim American Indian and Caucasian African and Caucasian	

(*Red, Yellow, Brown,* and *Black* are less commonly used to designate ethnic groups.)

ALSO IN CURRENT USE

For	Use
bureaucrat	official, civil servant, government employee
cop	police officer
the poor	disadvantaged
illegal alien	undocumented worker

For	*Use*
escapee	escaped convict *or* fugitive
prescription *or* over-the-counter drugs (to differentiate from illegal drugs)	medicine
the elderly *or* old	senior citizens
daughter-in-law, my	my son's wife
father-in-law, my	my husband's/wife's father
mother-in-law, my	my wife's/husband's mother
son-in-law, my	my daughter's husband
deceased spouse:	
man	survived by *or* leaves his wife (not *widow*)
woman	survived by *or* leaves her husband (not *widower*)

• 14 •

Computer & Internet Terms

*C*omputer, a 350-year-old word meaning *one who computes*, today refers to a programmable electronic device that can store, retrieve, and process data. *Computerese*, a word used since the early 1960s, refers to the technical terminology used by practitioners in this field—virtually a language in itself.

The following list of words and expressions represents only a sampling of the more than 24,000-word vocabulary of computer terms that grows as rapidly as the computer industry itself, and includes several printing and typographical terms commonly used in word processing.

accelerator	an expansion board or chip that speeds up the performance of a computer or monitor
access time	the time required by a computer to locate and transfer data to or from storage
active window	in a window environment, the currently selected window receiving mouse or keyboard input
add-in	individual chips inserted into circuit boards already installed in a computer

add-on
: a product such as a circuit board, cartridge, or program designed to enhance the capabilities of a computer

AI
: *artificial intelligence,* a group of technologies that attempt to emulate such aspects of human behavior as reasoning and communicating

ALGOL
: *algorithmic language,* an international high-level programming language used especially in mathematical and scientific applications

alphanumeric
: describing a combined set of characters including the letters of the alphabet and the numerals 0 through 9; describing terminals that only display characters and may include punctuation marks, mathematical symbols, and special characters exclusive to computers

alpha testing
: the preliminary testing of software or hardware products

ANSI
: *American National Standards Institute,* the organization that publishes standards for various aspects of the computer industry

anti-virus program
: a program designed to check for the presence of viruses in a computer system

application
: a set of instructions that enables a computer to perform a specific task (also known as a *program*)

applications software
: includes database programs, word processors, and spreadsheets; also called *end-user programs*

Archie
: a system for locating publicly available files by anonymous file transfer protocols (FTPs) on the Internet

archival
backup
: the copying of only those files modified since the last backup (also called *incremental backup*)

array
: an arrangement of similar elements of data or related items

ascender
: in printing, the part of some lowercase letters (e.g., *d* and *h*) that extends above the height of the letter *x*

ASCII
: *American Standard Code for Computer Information Interchange,* a standard code, consisting of 128 7-bit combinations, for characters stored in a computer or to be transmitted between computers

backup copy
: a copy of files on a disk or tape that is kept in case the original is changed, damaged, or destroyed

BASIC
: *Beginner's All-purpose Symbolic Instruction Code,* one of the earliest and simplest programming languages

baud
: named after J.M.E. Baudot (1845–1903), French inventor, a unit for measuring the speed of data transmission equal to the number of pulses or bits per second, such as 2,400 baud

BBS
: *bulletin board system,* an electronic message center, mainly used by specific interest groups and normally accessed by modem

benchmark
: a point of reference used to evaluate or compare speed results of devices or systems; the test itself

beta testing
: the final testing of software or hardware

binary	a number system having just two unique digits, usually *0* and *1*
BIOS chip	*basic input/output system* chip, a special chip that contains the instructions a computer needs to start working (pronounced *buy-ose*)
bit	*binary digit,* the smallest unit of computer information
bit map	a representation of a piece of text or drawing as a specific arrangement of screen dots
block	a group of data stored as a unit in an external storage medium and handled as a unit by the computer for input and output; a section of storage locations in a computer allocated to a particular set of instructions or data; on a flow chart, a symbol representing an operation, device, or instruction in a program
bomb	a concealed fault that can cause a program to hang or crash (end prematurely), the term normally used to describe the behavior of a program, i.e., as having "bombed"
Boolean logic	named after George Boole (1815–1864), English mathematician and logician, a form of algebra in which all numerical values are reduced to TRUE or FALSE
boot	to load the first software (operating system) that directs the computer's operation (short for *bootstrap*)
bps	*bits per second,* the standard measure of data transmission speed

browser	any program for reading hypertext on Internet's World Wide Web (WWW)
bug	an error or defect in software or hardware that causes a program or system to malfunction
bus	an electronic pathway through which data is transmitted
byte	a group of eight binary digits processed as a unit by a computer
cable connector	a device for connecting computer hardware
cache	[F, fr. *cacher* to hide, pronounced *kash*] part of memory that speeds up performance by holding the most recently accessed data from a disk, later allowing faster access than from the disk (also called *cache memory* or *RAM cache*)
cascading windows	an arrangement of windows that overlap vertically
CBT	*computer-based training*, a training program that uses the computer to present the information, evaluate the user's response, and direct the course of the instruction
CCITT	*Comité Consultatif Internationale Télégraphique et Téléphonique*, an organization that sets international communications standards
CD-ROM	*compact disc-read only memory*, a type of optical disk capable of storing large amounts of data
character	any single letter, numeral, or other symbol that requires one byte of storage

chip	a small piece of semiconducting material, usually silicon, in which an electronic circuit is embedded
circuit board	a rectangular plate on which chips and other electronic components are placed
CISC	*complex instruction set computer,* a computer whose central processing unit (CPU) recognizes a relatively large number of instructions
client/server	architecture in which the client, the requesting program, interfaces with the server, the answering program, which processes the client's request
COBOL	*common business oriented language,* the second-oldest high-level programming language (FORTRAN being the oldest), particularly popular for business applications that run on large computers
command	an instruction to a computer to perform a specific task
computerize	to carry out, control, or produce by means of a computer; to equip with computers; to store in a computer; to put into a form that a computer can use
cpi	*characters per inch,* a unit of measurement for the number of characters that will print in one horizontal inch (sometimes called *pitch*)
cps	*characters per second,* a unit of measurement for the speed of data transfer
CPU	*central processing unit,* in a microprocessor or processor, a chip that performs all the computer's calculations

crash	a system problem in which a computer fails to respond to any commands and requires rebooting
CRT	*cathode-ray tube,* a vacuum tube generating a focused beam of electrons that can be deflected by electric or magnetic fields or both, used to display alphanumeric and graphical information on computer screens
cursor	a flashing short segment or rectangle on a monitor that indicates the position for entering data
daisy chain	a general method of transmitting signals to a series of devices, in which the input to the first device is passed through to the next device
DAT	*digital audiotape,* a magnetic tape on which sound is digitally recorded with high fidelity for playback, and which may also be used for such functions as storing binary data for backups
data	information that can be digitally transmitted or processed
database	a usually large collection of data organized especially for rapid search and retrieval by a computer
data processing	the converting of raw data to machine-readable form and its subsequent processing by a computer
data structure	any of various methods of organizing data in a computer
daughterboard	a small printed circuit board that attaches to and adds capability to a larger main board (motherboard)

DBMS	*database management system,* software that controls the organization, storage, retrieval, security, and integrity of data as changes are made in the data
debug	to find and remove bugs (errors) from a program or system
dedicated	pertaining to a program, machine, or procedure reserved for just one use
descender	in printing, the part of some lowercase letters (e.g., *g* and *p*) that goes below the body of the letter
dialog box	a small box or window that displays options when a program needs additional information from the user
DIP switch	*dual in-line package* switch, a set of small on/off switches mounted on circuit boards to facilitate choice of options for use
directory	a list of a collection of files on a disk
disk drive	the "box" in which a hard or floppy disk operates
diskette	another term for *floppy disk*
display	an electronic device such as a cathode-ray tube that temporarily presents information in visual form; also, the display information
DMA	*direct memory access,* a technique for transferring data to and from external storage
DNS	*Domain Name System,* a distributed database system for translating computer names into numeric Internet addresses and the reverse

DOS	*disk operating system,* a program that provides the essential instructions for a computer's parts to function as a whole (pronounced *dawss*)
down	the state of a computer system currently not working or unavailable to users
download	to copy data from a main source to a peripheral device
dpi	*dots per inch,* a unit of measurement for the resolution of monitors, printers, and scanners
drag	to simultaneously hold down the mouse button and move the mouse to select a menu item or move an object around the screen
driver	computer software that controls input and output operations
DTP	*desktop publishing,* the use of a computer to design and print pages for publication, combining text and graphics on a single page
EDP	*electronic data processing,* the use of computers in the processing of data
e-mail	*electronic mail,* messages that are read and/or written on-screen and sent across a network or through a modem to other users at different terminals
end user	the final or ultimate user of a computer system
EPS	*Encapsulated PostScript,* a special file format, containing text and graphics, created using the PostScript programming language

execute   to run a program or enter a command

FAQ   *frequently asked question* or a list of questions and their answers, providing introductory information about a particular server's newsgroup (see *USENET*)

FAT   *file allocation table,* a record which is automatically generated on a floppy or hard disk to keep track of each file's location on the disk

fax/modem   a facsimile device that can be attached to a personal computer for transmission of electronic documents

file server   a disk storage device that each computer on a network can use to access or retrieve shared files

flame   a virulent and frequently personal attack against the originator of a USENET posting; a "flamer" is someone who often writes "flames"

floppy disk   a flexible plastic disk coated with magnetic material on which data for a computer can be stored

font   in printing, a set of characters of the same typeface (the design of the type) and type size

footer   a page number, date, author's name, or other information placed automatically at the bottom of every page of a document

FORTRAN   *formula translator,* the oldest high-level programming language, which resembles algebra in its notation and is widely used for scientific applications

Free-net	an organization to provide free Internet access to an urban community, either at public libraries or by dialing in
FTP	*File Transfer Protocol,* an Internet method for transferring files from one computer to another, regardless of their location, type of connection, or whether or not they use the same operating system
gigabyte	one billion bytes (approx)
Gopher	a menu-based system for exploring Internet resources
gppm	*graphics pages per minute*
grandfather file	the oldest backup file copy
graphics	visual images such as drawings, characters, or symbols produced on a display screen, plotter, or printer
GUI	*graphical user interface,* the component of an application that uses graphics to display information and provides the user with the ability to interact with the computer (pronounced *gooey*)
hacker	*slang,* a computer enthusiast; an expert at programming and problem-solving; a microcomputer user who illegally gains access to a proprietary system to tamper with information or break into other computer systems
handshaking	the process by which two devices initiate communication
hands-on	pertaining to the process of physically using a computer

hard copy   a printed paper copy of information stored in a computer (also called *printout*)

hard disk   a rigid disk that is sealed against dust and used as a high-capacity storage device for a computer

hardware   objects that can be touched, such as disks, disk drives, display screens, keyboards, printers, and chips

hardwired   implemented in the form of permanent electronic circuits

header   a page number, date, author's name, or other information placed automatically at the top of every page of a document

home page   the starting point for a series of linked documents on the Internet

hotlist   a user-generated list of favorite places on the World Wide Web that cross-references universal resource locators (URLs) used for repeated visitation

html   *hypertext markup language,* the language for writing World Wide Web documents on the Internet

http   *hypertext transfer protocol,* the standard for transferring hypertext data in Internet documents

hyperlink   a link in a given document to information within another document, usually represented by a highlighted word or image

IC   *integrated circuit,* a circuit of transistors, resistors, and capacitors constructed on a single semiconductor wafer or chip, in which the components are interconnected to perform a given function

icon   a picture or symbol on a display screen that represents a computer program or group of programs

input   to enter data into a computer

integrated circuit   See *IC.*

interface   a connection between two separate or independent systems, as between a computer and a typesetting machine

Internet   a multimillion-user worldwide network of computer networks that are connected to each other

I/O   *input/output,* any operation, program, or device whose purpose is to enter data into or extract data from a computer

IP   *Internet Protocol,* the most important of the protocols on which the Internet is based, allowing small chunks of data (see *packet*) to traverse multiple networks on the way to their ultimate destination

IRC   *Internet relay chat,* a service that allows multiple users to converse over the Internet

ISDN   *Integrated Services Digital Network,* telephone service in which phone lines to a person's residence carry digital rather than analog signals, allowing high-speed home access to the Internet

ISOC — *Internet Society,* an organization whose members support a worldwide information network

joystick — a lever that controls the movement of a cursor or other graphic element on a screen display (also used for playing video games)

keyboard — a group of systematically arranged keys by which a computer is operated

Knowbot — an experimental robotic information-retrieval tool

LAN — *local area network,* a group of cable-connected computers that are able to transfer files among themselves

laptop computer — a small personal computer for use on one's lap

laser printer — a printer that uses light and toner powder, like a photocopying machine, to print text and graphics onto paper (the industry standard for producing sharp and finely detailed images)

LCD — *liquid crystal display,* mostly commonly used to describe screens that come with laptop computers

leading — in printing, extra space inserted between each line of type to prevent descenders of one line from overlapping the ascenders of the following line (pronounced *led-ing*)

LED — *light-emitting diode,* a semiconductor diode that emits light when conducting current, used for displaying readings

LSD — *least significant digit,* the digit farthest to the right in a number

macro	resembling a small program, a recorded set of instructions for a frequently used task, activated by pressing a specified key combination (also called *macroinstruction*)
mainframe	a large, fast computer
matrix	a two-dimensional array
media	the material (such as hard disks, floppy disks, and tapes) on which data can be stored; in networks, the cables that link workstations together
megabyte	one million bytes (approx)
memory	an electronic storage area in which data can be inserted and stored subject to recall; components in which such data is stored (also called *computer memory, storage*)
menu	a list of options from which the user may choose
MICR	*magnetic ink character recognition,* a technique for reading and processing data printed with ink containing magnetic particles
micro	a microcomputer, a compact and relatively inexpensive computer that has less capacity and capability than a minicomputer
microchip	an integrated circuit (IC)
micro-computer	a personal computer
micro-processor	a silicon chip that contains a central processing unit (CPU)

MIDI — *Musical Instrument Digital Interface,* a standard means of sending digitally encoded musical information between electronic devices

MIME — *multipurpose Internet mail extensions,* a specification for automatically sending objects other than text in e-mail messages

minicomputer — a computer with processing and storage capabilities larger than those of a microcomputer but smaller than those of a mainframe

MIPS — *million instructions per second*

MIS — *management information system,* a system designed to support the activities and functions of company management

modem — *modulator/demodulator,* a device that allows computers to converse over telephone lines

monitor — a cathode-ray tube used for displaying computer information

monochrome monitor — a monitor that can display only one color (e.g., green or blue) on its background

motherboard — the main circuit board of a microcomputer to which every part connects

mouse — a small mobile manual device that controls movement of the cursor on a computer display

mousepad — a pad on which to move a mouse for better traction

MSD — *most significant digit,* the digit farthest to the left in a number

MUD | *Multi-User Dungeon,* a group of Internet role-playing games similar to the original "Dungeons and Dragons" games, which can also be used as conferencing tools and educational aids

multimedia | computer applications that combine audio, graphics, text, and video components with computer functions

multitasking | executing more than one computer program at once

network | an interconnected computer system containing any combination of computers, terminals, printers, audio/visual display devices, and the devices that connect them

noise | interference that destroys the integrity of signals on a line

NOT circuit | a circuit that is energized when its input is not (also called *NOT gate*)

ns | *nanosecond,* one-billionth of a second, the measure of the speed of a memory chip

OCR | *optical character reader, optical character recognition,* a program that can scan printed material, such as magazine or newspaper articles, and convert them into files for editing on a word processor

optical disk | a disk that employs a laser to read and write data

orphan | in printing, the first line of a paragraph when it appears alone at the bottom of a page (considered undesirable in page design)

packet   a bundle of data, varying from approximately 40 to 32,000 bytes long, that traverses the Internet independently

pagination   the feature that arranges a document into pages and numbers them

palette   a range of colors available in graphics programs

palmtop   a sublaptop portable computer weighing as little as one pound that literally fits into the palm of the hand

PASCAL   a computer programming language

path   the hierarchy of directories that must be traversed to access a specific file

PC   *personal computer,* a microcomputer designed for a person to use in the office, home, or school, which includes applications for word processing, data management, financial analysis, or computer games

peripheral   an external device or unit that attaches to but operates separately from the CPU to provide input and output or auxiliary functions such as additional storage

personal computer   a small, inexpensive computer designed for one user at a time (also called *microcomputer*)

PIM   *personal information manager*

pixel   *picture element,* the smallest element of an image that can be individually processed in a video display system

pointer   an arrow-shaped icon controlled by a mouse

port	a receptacle, usually on the back of a computer, to which a peripheral device or a transmission line from a remote terminal can be attached
PPP	*Point-to-Point Protocol,* an Internet protocol method allowing World Wide Web access with a standard telephone line and a high-speed modem
printer	an output device that produces hard copy (a printout), a paper copy of alphanumeric and/or graphic data
PROM	*programmable read-only memory,* a memory chip whose contents can be programmed by a user or manufacturer for a specific purpose
RAM	*random-access memory,* which holds data that is lost when power is interrupted
raw data	data not yet processed
real time	the actual time during which a process takes place
resolution	the sharpness of an image on a screen or in print (the higher the resolution, the sharper the image)
RGB monitor	*red, green, blue* display system
RISC	*reduced instruction set computer,* a computer whose central processing unit (CPU) recognizes a relatively small number of instructions
ROM	*read-only memory,* which holds data that is permanent and cannot be changed by the computer user

run   to execute a program

save   to store a file for future use on a disk or
               tape

scanner   a device that converts images, both printed
               text and graphics such as photographs, into
               an electronic format for computer use

scroll   to move data, text, or graphics up/down or
               right/left on a display screen

scroll bar   in windows, the rectangular bar that
               appears at the right and bottom of some
               windows to indicate which part of a
               document is currently in the window's
               frame

SCSI   *small computer systems interface,* a
               standard for computer interface ports
               featuring faster data transmission and
               greater flexibility than normal ports
               (pronounced *scuzzy*)

server   a computer that serves information and
               software to the Internet community

SLIP   *Serial Line Internet Protocol,* a protocol
               that allows a computer to use the Internet
               protocols—and become a full-fledged
               Internet member—with a standard
               telephone line and a high-speed modem

software   information stored as electrical signals on
               disks or tapes

stand-alone   pertaining to a self-contained unit, such as
               a word processing typewriter, capable of
               operating independently (without other
               hardware or software)

storage   memory that exists on disks and tapes

submenu	an additional set of options offering variants of the main menu choice
supercomputer	the fastest type of computer, used for specified applications requiring immense amounts of mathematical calculations as in weather forecasting, nuclear energy research, and petroleum exploration (the least expensive costs more than $1 million)
TCP	*Transmission Control Protocol,* a set of rules that establish the method with which data is transmitted over the Internet between two computers
TELNET	an application program allowing a user to log in to other computer systems on the Internet
terminal	a combination of a keyboard and video display
trackball	an input device, essentially a mouse lying on its back, used to move the cursor around on a computer display screen
truth table	a systematic tabulation of all the possible input/output combinations produced by a binary circuit
TSR	*terminate and stay resident,* a program that remains on-call after the user has left it (also known as *memory resident*)
typeface	in printing, a design for a set of alphanumeric characters
upload	to transmit a file from one's computer to a BBS or other host computer

UPS   *uninterruptible power supply,* a battery-powered device that protects against power spikes and outages

URL   *universal resource locator,* the standardized format for identifying resources on the Internet that include document location and transfer protocol

USENET   neither a computer network nor software, but a set of voluntary rules for passing and maintaining newsgroups; also a set of volunteers who use and respect those rules

user-friendly   applied to computer programs that are easy to learn

user group   a group of local computer users who exchange information, share programs, and trade equipment

vaporware   a software product that has been announced, discussed, or promoted but is not yet publicly available

VDT   *video display terminal,* a screen on which data or graphics can be displayed

vector   a one-dimensional array

Veronica   an Internet service similar to Archie, that is built into Gopher, allowing searching all Gopher sites for menu items

video adapter   an expansion board used in conjunction with a monitor to enhance display capabilities

virus   a self-duplicating computer program that copies itself into computer systems with which it comes into contact—can be spread by floppy disk, transmit itself across networks, bypass security systems, and perform malicious actions such as destroying data

volume	another name for a hard or floppy disk
WAIS	*Wide Area Information Service,* a powerful system that searches Internet databases or libraries for information (pronounced *wayz*)
WAN	*wide-area network,* a network that spans a relatively large geographical area
widow	in printing, a short last line of a paragraph, especially one less than half the line's full measure or consisting of only a single word; the last line of a paragraph that appears alone at the top of the next page (considered undesirable in page design)
wild card	a special symbol, such as an asterisk (*) or question mark (?) that takes the place of one or more characters
windowing	displaying two or more files or different portions of the same file on the screen at the same time
word processing	the most common computer application, used to create, edit, and print documents
word wrap	a word processor's capability of placing a word at the beginning of the next line as soon as the first line becomes full (also called *wraparound*)
WORM	*write once, read many* (times), a type of optical storage; in lowercase, a special type of virus
WPM	*words per minute,* a measure of data transmission speed
WWW	*World Wide Web,* a hypertext-based system for locating and accessing Internet resources

WYSIWYG   *what you see is what you get,* a word processor that displays on the screen exactly what the printed text will look like (pronounced *wizzy-wig*)

x-line   in printing, the vertical space filled by a lowercase *x*

zone   a single area or location in a network

APPENDICES

Names of Animals & Their Families

Each species of all major groups that comprise the animal kingdom—mammals, birds, fish, reptiles, amphibians, and insects—has a scientific name of two terms. Known in zoology and biology as *binomial nomenclature,* the first identifies the genus to which it belongs and the second the species itself—e.g., *Homo sapiens* [NL rational man] is the name for humankind.

While not nearly as complex as binomial nomenclature, *nonscientific* terminology of animals can be confusing, especially the names that indicate gender, age, and group. The following list contains species commonly referred to, along with the adjectives that pertain to them (when available). For many animals, *like* is added to the name: *antlike, batlike, butterflylike, camellike, cricketlike, porpoiselike, sharklike, snaillike, snakelike, spiderlike, squirrelish* or *squirrellike, tigerlike, wasplike.* **EXCEPTIONS:** *crocodiloid, insectival, ranid* (frog).

Terms that refer to the young of certain carnivorous mammals include *cub,* as of the bear, fox, lion, or tiger (also a young shark), and *whelp,* especially of the dog, as well as the bear, lion, seal, tiger, and wolf.

Terms that refer to groups of young creatures include *brood,* pertaining to birds (or insects) produced or hatched from eggs at one time; *clutch,* a nest of eggs or a brood of chicks; and *litter,* the offspring of a multiparous animal, one producing many or more than one at a birth, as the cat, dog, pig, and lion.

Animal	Adjective	Male	Female	Young	Group
Antelope	antelopian antelopine	buck	doe	kid	herd
Bear	ursine	boar	sow	cub	sloth
Beaver	beaverlike beaverish	buck	doe	kit pup	colony family
Bee	apian apiarian (applies to beekeeping)	drone	queen worker	larva to pupa	colony
Bird*	avian	cock	hen	nestling fledgling	flock
Bison (buffalo)	bisontine	bull	cow	calf	herd
Bobcat	feline	tom	lioness	kitten	clowder
Cat	feline	tom	queen	kitten	clowder
Cattle	bovine taurine (applies to bull only)	bull	cow	calf	herd drove

* Adjectives include *grouselike, partridgelike,* and *quaillike.* Group names include *brace,* a pair, as *a brace of grouse; bevy,* a group of birds, as larks or quail (or animals, as roebuck); and *covey,* a brood or small flock of partridges or similar birds. A young penguin is called a *chick;* a group of these flightless, aquatic birds, a *colony.*

Animal	Adjective	Male	Female	Young	Group
Chicken		cock rooster	hen	chick cockerel (male less than one year old) pullet (female less than one year old)	flock
Deer	cervine	buck hart stag	doe hind roe	fawn	herd
Dog	canine	dog	bitch	pup whelp	kennel pack
Donkey	asinine	jackass	jenny jennet	foal	pace
Duck	ducklike (*not* ducky *or* duckie)	drake	duck	duckling	flock
Elephant	elephantine	bull	cow	calf	herd
Fish*	piscine			fry	school
Fox	vulpine	dog	vixen	cub pup kit	skulk
Giraffe		bull	cow	calf	herd

* *Crustacean* is both a noun and adjective, and pertains to aquatic arthropods whose bodies are covered with a hard shell or crust, including *crabs, lobsters, shrimps,* and *barnacles* (also applies to the small, terrestrial *wood louse*).

Animal	Adjective	Male	Female	Young	Group
Goat	caprine	billy buck	nanny doe	kid	herd
Goose	anserine	gander	goose	gosling	flock gaggle (when not in flight)
Hog Pig Swine	porcine	boar	sow	shoat piglet gilt (a pig less than one year old that has not given birth)	herd drove
Horse	equine	stallion stud colt (less than four years old)	dam mare filly (less than four years old)	foal (a horse of either sex less than one year old)	herd
Kangaroo	kangaroolike	buck boomer	doe flier	joey	herd troop mob
Lion	leonine	lion	lioness	cub	pride
Ostrich	ostrichlike	cock	hen	chick	flock
Owl	owllike owlish	owl	jenny howlet	owlet howlet	flock
Peafowl	peacockish	peacock	peahen	peachick	muster

Animal	Adjective	Male	Female	Young	Group
Rabbit	rabbitlike rabbity	buck	doe	kit leveret (a hare less than one year old)	warren
Rat	murine	buck	doe	pup	colony
Seal	seallike	bull	cow	pup whelp	pod herd trip harem (during breeding season)
Sheep	ovine	buck ram	ewe dam	lamb lambkin teg (an unshorn two-year-old)	flock herd
Swan	swanlike	cob	pen	cygnet	flock
Turkey		cock gobbler tom	hen	poult	flock
Walrus		bull	cow	cub	herd
Whale	cetacean	bull	cow	calf	herd pod gam school
Wolf	lupine	wolf	bitch	cub	pack
Zebra	zebrine	stallion	mare	colt	herd

Proofreaders' Marks

The use of proofreaders' marks—a set of symbols for marking a variety of errors found in a printed trial copy, or *proof,* of an original manuscript—is almost as old as printing itself. German printer Johannes Gutenberg invented movable type *ca* 1440, and by 1499 there were contracts holding the author responsible for corrections of the proof.

All printed matter—from books, magazines, and newspapers to fliers, personalized stationery, and business cards—should be carefully proofread for errors and corrected before production.

The following marks are used in both preparing a manuscript to be typeset and in proofreading or revising printed material. While there are several styles of certain marks and their use may differ from person to person, it is essential to write marks legibly and to place them where there is no mistaking their meanings.

LETTERS, WORDS, AND SPACING

In Margin	*In Copy*	*Meaning*
∧ or ⌄or ⅄	smrt	Insert
ℰ or ᵧ	take it out	Delete
◡	Sm art English	Close up
ℰ	Smart Englissh	Delete and close up
(stet)	English-language	Let it stand
(tr)	guide instant-access	Transpose
#	SmartEnglish	Insert one letter space
(hr#)	language	Insert hairspace (very thin space) between letters
(eq#)	written and spoken English	Space evenly between words (or lines)
out: see copy	instant- guide	Something left out
(line #)	Pulitzer Prizes # Pulitzer Prize in fiction Pulitzer Prize in public service	Insert line space
⊏	⊏Smart	Move left
⊐	English⊐	Move right
⊓	Smart English	Move up
⊔	Smart English	Move down

In Margin	In Copy	Meaning
]𝄔	]"A Dictionary of the English[Language"	Center (title, heading)
¶	public buildings. Lowercase roman numerals^	Start a new paragraph
no ¶ or run in	and finally the units.⌐ ⌐The principle	No new paragraph
run over	sequence for people and⌐ani-mals;	Start new line
☐	☐The trend in recent years	Indent or insert one em-dash space
☐☐	☐☐The Use of Arabic Numerals	Indent or insert two em spaces
fl	⌐1. to set off an appositive	Flush left; do not indent
fr	Total: $72.50]	Flush right; do not indent
sp	3rd Avenue	Spell out; use letters
fig	There are sixteen guidelines in this chapter.	Use figures for numbers
wf	Smart English	Wrong font
X	Smart English	Broken (damaged) letter of type
⑨	Smart English	Turn letter right side up

PUNCTUATION MARKS

In Margin	*In Copy*	*Meaning*
⊙	The usage is correct₎	Insert period
⋋	books, books₎books	Insert comma
⋋ or ; or ;/	Check the spelling look it up.	Insert semicolon
⊙or :	The following books₎	Insert colon
?	Have you proofread the copy yet.	Insert question mark
⋁	the Kings English	Insert apostrophe
ᵛᵛ/ᵛᵛ or ᵛᵛ ᵛᵛ	*Smart* ᵛAmerican ᵛ*English*	Insert quotation marks
ᵛᵛ/ᵛ or ᵛ ᵛ	She said, "Read ᵛEvangeline ᵛ tonight."	Insert single quotation marks
!	Be careful₎	Insert exclamation point
/	neither₎nor	Insert slash (virgule)
...	Every proofreader₎ every typesetter knows these marks.	Insert ellipses
⸗ or -	easy₎to₎use reference book	Insert hyphen(s)
⸗	Rogers received three⸗ quarters of the vote.	End-of-line hyphen is part of word
1/m or em or /M/	This book₎an aid to students and editors alike₎belongs on every desk.	Insert em dashes

In Margin	*In Copy*	*Meaning*
1/N or en or /N/	See pages 90∧112.	Insert en dash
(/) or {/}	Enclosed is a check for one hundred dollars∧$100.00∧.	Insert parentheses
[/] or {/}	"This statue∧Michelangelo's *David*∧is in Florence, Italy."	Insert brackets
&	Brazelton ~~and~~ Sons∧	Insert ampersand
⁎	grammar∧	Insert asterisk
†	preferred spelling∧	Insert dagger
‡	parts of speech∧	Insert double dagger
§	∧Book Reviews	Insert section mark (symbol)

TYPOGRAPHIC CASE AND STYLE

Cap or caps	the american role in Gatt	Use CAPITAL letter(s)
sc or Sm cap	The Chinese probably invented wood-block printing before A.D. 770.	Use small CAPITAL letter(s)
lc or lc	*Lowercase* means Small LETTERS.	Use lowercase letters
U+lc or c+lc or uc+lc	BRAVO! BRAVO!	Use uppercase and lowercase letters
ital	Romeo and Juliet is my favorite Shakespearean play.	Use *italic* type

In Margin	*In Copy*	*Meaning*
(rom)	from *alpha*	Use roman type (not *italic*)
(bf)	Abbreviate degrees only after a full name.	Use **boldface** type
(lf)	Lowercase *prize* when used without the word *Nobel*.	Use lightface (standard type)
∧	H₂0	Use subscript or inferior figure (or letter)
∨	4²⁄ = 16	Use superscript or superior figure (or letter)

ADJUSTMENTS AND QUERIES

═══	*Smart* English	Align horizontally
‖	*Smart English* *Smart English* *Smart English*	Align vertically
(OK?) or (OK/?) or (?)	by Jean T. Sutton. He wrote	Is this correct?
(set?)	was published in 1897 wrong date and	Is this part of copy to be set or only a marginal note?
(by/?)	the invention of stereotyping in 1725∧English goldsmith William Ged	Insert this word here?
(out: see copy)	Walter Morey, invented the teletypesetter in 1918.	Something left out in typesetting

BEFORE CORRECTIONS

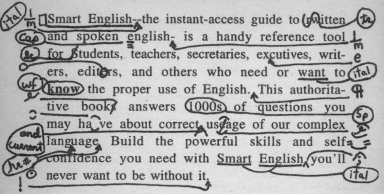

AFTER CORRECTIONS

Smart English—the instant-access guide to written and spoken English—is a handy reference tool for students, teachers, secretaries, executives, writers, editors, and others who need or *want* to know the proper use of English.

This authoritative book answers thousands of questions you may have about correct and current usage of our complex language. Build the powerful skills and self-confidence you need with *Smart English;* you'll never want to be without it!

Bibliography

The two following reference books were not only used in the preparation of *Smart English,* but are also the accepted reference sources for material not covered by this book.

Merriam-Webster's Collegiate Dictionary. Springfield, Mass.: Merriam-Webster, 10th ed., 1993.

The Random House Dictionary of the English Language. New York: Random House, unabr., 3rd ed., 1993.

Other references consulted in the preparation of *Smart English*:

Cappon, Rene J. *The Word.* New York: The Associated Press, 1989.

Crowley, Tony. *Proper English?* London and New York: Routledge, 1991.

Dorland's Pocket Medical Dictionary. Philadelphia: W. B. Saunders, 24th ed., 1982.

Freedman, Alan. *Computer Words You Gotta Know.* New York: AMACOM, 1993.

French, Christopher W., ed. *The Associated Press Style-*

book and Libel Manual. Reading, Mass.: Addison-Wesley, rev. ed., 1990.

Iverson, Cheryl, et al. *American Medical Association Manual of Style*. Baltimore: Williams & Wilkins, 8th ed., 1989.

Kraynak, Joe, et al. *The First Book of Personal Computing*. Carmel, Indiana: Alpha Books, 3rd (best-seller) ed., 1992.

Krol, Ed. *The Whole Internet User's Guide & Catalog*. Sebastopol, Calif.: O'Reilly & Associates, Inc., 2nd ed., 1994.

Margolis, Philip E., ed. *The Random House Personal Computer Dictionary*. New York: Random House, 1991.

McDaniel, George, ed. *IBM Dictionary of Computing*. New York: McGraw-Hill, 1994.

Mossman, Jennifer, ed. *Acronyms, Initialisms & Abbreviations Dictionary*. Detroit: Gale Research Inc., 18th ed., 1994.

Paxson, William C. *The New American Dictionary of Confusing Words*. New York: Signet, 1990.

Pogue, David and Joseph Schorr. *Macworld Macintosh Secrets*. San Mateo, Calif.: IDG Books, 1993.

Safire, William. *Fumblerules*. New York: Doubleday, 1990.

Safire, William. *On Language*. New York: Avon, 1981.

Seldes, George, ed. *The Great Thoughts*. New York: Ballantine, 1985.

Shakespeare, William. *The Complete Works of William Shakespeare*. New York: Doubleday, 1936.

Spenser, Donald, ed. *Webster's New World Dictionary of Computer Terms.* New York: Prentice Hall, 4th ed., 1992.

Stedman's Medical Dictionary. Baltimore: Williams & Wilkins, 24th ed., 1982.

Strunk, William, Jr., and E. B. White. *The Elements of Style.* New York: Macmillan Co., 3rd ed., 1973.

Sturgeon, Linda B. and Anne R. Hagler. *Personal Letters That Mean Business.* Englewood Cliffs: Prentice Hall, 1991.

The Chicago Manual of Style. Chicago: University of Chicago Press, 14th ed., 1993.

The World Almanac and Book of Facts 1995. Mahwah, N.J.: Funk & Wagnalls, 1994.

The World Book Encyclopedia. Chicago: World Book, Inc., 1993 ed.

U.S. Postal Service Directory of Post Offices. Washington, D.C.: U.S. Postal Service.

Index

Computer-related terms are set in boldface type; Latin and French words, phrases, and abbreviations are set in italics.

Annette Francis began her career as continuity editor at radio station WSAI in Cincinnati, where she was also associated with WKRC-TV and WCPO-TV. Upon moving to New York, she became assistant promotion manager of WOR Radio and WOR-TV (now WWOR-TV), and subsequently worked as audience promotion manager at NBC-TV and copy supervisor at RKO Teleradio Pictures, Inc. She also worked in editorial and promotional capacities for *McCall's, Seventeen,* and *Country Inns/Bed & Breakfast* magazines, and wrote her own column—"Health in the Home"—for *American Home* magazine.

In 1985 Ms. Francis moved to South Florida, where she served as founding editor of *Palm Beach County ARTS* (now called *CULTURE,* the quarterly magazine of the Palm Beach County Cultural Council) and opened an office for editorial and communications consulting. Her clients included physicians, attorneys, concert artists, and such organizations and institutions as the National Foundation for Advancement in the Arts (Miami), the Chopin Foundation (Miami), the Morikami Museum and Japanese Gardens (Delray Beach), Palm Beach Community College (Lake Worth), the Palm Beach Opera, the Palm Beach Festival, and the Palm Beach County Health Care District.

Annette Francis is coauthor with Bry Benjamin, M.D., of *IN CASE OF EMERGENCY: What to Do Until the Doctor Arrives* (Doubleday) and *New Facts of Life for Women* (Prentice Hall). In 1988 she cofounded Bravo! Books Inc. with graphic artist Paula Hober and established an international market for their books, *The Mozart Diet* and *Cooking with Shakespeare.* An accomplished pianist, composer, and lyricist, Ms. Francis is a member of the American Society of Composers, Authors & Publishers (ASCAP) as well as the Harvard Musical Association in Boston, where she now resides.